Narrating Colonialism

Postcolonial Images of the British in Indian English Fiction

In the same series

Indian Women Novelists, 18 vols.
R.K. Dhawan, ed.

Women's Voices: The Novels of Indian Women Writers
K. Meera Bai

New Perspectives on Indian Writing
V.L.V.N. Narendra Kumar, ed.

Fiction of the Nineties
R.K. Dhawan and Veena Noble Dass, ed.

Indian Literature Today, 2 vols.
R.K. Dhawan, ed.

Style in Indian English Fiction
Z.N. Patil

Recent Indian Fiction
R.S.. Pathak, ed.

Comparative Perspectives on Indian Literature
A. Ramakrishna Rao, ed.

Studies in Indian Writing in English
P. Bayapa Reddy

Major Indian Novelists
K. Venkata Reddy

Postcolonial Discourse
R.K. Dhawan, ed.

Narrating Colonialism

Postcolonial Images of the British
in
Indian English Fiction

D. MAYA

Foreword

by

Professor K. Ayyappa Paniker

PRESTIGE

Published by
Prestige Books
3/28, East Patel Nagar
New Delhi 110 008

ISBN: 81-7551-029-3

1997

Photo Typesetting by
Pivot Computers
Delhi 110 006
Ph. 293 4490

Printed at
Chaman Offset Press
New Delhi 110 002

Contents

Foreword

Self-Conscious Fictionalization

The story of what happened to Clive of India when he returned to England after laying the foundations of an empire in the East, as told by Nirad. C. Chaudhuri, reveals the highly complex nature of the experiences of the natives as well as the colonizers in India. Maya's attempt in this book is to explore and analyse these complexities as they are presented in the works of post-Independence Indian novelists through a study of the way in which the British have been portrayed in them. Without any effort to stereotype and oversimplify issues, she prepares a rational basis for understanding and explaining the behaviour of the British in India—both before and after independence. While all the works studied here wer written during the post-Independence era, some of them relate to events and situations before Independence. The implicit fallacy in invoking Prospero and Caliban as the prototypes of the colonizer and the colonized comes through in this in-depth examination of the multiple role models available to the British who came to India as rulers as well as to the novelists who try to create living examples to illustrate these models.

Narrating Colonialism becomes an interesting exploration in the context of the question sometimes raised among Indian literary scholars—why India has not produced in modern times an epic of the magnitude of *Ramayana* or *Mahabharata* in spite of a prolonged struggle for national freedom conducted in a series of pitched battles all over the country under the leadership of the greatest man of our times ably supported by stalwarts next only to him in stature. A great theme, a host of heroic characters, blood-curdling incidents—and yet—have our writers failed to take up the challenge? If we take all the fictional writings in Indian English (or for that matter, in all Indian languages), will it be possible for us to say that the cumulative multi-authored text(s) like those under discussion here gives us a panoramic view of this epic story, equivalent in breadth and depth to the classics of bygone days? For her part, the author of this study has brought into focus the fascinating galaxy or gallery of British citizens who have been portrayed in the post-Independence novels in English by Indians. It is an impressive array of diverse characters who display archetypal patterns of behaviour and have dispensed the destiny of the vast mass of people of a subcontinent for a considerable length of time.

Throughout this book we find certain basic ideas in operation behind the narrative controlled and communicated by the dominant image of postcolonial reality. One of these is the interconnectedness of socio-political domains of life in a country still haunted by Anglophobia and Anglophilia. Another point is the observation that the response of the Indian novelists to the British, as seen in their works, is not as vehement as in African fiction. A third feature is the classification of these British characters into two major groups of colonizer-conformists and de-colonized nonconformists. The conformists consist of two further subdivisions: those who are passive and those active in their conformism. The nonconformists also display different shades of decolonization. The relative insularity of the British women as portrayed in the novels confirms the natural sense of alienation experienced by them. The contrast with Indian women characters in these novels very effectively projects this.

The writer reveals very close familiarity with the texts examined. There is a thoroughgoing analysis of the rôle models before the white population until independence in contrast with those after independence. The contrast between the behaviour of the white rulers in their exclusive clubs and that outside the clubs in contrast with Indians is convincingly brought out. In every chapter we find perceptive discussions of how the British appeared in the eyes of these postcolonial authors of Indian fiction. Fictional images are not the products of dry documentation. The distortion in the perception of characters on account of their self-alienation in a country so different from their own is sympathetically presented.

Another valuable contribution of this study is the explanation for the divergent portraits given by different Indian novelists. Four major categories have been identified among Indian novelists—the Anglophiles, the ambivalent, the compromisers and those committed to Indian value systems. The Indian writers are also studied in relation to writers from other Third World nations. The author points out by way of resumé that the Indian English novelists of the past fifty years who have been deeply concerned with the colonial hangover, are now moving towards a gradual release from it.

Her final assessment reveals her understanding of the dynamic nature of the involvement of these novelists with contemporary socio-political reality. This reality is not static nor is the perception of the new generation of writers static. She comments:

> The Indian English novelists' attempt to reevaluate colonial experience and the relationship between the Indians and the British forms a part of his endeavour to strike against the imperial centre. The dominant features of post-independence fiction—the displacement of the idols of the Empire by national heroes, the appropriating of frames of power, the reversal of the colonial perspective and even the liberation of the linguistic medium from the emotional tags of colonial authority—establish its oneness with other postcolonial literatures.

This study begins with the contention that "the withdrawal of British power in 1947 under the pressure of a massive national movement did not neutralize the impact of colonialism. The colonial hangover lingers on in the nation even today." The continued presence of the British in the Indian English novel, according to the author, is explained by the fact that the novelists are attempting to narrate the colonial past in a retrospective vision. They are narrating colonialism from the vantage point of postcolonialism.

Such thorough-going analysis as found in this book is sure to attract the attention of all scholars and readers interested either in colonialist aesthetics or in postcolonial politics or in the Indian attempt to fictionalize the erstwhile colonial experience. Together the novelists discussed here have achieved remarkable success in grappling with the emergent politics of decolonization through self-conscious fictionalization.

K. AYYAPPA PANIKER

Preface

Preoccupation with the colonial past is a persisting phenomenon in postcolonial narratives. The tendency to remap the cartography of the nation's political and cultural past is a vital concern in them. Indian English fiction of the post-Independence period—itself an off-shoot of colonialism—struggles to evolve a liberated discourse that can break free from the cultural imperialism of the west. Positioning himself as the liberated self, the Indian writer views the 'imperialist' who exercised his hegemony over the 'native' giving rise to the complexities and tensions of a coloniser-colonised, Prospero-Caliban, self-other, civilized-savage relationship. This book is an earnest endeavour to capture the images of the British mirrored in postcolonial imagination as it narrates the colonial past. I have attempted to include within my canvas the entire spectrum of Indian English fiction ranging from the works of Mulk Raj Anand to Salman Rushdie (works published from 1947 to 1990). The socio-cultural and psychological dimensions of the subject have made this exploration into fiction challenging and exciting. I hope this becomes shared experience as the readers go through the book.

On this occasion I remember with extreme gratitude Dr. K.P.K. Menon, former Head of the Institute of English, University of Kerala, who inspired me to take up the work, but did not live to see its completion. I am deeply indebted to Dr. K. Radha, Professor and Head of the Institute of English, University of Kerala, for supervising the original research and encouraging me with her valuable suggestions and painstaking guidance. I acknowledge my gratitude to Dr. K. Ayyappa Paniker, the well-known poet and critic, and former Head of the Institute of English, University of Kerala, for his kind encouragement and valuable counsel in the writing of this book, and for contributing the Foreword. I have greatly benefited from the stimulating discussions on the subject with Prof. C.D. Narasimhaiah, Director, The Literary Criterion Centre, Dhvanyaloka, Mysore. I appreciate the help rendered by Dr. Paul Love, the Director, SCILET, American College, Madurai, and the librarians of Literary Criterion Centre, Dhvanyaloka, Mysore, SCILET, Madurai, the C.I.E.F.L., Hyderabad, The British Council Library, Trivandrum, Library of the Institute of English, Trivandrum, University of Kerala, Trivandrum, and The Public Library, Trivandrum.

I am thankful to the University Grants Commission for offering assistance through the Faculty Improvement Scheme and to the Govt. of Kerala for granting leave for the completion of the work. I place on record my deep gratitude to the Professor and Head of the Institute of English and the University of Kerala for providing the facilities for research.

This work would not have been possible without the enormous help and encouragement given by my husband Er. Raghavan Nair in the collection of material for research and in the painstaking exercise of proofreading the manuscript. The moral support of my parents and children was a source of great encouragement to me.

Finally I am grateful to Ms. D. Renu of Prestige Books for bringing out this book so expeditiously and elegantly.

Introduction

The occupation of India by the British for centuries has left its lasting impact on the soul of the nation. The saga of British rule starting with Clive's victory in the Battle of Plassey in 1757, leading to colonial expansion and the establishment of the British Empire, presents one of the most unusual phenomena in history—the political, cultural and social domination of a large populace with an ancient culture, by a much smaller and alien country. The withdrawal of British power in 1947 under the pressure of a massive national movement did not neutralize the impact of colonialism. The colonial hangover lingers on in the nation even today.

"Historical situations create cultural consequences,"[1] says the famous Indian poet Nissim Ezekiel. The emergence of Indian English fiction in the thirties under the influence of western thought and writing fully endorses the poet's statement. With Independence, the novel became a liberated medium for the Indian writer who did not any longer feel the constraints of nationalism and pan-Indianism. This explains the Indian English novelist's continued preoccupation with the socio-political issues of the period before Independence. Retrospective narration of India's eventful past accounts for the compelling British presence in the Indian English novel.

History is a witness to the spirit of mutual discovery and accommodation that marked the first phase of Indo-British relations. British romantics like Thomas Munro, Mountstuart Elphinstone, John Malcolm and Charles Metcalfe understood India and tried to preserve her spirit by resisting all efforts to impose British constitutional principles on her. They did not try to tamper with Indian customs, tradition or religious beliefs. They realized that even foreign domination "should be administered on a principle of humility, not pride."[2] In the beginning of the nineteenth century, the Evangelical movement in England set in motion a burning zeal for reform and religious conversion. Missionaries who were permitted entry into India for the first time tried to convert the Indians by educating and reforming them. Sir Charles Edward Trevelyan suggested introducing English education as a diplomatic means of achieving permanent political power through the cultural subjection of Indians. He dreamt of an India which "is trained by us to happiness and independence and endowed with our learning and political institutions"[3] and which "will remain the proudest monument of British benevolence."[4] Macaulay's celebrated Minute of 1853 translated Trevelyan's dream into policy and English became the official language of India. With this the stamp of power was affixed on the anglicization of the educated classes.

The first rebuff to British power was described by British historians as "the Sepoy Mutiny" and celebrated by Indians as "the First War of Independence." With the British success in quelling the rebellion, the rule of the Company was replaced by the direct rule of the Crown, heralding a new era of arrogant racism—a period that marked "the final flowering of Western imperialism in Asia."[5] Communication between the races almost ceased with the growing aloofness of the rulers. Though India had been ravaged and conquered many times before, the British were the only invaders who remained to the last "absentee masters alienating themselves in pastime and profession with a smug air of superiority from the native masses all the while."[6]

However, the growth of English education indirectly led to the spread of Indian nationalism. As the wind of revolutionary thought swept through the country with the appearance of Gandhi on the national scene, a growing sense of uneasiness became obvious in English administrators as to the justification of their presence in India. Liberal humanist thought popular in England undermined the earlier notions of divine authority and moral superiority. The non-violent struggle of the masses that finally resulted in the emancipation of Indians served to create on attitude of humility in the nobler Englishmen of the day.

The impact of colonized experience on native consciousness, the social problems of the newly liberated nation, the erosion of indigenous culture and values through continued western domination, the dilemma posed by biculturalism, the search for identity and alienation in the products of a dual culture and the strident self-assertion and urge for decolonization in the liberated Indian—all these are persistent themes in post-Independence writing. They are areas of experience common to Commonwealth nations whose literature manifests, according to Srinivasa Iyengar, three main stages in its evolution: "In most Commonwealth countries, parallel to the movement from Colonial to Commonwealth status, there has been witnessed also the movement, at the cultural level, from imitation and immaturity to creative experimentation and conscious adulthood."[7] In its effort to break free from its colonial legacy and to stand on its own legs, Indian English fiction too passes through the same leading to self-discovery. This journey to self-realization involves a review of the colonial past, the rejection of the imperial connections and the rediscovery of one's own cultural moorings. The story of alien domination is narrated from different angles and the British are presented in the context of their political, social and cultural relations with the Indian.

This study attempts to explore the nature of the Englishman who came to India as part of the imperial machinery, his behaviour in the imperial cast, the problems of alienation suffered by those who did not identify themselves with the imperial role and the cultural tension issuing from the encounters between the English and the Indians as found in Indian English novels. The attitude of the Indian writer to the former colonizer is examined in the light of the privations imposed by his colonized past. Cultural polarities that curb the Indian vision and also the areas of human experience shared by both races, transcending the barriers of culture and race, come within the scope of the study.

The British as portrayed in Indian English fiction of the Post-Independence era have not been made the subject of any comprehensive and full-length study, though they continue to figure prominently in Indian novels written in English. However, mention should be made of a few critical works that give importance to the theme—some, as the central issue, and others, at least as a major concern. Kai Nicholson's *Social Problems in Indo-Anglian and Anglo-Indian Fiction* (1972) devotes a chapter to the Sahib in Indo-Anglian and Anglo-Indian novels. Gomathi Narayanan concentrates on certain aspects of the complex subject of the Indo-British nexus in her work *The Sahibs and the Natives: A Study of Guilt and Pride in Anglo-Indian and Indo-Anglian Novels* (1982)—guilt, shame and pride in the Indo-British relationship. Dieter Riemenschneider has made a brief study in his article titled "British Characters in Indo-English Fiction." The East-West encounter, which is a consequence of Indo-British contact and cultural interaction, as projected by individual novelists of the post-Independence era, has drawn the attention of many critics. Meenakshi Mukherjee makes it the theme of a chapter in his work, *Twice-Born Fiction* (1971). Articles dealing with individual aspects of the theme are comparatively large in number. So far no exhaustive study of the fictional representation of the British by the post-Independence Indian novelist in English has come out. This work hopes to fill the gap.

In the exploration of the British in Indian English fiction, the novelist's preoccupation with the theme has become the deciding factor in the selection of works for detailed investigation. An exhaustive survey of all the novels being impossible, the study is restricted to relevant works published before 1990. The authors who have given prominence to the British are, Mulk Raj Anand, Manohar Malgonkar, Chaman Nahal, Kamala Markandaya, Timeri Murari and Nayantara Sahgal. Though not so conspicuously, the British do figure in the novels of Khushwant Singh, B. Rajan, and K.A. Abbas. The cultural encounter resulting from Indo-British relations is one of the issues dealt with in the works R.K. Narayan and Bhabani Bhattacharya. In Raja Rao, the Indian and French sensibilities are at loggerheads and cultural conflict is raised to higher planes and given larger dimensions. The immigrant Indian in England counteracting with his cultural opposite is a thematic concern in certain works of Kamala Markandaya, Anita Desai and Timeri Murari. The historical novelist's role in debunking the myths that sustained the Empire and gilded British history is analyzed through a study of the novels dealing with India's colonial experiences. The use of style as iconoclastic device by writers like G.V. Desani and Salman Rushdie is taken up in this connection. Their works assume significance as part of the reaction of the post-Independence writer towards his colonized past. In a brief study it would not have been possible to do justice to the subject chosen and the social and psychological issues involved because a large number of authors and works had to be examined.

The historical nature of the topic has necessitated a comprehensive study of India's colonial past and the major political theories that had dominated British thought. An exploration of modern psychological research in colonial behaviour has helped to sharpen perception and has afforded an insight into British behaviour in India. Sociological studies of British life in India and studies of the Englishwomen of the colonial era have also been enlightening. What started as a literary study has thus encroached upon different disciplines and formulated an interdisciplinary approach to the theme.

An exploration of the works leads to the premise that political freedom has not brought about the liberation of the Indian English novelist from colonial predilections and the emotional restraints it imposes on the colonized mind. Three major tendencies can be identified in the Indian fictional approach to the British:

1. A tendency to place the British in terms of a colonial relationship—branding him either as imperialist or anti-imperialist.
2. An ambivalent attitude towards the British which involves an overt expression of admiration of the British system of values on the one hand and antagonism towards the former ruler on the other.
3. The post-Independent reaction against British colonialism manifesting itself in the decolonizing urge of the Indian artist who adopts the role of an iconoclast.

The psychology of colonial behaviour and its reflection in literature have influenced the perspective of the Indian novelist. In literature, Shakespeare had first provided the typical colonizer image through his Prospero: "Prospero at his best stands for many a man conscious of powers which he cannot exert to the full among his peers, a magnificent leader among people who give him unquestioning homage and do not compete with his greatness."[8]

Colonial history is full of Prosperos who instilled in the colonized, a complex of dependency and sense of inferiority. The Prospero-complex of the European has given birth to a corporate body of orientalist discourse which dealt with the Orient, "by making statements about it, authorizing views of it, describing it, by teaching it, settling it, ruling over it,"[9] and "postitioning" the Orient "as a sort of surrogate and even underground self."[10] The cultivated theory and practice of Orientalism which depends for its strategy on the "flexible positional superiority"[11] of the Westerner in all his relationships with the Orient, has grown and strengthened through the years, developing into a system of knowledge. Oriental discourse has infiltrated western consciousness and coloured all writings—historical, political, social and literary—about the Orient. The Indian English writer of the post-Independence era has to counteract this deeply established horde, to re-establish the cultural identity of his nation and of his race.

The entire range of post-Independence Indian fiction in English can thus be viewed as a corporate body of literature, in its reaction and response to the colonial experience. The emotional restraints conditioning the novelist's approach and the cultural bondage lingering from the colonized past form important moulding factors in the Indian novelist's treatment of the British. Though the bitterness of the pre-Independence perspective is noticed as softening in the post-Independence novelists, their judgement seems to be still coloured by the denigrating discourse of orientalism. A pronounced trend emerging in the liberated novelists is the tendency to strike back at the Empire, refuting the ideology of containment with an ideology of liberation. Fawzia Afzal-Khan explains it thus: "By such an ideology I mean one that allows 'colonized' writers to transform their past, their culture and their people, from being determinate objects, to becoming living subjects, from constituting the antagonistic 'other' to becoming a sympathetic 'self.'"[12] It can be noted that the general Indian reaction against colonialism and cultural subjection is not as pronounced as it ought to be, unlike the vehement reaction that permeates modern African fiction.

The largest single group of the British present in Indian English fiction comprises the imperialists who came to India, authorized to govern the conquered country. Their behaviour patterns as determined by the roles provided by the Empire and fostered by the public school ethos and Victorian values form the subject of exploration in Chapter II of this book. Imperialist tendencies persist in some, even after Independence and identical attitudes are recognized. Loss of identity involved in identification with the imperial role and the resulting alienation from the native and from one's own self also become issues of concern in this chapter.

The insularity of the colonizer manifests itself more obviously in the Englishwomen in India, who form a stereotyped group in Indian English fiction. The Indian English novelist's treatment of the imperialistic English women in India forms the topic of discussion in Chapter III.

Chapter IV brings within its scope the British who refused to sacrifice individual values to the demands of the Imperial role and suffered consequent alienation from the English community, while failing to achieve complete identification with the Indian ethos and remain suspended between two worlds. The process of decolonization operates in a few Englishmen of the post-Independence era who have emancipated themselves completely from the colonial hang-over.

The Indian writer's endeavour to destructure history coloured by oriental thought and to restore the values sabotaged by western cultural imperialism, is a feature of the Indian historical novels in English. The process is illustrated through the major Indian English historical novels in Chapter V.

Chapter VI tries to define the bicultural situation and the resulting tension and to identify the different approaches of the Indian English novelists to the cultural conflict engendered by Indo-British relations. The stance of the Indian expatriate writer to the cultural issue is examined in relation to Indian English fiction. The solutions offered are also considered.

Chapter VII, the conclusion, records the findings of the exploration conducted into the post-Independence novel and examines the style of the Indian English novelists, their use of the alien medium and the degree of authenticity achieved in the portrayal of the British.

NOTES

1. Quoted in William Walsh, "India and the Novel," *The New Pelican Guide to English Literature: The Present,* Vol. 8, ed. Boris Ford (1956;

England: Penguin, 1984) 245.

2. Michael Edwardes, *Glorious Sahibs: The Romantic as Empire- builder 1799-1938* (London: Eyre and Spottiswoode, 1968) 237.
3. Quoted in Peggy Woodford, *Rise of the Raj* (Kent: Midas Books, 1978) 110.
4. *Ibid.*
5. Rhoads Murphey, *The Outsiders: The Western Experience in India and China* (USA: Univ. of Michigan Press, 1977) 67.
6. Swapan Majumdar, *Comparative Literature: Indian Dimensions* (Calcutta: Papyrus, 1987) 97.
7. K.R. Srinivasa Iyengar, "The Colonial and Neo-Colonial Encounters in Commonwealth Literature." *The Colonial and Neo-Colonial Encounters in Commonwealth Literature*, ed. Anniah Gowda (Mysore: Univ. of Mysore, 1983) 9-20.
8. Philip Mason, "Foreword," D. Mannoni, *Prospero and Caliban: The Psychology of Colonization* (London: Methuen, 1960) 12.
9. Edward W. Said, *Orientalism* (London: Routledge and Kegan Paul, 1978) 3.
10. *Ibid.*
11. *Ibid.*
12. Fawzia Afzal-Khan, "Myth De-bunked: Genre and Ideology in Rushdie's *Midnight's Children* and *Shame*," *Journal of Indian Writing in English*, 14, No. 1. (Jan. 1986) 50.

The Imperial Role

This chapter focuses on the fictional representation of the British who functioned in colonial India as exponents of a system of values and a code of behaviour that provided the moral base for the edifice of the British Empire. Their behaviour in India was conditioned by the imperial role founded on the myth of Britain's racial and cultural superiority and moulded by the colonial ethos. They tried to identify themselves completely with the role, losing their own individual self-hood in the process. It is an instance of the role taking over the role-player. The tendency of the individual to identify himself with the role and its requirements, to the extent of deindividuation or loss of identity is an accepted theory in psycho-analysis. Ralph Ruddock says: "In a sociological perspective, identity is socially bestowed, socially sustained, socially transformed."[1] Most of the British who figure in Indian English fiction are men cast in imperial roles, functioning as cogs in the imperial machinery. For convenience of categorization and reference, they are often described here as "Imperialists," using the term with all its colonial connotations of usurped authority, pride of racial, cultural and intellectual superiority and consequent contempt for the native.

Studies on British character and colonial psychology have revealed how colonialism generated an imperial myth of racial superiority and divine authority which transformed the nature of the Englishman when he came to India. The word "Imperialism" which initially saw the light of day only in the nineteenth century, came to be associated in people's minds with trusteeship and the governing of colonies for human purposes. These were the values that were given visibility in England by an extensive imperial literature, especially by Charles D. Dilke (*Great Britain*); John R. Seeley (*The Expansion of England*) and J.A. Froude (*Oceana*). Kipling propagated the idea of the whiteman's civilizing mission in India, towards the less advanced peoples of the world. In the 1880's Sir John Strachey declared: "We . . . to use Sir James Stephen's expression, are the representatives of a belligerent civilization which has to wage constant warfare against strange barbarisms, horrid customs and cruel superstitions, ancient survivals, ready at any moment to start into activity."[2]

The words "Imperialism" and "Imperial role" as used in this study include the awareness of cultural and racial superiority that came with political authority and provided the British a moral justification for their presence in India as expounded in the statement quoted above. The idea that the British race is "the greatest of governing races that the world has ever seen"[3] was received opinion among the English in India.

The rhetoric of power based on the destiny of the British as a governing race, generated an imperial mystique which provided an image of the ideal ruler and offered him a role to play. The brave, daring and masculine Englishman—"the man who knew how to command"[4] —was the heroic ideal to be projected before the savage and uncivilized native. The right to rule was a normal prerogative sanctioned by racial superiority and ingrained leadership qualities to the British. In course of time the English in India completely identified themselves with the imperial role. Benita Parry writes: "Hypnotised by belief in their Messianic role or infatuated with vanity at wielding great power, Anglo-Indians expunged from their writings the material interests which Britain had in India and detached the idea of a mission from the complex and equivocal motives which brought them to India and which are gratified in ruling over Indians."[5]

Mannoni has recognized this tendency to glorify one's role in the occupied country as a typical colonial trait. The change wrought on the character of the average European in the colonial atmosphere is, according to him, a surfacing of suppressed complexes in the European psyche:

> . . . the personality of the colonial is made up, not of characteristics acquired during and through experience of the colonies, but of traits, very often in the nature of a complex, already in existence in a latent and repressed form in the European psyche, traits which the colonial experience has simply brought to the surface and made manifest. Social life in Europe exerts a certain pressure on the individual and that pressure keeps the personality in a given shape: once it is removed, however, the outlines of the personality change and swell, thus revealing the existence of internal pressures which had upto then passed unnoticed.[6]

The British in Indian fiction are mainly drawn from the social and political milieu of British India and in fiction they are realized in their imperial roles. As in any colonial situation, the imperial code determines their character and social behaviour. The Indian novelists have drawn them from the period spanning the entire duration of the British Raj (1858-1947), as well as the post-Independent era.

The novelists try to expose the illusion of a permanent and belligerent mission that had got deeply entrenched in the British consciousness, after the first war of Indian Independence in 1857. The illusion lent a halo to the British rulers in India, wedging permanent cleavages of cultural and emotional alienation from the Indians. The imperial cult had seeped into the British consciousness, so that not only the bureaucrats, who directly wielded the administrative machinery, but the officials of all classes, planters, educationists and even the missionaries embodied its values. The representative nature of their function in the Indian novel inhibits the individual development of the characters. The imperialists in fiction, therefore, largely remain stereotyed figures manifesting a class consciousness in itself representative of colonial behaviour. Their significance derives from the ideals and values they represent. Here typification becomes an effective instrument since it is employed by the novelist with the definite intention of revealing the sentiments and values of an alien race of rulers.

A comparative analysis of the portrayal of the British imperialists in Indian English fiction before and after Independence, brings into view a definite shift in the approach of the novelist of the postcolonial era. The pre-Independence writer gives vent to his bitterness through the highly coloured portraits of imperial exploiters. Their villainy is contextualized in the socio-political climate of the occupied nation. They remain dark figures of unrelieved evil. They mainly project colonial tendencies and function as representatives of the value system of the empire. Himself a suffering victim of the occupied nation, the novelist employs these characters to direct his invective against the Empire. The British rulers figure invariably as exploiters. As capitalists or planters, they exploit the native labourers; reduce them to poverty; trample on their women and expose themselves as morally depraved and corrupt individuals. As policemen or soldiers, they act as instruments of imperial oppression in trying to crush the rising tide of Indian nationalism. The works of prominent Indian English novelists like Mulk Raj Anand and Raja Rao provide ample illustrations. Mulk Raj Anand's novels of social protest like *Coolie, Untouchable* and *Two Leaves and a Bud* depict the role of the British in bringing about the gulf between the haves and the have-nots, the rulers and the ruled. The planters like Croft Cooke and Reggie Hunt (*Two Leaves and a Bud*) symbolize the cruelty and carnality of the affluent planter class. They strike a glaring contrast to the impoverished plight of the labourers.

The typical English bureaucrat W.P. England (*Coolie*) who scrupulously avoids familiarity with the native, the missionary Col. Hutchinson (*Untouchable*) who hides behind rubbish heaps waiting for some troubled outcaste who would listen in his despair to the Gospel of Christ, the Headmaster Father Annandale who converts sweepers and heathen workers in a proselytizing mission (*Village*), and the capitalist exploiters Croft Cooke and Reggie Hunt (*Two Leaves and a Bud*) who are embodiments of undiluted villainy—all of them are representative figures suffused with imperial sentiments whom the novelist denies complete development within the framework of the novel. They are either partial portraits or living manifestations of the oppressive aspects of colonialism. By reducing the English to symbolic roles, the novelist denies them rounded characterization. R.S. Singh's comment on the dark portrayal of Reggie Hunt is applicable in all these cases: "Anand's bitterness against the inhuman imperialists gets here the better of him, as a consequence of which the artistic balance is lost."[7]

Raja Rao's *Kanthapura*, written in the wake of nationalism, provides a lurid picture of the British planters and the tormented Indian labourers in Skeffington Coffee Estate. The story of exploitation described at length in *Two Leaves and a Bud* is only hurriedly glanced at in *Kanthapura*: but the approach of the writers remains the same. Even R.K. Narayan, who is content with "his little bit of ivory" and confines his art to the serenity of Malgudi, cannot refrain from creating the imperial-minded English Principal Mr. Brown (*Bachelor of Arts*) who feels all important and puts the blame for everything on Indians. Whereas Anand's novels abound in sweeping statements of condemnation of British like "The British had never done anything for anybody without seeing to what they could get out of it" (*Two Leaves and a Bud* 76) and "the British had exaggerated the worst instinct in their own character and called out the worst in the Indian," (117) R.K. Narayan's pre-Independence works carry the underlying theme of the disillusionment of the Indian mind during the British regime.

A comparative study of the approach to the British in the novels before and after Independence brings to focus a perceptible shift in stance. Though the tendency to portray the British as typical representatives of the imperial code continues, there is a larger awareness of their individual status within the colonial framework. They cease to be dark figures of villainy. There is a sincere effort on the part of the post-colonial writer to understand the colonial ethos that had imposed restrictions on the British in India and moulded their behavioural pattern. Some novelists have even attempted to understand the working of the alien psyche in the light of modern psychological research on colonial behaviour.

This psychological probing into individual personality reflects a common trend in the writers of the generation.

The distance of time might also have been a favourable factor that helped the post-Independence novelist to attain a deeper perspective. It can be perceived that there is a greater concern regarding the problems of alienation suffered by the colonial. Two types of alienation have been identified and represented in fiction by post-Independence novelists like Kamala Markandaya, Chaman Nahal, Nayantara Sahgal and Manohar Malgonkar. On the one hand, there is the emotional and cultural alienation brought about by the totally unfamiliar cultural ethos of the country in which he is domiciled. The Indian novelists have projected the English club and hill-stations as symbols of their alienation from native life. On the other, there is the alienation from the colonial's own real self, through total identification with the imperial role he has adopted. It involves loss of individual values and a dispossessing of identity. It is an instance where one finds the role-player merging with the role so that his inner self loses its identity and becomes non-existent. This explains the transformation undergone by the Englishman when he comes to India.

The British imperialists in Indian English novels mainly represent a cross-section of the British bureaucracy that formed the administrative machinery of the Raj in the post-mutiny era. British officialdom with its rigid hierarchy of Viceroys, Political Agents (Residents), Commissioners, Deputy Commissioners, Judges and educationists people the world of British India contextualized in Indian English novels. Imperial values, the myth of racial superiority and the illusion of a beneficent mission in India were deeply entrenched in their minds. Colonialism in the post-mutiny era was a moral force that had established itself within the consciousness of the Englishman and the Indian. The imperial mystique provided both with images of the ideal ruler and the ruled. Modern research has come out with the theory that colonialism is a psychological state in which the colonizer and the colonized accept certain well-defined stances, disturbing original cultural priorities.[8] In any colonial situation the colonizer formulates an ideology as camouflage for his imperial policies. Feelings of guilt are warded off by a self-imposed illusion of moral superiority, divine authority and a sense of duty. The Englishman's illusion of superiority was strengthened by the writings of Evangelists and Utilitarians who invested the conquests made by the merchant adventurers with an aura of glory. The Evangelical reformer Charles Grant recorded his conviction that conquest has been made in British hands "the means not merely of displaying a government unequalled in India for administrative justice, kindness and moderation, not merely of increasing the security of the subjects and prosperity of the country, but of advancing social happiness, of meliorating the moral state of man, and of extending a superior light."[9] The British historian James Mill avoided justifying conquest, but stressed the possibility of compensating "the people of India, for the miseries of that misgovernment which they had so long endured."[10] The edifice of the Raj rested on the moral props provided by these prominent social reformers.

In the princely states under the British Raj, imperial authority was represented by the Political Agents (Residents) who managed to sustain a delicate love-hate relationship with the Indian princes, which is symbolic of the complex and ambivalent relationship between the two races. The Political Agents figuring in *The Golden Honeycomb*, *The Princes* and *The Private Life of an Indian Prince*—the three Indian English novels dealing with princely India—are representative figures occupying the highest ranks of the imperial hierarchy. Through them are revealed the subtle methods employed by the imperial machinery to reduce the unsuspecting prince to a state of subjection. Any delicacy caused by their presence within the ostensibly independent princely states was warded off by what Kamala Markandaya called "the catch 22 arrangement"[11] employed by the British. A British-controlled force was kept in the states apparently for the protection of the ruling prince: it was maintained at the expense of the state treasury and was effectively employed against the princes to guarantee their subjection, in case they failed to pay the subsidy to the British. The relationship between the prince and the Resident was virtually that of vassal and lord. The Residents held the reins and the princes sought eagerly to please them. As agents of the King Emperor and the Viceroy they posed as King-makers and watched over every independent move of the princes to ensure that there was no infringement on British interests. In every important policy matter of the state, the Resident's approval was to be solicited in entering into treaties, levying taxes, filling important offices and even in arranging the marriages of princes.

A detailed investigation of Kamala Markandaya's portrayal of the three British Political Agents against the vicissitudes of fortune that befell the princely state of Devapur (between the last years of the nineteenth century and the post 1914-18 war period) helps to reveal their role in moulding the destiny of the princely states. Their roles are extremely significant in that they expose the attitudes determined by the imperial ethos of the times, the conflicting values within the individual psyche, the cultural alienation and the loss of identity suffered by imperialists.

The Empire-building ethos clashes with human values in a rather unobtrusive way in the first Political Agent (unnamed), at times giving way to softer human sentiments. In the second, Sir Arthur Copeland, Markandaya portrays "the predicament of identity," "affected by the east-west clash of codes that is part of modern India."[12] In him we see the struggle of the self caught in the conflict between real and assumed identities because his human values refuse to make compromises for his imperial role. He is therefore grouped with the Englishmen who passively submitted to the imperial role, at the same time rejecting it emotionally (Chapter IV). The third Resident, the Hon. Mr. Buckridge is an emblem of imperial brashness, as the name itself suggests. He embodies the unsympathetic authoritative attitude of the British imperialist, a person who has sacrificed his real self for the imperial role and its values.

The clever diplomacy and expert manoeuvering employed by the agents of imperial machinery are illustrated through the first Political Agent of Devapur state. He manages to dethrone and imprison Bawajiraj, the existing ruler of Devapur and install in his place "an accommodative puppet who could be trained to function according to imperial requirements" (*The Golden Honeycomb* 3-10). The British Resident's clever choice of a victualling "bania" who supplies grain for men and fodder for cattle is averted only by the timely interference of the shrewd Brahmin minister of Devapur. He suggested a scion of the ruling house as a better candidate since he belongs to the ruling caste and is a youth of irreproachable character. The mob clamouring for the dethroned king is kept happy by the Agent's interpretation of the Roman numeral attached to the new king's name—Bawajiraj II—as a symbol of continuity of the royal race. The Resident also manages to keep the prince happy by occasionally acceding to his whims, like improving the conditions of the peasantry, striving thereby to keep the chances of a revolution at bay. Ironically enough, the Resident considers it his prime responsibility to safeguard the coffers of the state from indiscriminate dissipation by the prince!

In the portrayal of the Political Agents Markandaya's achievement is remarkable in that she has been able to individualize the three representatives of the Crown. She sketches them without bitterness and hatred, "With the rapprochement afforded by the passing of time,"[13] so that even those who do ill are not villains. Through subtle strokes of her poignant irony, she reveals the concealed motive behind apparantly innocent actions, unveiling in the process the entire saga of Indo-British relations.

The hardened imperialist (the first Political Agent) responsible for the dethroning of the ruling Maharajah of Devapur State is revealed as one who has his moments of longing for his lost home. Sometimes "his heart flits back to England, his green and gentle birthplace, in which wife, children, an entire supporting web of blood relations reside. In such moments not all the pomp and power of his Indian position—which for the rest of the time suffice—can compensate the angular Agent for the voids and losses of his life." (13-14) The Political Agent is assigned a definite role in the imperial system that does not call for humanity in lesser human beings. But the unnamed Political Agent of Devapur State cannot help infusing warmth into certain functions his role assigns to him. When Bawajiraj III is born, in spite of the Minister's objections, he goes to the Maharani's chamber to felicitate the glowing pair and as he delivers his carefully prepared oration, cannot help being touched by their unaffected and radiant happiness.

The power enjoyed by the Political Agent in the alien country and the luxuries afforded by his enviable official status hardly compensate for the discomfort of the Indian climate and the various pressures that threaten to flout the interests of the Crown. The Political Agent thus passes through moments of anxiety as the minister and Mother search for a suitable alliance for the prince. His essential otherness makes it impossible to interfere in such a family affair, though loyalty to the Empire cautions against sanctioning a union whose combined strength could threaten British power. He is wary of exercising the power of veto because it can very well turn into a blunderbuss. He is fated to ride tandem with the "stringy" minister who loses no opportunity to remind him of his alienness in contrast to his oneness with land and its people. The announcement to conduct the marriage in June is like a slap on the face for the Resident for he always takes refuge in the hills in June, the hottest month of the year. His English constitution would "wilt" in the "scenes of unremitting enthusiasm" of the oriental festivities in the scorching Indian climate. (22)

Kamala Markandaya manages to dilute the villainy of the colonizer as usurper by the exposure of innate human weakness. The Agent cherishes a nostalgic dream like a pearl in an oyster. He brings it out shyly to exhibit before the Indian Dewan, Narasimha Rao, in a moment of communion when the barriers posed by racial and cultural differences fall off temporarily. "A place in the country. Really quite small, a few acres. Nothing as all this, of course." "There's a trout stream, well-stocked. I'm told and the shooting is excellent. . . . I hope to . . . " (23-24) Though the Indian Minister too has his pearl of a dream—of retiring to an ashram—he refrains from disclosing it because the Englishman may not be able to appreciate it. The spiritual yearning to get away from the din and glory of life to the tranquillity of a dilapidated ashram might not appeal to an Englishman whose dreams still have relevance only to the material world of shooting and fishing. In spite of the yawning cultural gulf projected through the situation, Kamala Markandaya comments that such rare moments of confession melt the walls between the races. About Agent and the Minister—the off-shoots of two entirely different cultures—she says: "They are of the same calibre and, basically informed by the same decencies. It is possible, even likely that had they been permitted to meet as equals they would have been friends, but the dominant/subservient roles written into and essential for the survival of Empire, of which this kingdom is a part, preclude such meeting. In the circumstances each man has done the best he can." (24)

The Hon. Mr. Buckridge is a weathered imperialist, determined to make his unpleasant presence felt in the foreign soil. The self is submerged beneath the adopted role and he is revealed as an embodiment of imperial arrogance and racism. The people's reaction to the new Resident speaks for itself: "Few felicities, it seemed to some, the tentative tendrils they had put on withdrawn, or withering: no charm and hardly a grace to redeem the saturnine figure that stalked about the place straightlipped." (326)

Mr. Buckridge was appointed after the outbreak of hostilities between India and Britain and he had come to India bristling with the awareness of the duties and responsibilities vested in him. The brash Mr. Buckridge "dripping with authority" (338) is exposed in his uncompromising imperialistic attitude by striking a contrast with the more sensitive and humane Sir Arthur Copeland and the shrewd, severe Brahmin minister. The battle of wits takes the form of an East-West conflict where the Englishman's prosaic, practical wisdom is overpowered by the sharper wits and serene complacence of the Brahmin. A typical instance is afforded by the Resident arguing at a high pitch about the need to levy more taxes and the Minister reacting, silently by producing an army of writers, clerks and chaprasies with bundles of files telling the staggering tale of exploitation through tolls, taxes, imposts and levies, under which the citizens of the state groaned and somehow contrived to pursue their activities. Buckridge remains undaunted and places his finger on the one essential commodity that had not been taxed—salt. When the Minister protests, he exercises his pressure over the weaker Maharajah, by withholding honours and imposing a curb on his fond plan of a grand tour. Mr. Buckridge proves that he has the upper hand and the Minister quietly retreats into a period of silent prayer and self-purification in penance for the crime of the exploitation of the poor. In spite of his apparent triumph over the Minister, Mr. Buckridge's inflated ego is pricked at the infinite spiritual resources of the Indian. The mystery that shrouds the Minister's thoughts and actions, the peaceful composure with which he tackles the irritant, impatient and boisterous Englishman, make the latter feel out of depths in his presence. He writes in his diary: "There is something about the Indian Mind that is Absolutely Unintelligible." (348) Later he substitutes "Hindoo" for Indian.

Buckridge displays the closed mind of the colonizer making every Indian encounter a disaster. He is furious at the children's stage representation of the state's misery under a bad ruler; he deals a harsh blow to the gentle Bawajiraj by deferring the decision for the final transfer of power from Dewan to Maharajkumar. Buckridge's career in Devapur State represents the corrosive aspects of British-Indian relationship. On his departure people of all ranks heave a sigh of relief, because all people from sweeper to Dewan had suffered in some degree, the general opinion being that the already unhappy state of affairs in Devapur would have been rendered intolerable by Mr. Buckridge.

Kamala Markandaya brings out through the attitudes of Buckridge and Arthur Copeland the subtle difference between the imperialist who has fully identified himself with the role and the one caught in the conflict between natural impulses and the demands of the artificial code. It is in the exercise of authority that they vary markedly. Whereas Mr. Buckridge revels in the use of power and exercises authority with sadistic pleasure, Sir Arthur is extremely cautious in indulging himself.

None of the other Indian English novelists have provided such full portraits of that difficult phenomenon of the British Empire—the Political Agent, whose presence and interference the princes had to put up with. Atrocities of Political Agents in the flush of imperial power are mentioned in many novels. Malgonkar refers to Edward Burton (*The Princes*), The Resident of Padmakoshal, who wantonly blew up the Begwad fort for alleged sympathy with the mutineers and then went on to annex the district of Katur. One of the Begwad kings; the second Hiroji (*The Princes*), was deposed because he had an indigo planter's moustache shaved off in public for abducting a girl from the Bulwara valley. The Resident was the one who proclaimed Ashokraj (*The Princes*) insane because he had refused to call on him when he came to visit Begwad. The prince's contention was that according to the treaty it was upto the Resident to call on him first. In *The Private Life of an Indian Prince*, Mulk Raj Anand's hero Prince Victor is mortally afraid of the Imperial Agents Col. Jevons and Col. Burton. His very assertions of nonchalance only confirm his fear of them. Prince Victor is a typical example of the weak products of a mixed heritage—of Indian culture and English public school values. He can be considered a victim of the imperial system represented by the Political Agents. By wielding imperial power, they sedulously crush his will to harness the warring powers in his mind—a perpetual battleground between old values and new demons—and reduce him to an ineffective state of servility.

The figures from British bureaucracy are mainly typecast and serve as emblems of the imperial cult that had controlled the British consciousness. They represent patterns of colonial behaviour—a subject that has aroused much interest among psychologists because of the factors that pre-determine its nature—creating a rigid mould to which the individuals are expected to conform. The Indian novelist has tried to impart some strains of individuality to these representatives of the imperial machinery, who like dummy figures play the role of the "sahib" in India, becoming dispossessed of their own individual identity, and alienating themselves from their real selves in the process.

The same behaviour patterns can be identified in the planters and missionaries who came and settled down in India—the occupied land. The shared beliefs and values emanating from a common culture and the ethnic consciousness of the English race, often resulting in herd-behaviour, are identified and examined.

The postcolonial novelist has drawn his characters from every field of activity in which the Englishman made his presence felt in India. Among the bureaucrats there are hardened jingoists like Charles Tenor (Nahal, *The Crown and the Loincloth*), Hartman (K. Nagarajan, *Chronicles of Kedaram*), Patrick Mulligan (Malgonkar, *A Bend in the Ganges*), Robert Pryor (Sahgal, *Plans for Departure*), Cyril Weatherby and Tom Granges (Sahgal, *A Time to be Happy*). They hardly suffer from any uneasy thoughts about the moral justification of their presence in India, because they are deeply convinced of their role as benefactors. They live by an inflexible code of values dictated by the imperial ethos and sustained by it. The basic tenets of their value system are moulded by the colonial ideology that believes in the moral superiority of the British and morally justifies the physical and moral subjection of the Indian by relegating him to the status of the "native"—a term that has come to acquire connotations of cultural and moral inferiority in the colonial context. Imperialism and myths of the whiteman's superiority propagated by writers like Kipling had generated a dream of empire and an illusion of sacrifice that provided the inspiration to come to India. From the Indian perspective, the imperialists's role can only be described, as Benita Parry has aptly termed it, as an instance of "superb insolence," blind "ethnocentricity" and "total egocentricity."[14] Naturally, the hardened imperialists, who are embodiments of these qualities figure as villains or anti-heroes in the Indian novel.

The edifice of the Raj as presented in Indian fiction has, as its central figurehead of authority, the Viceroy. Whereas the Political Agents reign supreme in the princely states, in those directly under British reign, civil and military officers form the props of the Raj. The higher echelons of authority are occupied by the much-celebrated ICS officers from England. As a class the English bureaucrats impress us by their high regard for duty. The fictional representation reflects the larger reality outside for they live upto the reputation of the British officers in India, who have been acclaimed as first-rate officers, unbelievably earnest in the discharge of their duties and in preserving the image of the efficient ruler. Gokhale's comment about the British officials in India is applicable to each one of them. According to him, they are "a body of picked men: . . . man for man they are better than ourselves: they have a higher standard of duty, higher notions of patriotism, higher notions of loyalty to each other, higher notions of organised work and discipline."[15]

In spite of the common attributes of the British bureaucrats in India, in the Indian English novels a sharp line of demarcation emerges between the hardened imperialists who completely identify themselves with their role and those who function passively and reject the imperial values morally and emotionally. The former group represents the colonial ethos and become the spokesmen of the Raj. Among them there are a few who experience the dilemma posed by the dichotomy of selves, like Arthur Copeland (*The Golden Honeycomb*).

Sir Charles Tenor, the Commissioner of Lahore in Nahal's *The Crown and the Loincloth* is perhaps the most undiluted picture of imperialism incarnate. He is an ego-centric bully, so steeped in the arrogance of power that he is not only alienated from the natives, but is estranged even from his white subordinates. A huge, garrulous man, he infuriates his subordinates by making snide comments on their reports, as though he is reprimanding them not only for lack of judgement but for lack of proficiency in the language as well. Tenor's contemptuous disregard for his subordinate Ashby's warnings against the public appearance of the Prince of Wales, finally lands him in trouble. The Indian English novelist cites his failure as an example of the consequence of uncompromising imperial aloofness and insolence.

Hartman, the Collector of Kedaram in K. Nagarajan's *Chronicles of Kedaram* too has to smart under the jolt of the people's organized protest (against the Simon Commission) because of his deliberate distancing from popular sentiments. Both are instances of the alienated ruler failing in the task of administration due to voids in understanding. Nagarjan drives this home by contrasting Hartman's failure with the success of the Collector of the neighbouring district, Poppali. He was able to make a success of the visit of the Simon Commission because he was a man who knew his India and went the right way to work. An unstated code of judgement implicit in the Indian novelist's perspective can be seen operating in all these cases. According to the code, the British officers who are sympathetic to India emerge as the virtuous men or heroes and those who alienate themselves turn out to be the villains. The attitude is warranted by the prejudices issuing from a colonial relationship.

T.N. Murari has provided another example of a power-corrupt English imperialist in *The Imperial Agent.* Col. Creighton believes that the English would rule India "for ever" and does not even think it necessary to set a good example before the native because according to him, "We are his rulers. We do as we please."[16] He yearns for more stringent laws that would permit oppressive measures against the Indians and even stages a fake attempt on the Prince's life causing the death of an innocent police officer, in order to impress upon the new Viceroy Lord Minto, the need for additional powers to suppress seditious activities. The innocent Anil Ray, an England-educated brilliant young lawyer becomes a pawn in his hands, to be used as an example to prove that education was wasted on a native and that severe punishment would be meted out to even an educated and aristocratic youth on suspicion of sedition. As he plays the power-game, he continues to believe staunchly that he is serving the country and fostering its interests. He has so deluded himself by the illusion of the Englishman's civilizing mission in India that "if he had been told that he was in fact an enemy of the land, an occupier, he could have stared in disbelief." (49) When it comes to safeguarding his imperial interests, the Colonel suffers from hardly any moral compunctions. Thus he sets his men to kill Kim, who had always served him and regarded him as his foster-father, once he opts not to do the dirty spy work against the Indians he loved. His wife Alice is rudely expelled from his life and his home and is denied permission to meet her children because she takes interest in the natives and gets attached to a more humane person. The greatest cruelty is the deliberate concealment of the mother's existence from the children. He is a clever manipulator who manoeuvres the rift between the Congress and the Muslim League by nurturing venomous politicians like Bahadur Sahib. He promises to make him "the first Indian" in the legislative Council if he works as a spy for the Colonel within the Congress. The author saves this picture of crooked political cunning and arrogant oppression from being reduced to a mere symbol of imperialism, by attributing him an unexpected quality—a faculty for appreciating Urdu poetry which he avidly reads and translates into English.

Patrick Mulligan (Malgonkar, *A Bend in the Ganges*), the Superintendent of the Silver Jail in Andaman Islands, is a more confirmed imperialist than the British officials in India. In him we find the perfect blend of imperial sentiments and the Victorian public school ethos, which have gone into the making of the British imperialists in India. He is presented as a conscientious and self-righteous officer who discharges his duties so meritoriously that he is promoted to the post of Superintendent of the cellular jail. He suffers no qualms about the moral validity of his presence and role in India. The Jail Manual is his gospel and he openly boasts that he has never read any other book. Together with the other imperialists in India, he glories in the possession of what E.M. Forster described as "the undeveloped heart"[17] that has narrowed down his vision to a few artificial values and drilled-in sentiments. He can never visualize anything beyond the Empire. Therefore he safeguards its interest rigorously by banning references in prisoners' letters to England's war with Germany and punishing those who dare to hail Hitler through writings on the walls. He comes down on Debi Dayal with an iron hand, when he spots him assaulting the Gurkha and trying to escape. This staunch devotee of the Empire makes an example of Debi Dayal by giving him twenty-five cane lashes in front of all the convicts. The glory of the British Empire is a myth he cannot discard, even when Britain is suffering setbacks from Germany and he desperately tries to keep up the morale of the convicts by giving reassuring talks about the undying glory of the British empire.

The Indian novelists have tried to expose the underlying system of values that shaped and moulded the character of the British imperialists. It is the Victorian public school ethos that instilled into them a zealous regard for an artificial code of values that warped the development of their natural sensibility. These values manifest themselves in Cyril Weatherby's (*A Time to be Happy*) abnormal addiction to work; Mulligan's pride in his capacity to "lick any man of his own age" and to drink any man of any age under the table;[18] Mr. Drinkwater's desperate effort to avoid losing face by sending Narayan, a normal college teacher to the lunatic asylum (*The Nowhere Man*); the English community's unusual recognition of an Indian, Sanad, (*A Time to be Happy*) as gentleman because he plays tennis; Weatherby's punctilious regard for the correct office gear—with the tie included—even on the hottest day and Mulligan's preference for torture and death at the hands of the Jaores in the jungle to "losing face" working as a manual labourer before the natives under the Japanese. Ethel M. Dell has summed up the canons of the ideal hero of Victorian England.[19] He "works like an ox" and is "indomitable, unfailing, always fulfilling his duties with a machine-like regularity, stern, impenetrable, hard as granite."[20] Allen J. Greenberger calls the Englishman in India "an overgrown public schoolboy."[21] The public school code was the major factor that shaped Victorian morality. Francis G. Hutchins describes the Victorian age as "a time of great moral seriousness" in which "an almost infinite number of systems and schemes evolved through attempts to find underpinnings for ethical obligations." (*The Illusion of Permanence* 21-22) Among the systems which contributed to the ideology of permanence were nationalism, racism, the worship of material progress and force, and the cult of good conduct. "For the majority of Englishmen it [the cult] meant little more than a vague sense that hard work and sportsmanlike play helped form character. Character itself was not associated with intelligence or learning but 'with the ability to deal with other people.'" (*Illusion of Permanence* 25) Sir Jeffrey Dart, Resident Director of the Brindan Tea Company reminds Henry Winton, the planter, of his responsibility to the Empire, with these enlightening words: "Remember that the Empire is a hellish big thing, but in the last analysis it is nothing more than a few thousand of . . . hardcoremen like you and me, doing our jobs and taking care not to let the side down."[22]

Ronny's (E.M. Forster, *A Passage to India*) view about the role of the Englishman in India expresses the ideology of each one of these bureaucrats. "I am out here to work, mind, to hold this wretched country by force. I am not a missionary or a Labour Member or a vague sentimental, sympathetic literary man. I'm just a servant of the Government; . . . We're not pleasant in India, and we don't intend to be pleasant. We've something more important to do."[23] These words could be put into the mouth of any of these supercilious, haughty officials of the Raj.

Public school education in itself was enough qualification for an Englishman to be selected to an authoritative office under the Raj. Malgonkar's comments on Henry Winton (*Combat of Shadows*) reveal the criterion for selection of British officers to India. Henry Winton, who was a failure in England, "had put on his old school tie and had gone to the London office of the Brindan Tea Company, and as soon as they had discovered that he had played rugger for his school, they had stopped asking him any further questions. They sent him off to Calcutta, first class all the way." (57) Winton's ambition and moral rectitude imbibed from the English public school, crumble in the encounter with India, bringing about complete moral disintegration. The public school products in every field—bureaucrats, missionaries or civil servants—are seen to undergo a similar change, though not perhaps to the same extent. This can be explained only by analyzing the economic and social factors that transform the life of the young, middle class Englishman when he comes to India. There is a sudden change in social status, at the first introduction to power and authority and initiation into a luxurious, indulgent style of living. Francis G. Hutchins writes: "Englishmen in India were [thus] committed, by the unwritten terms of the understanding which had brought them to India, to living in a manner well above the station from which they had sprung in England. India's function was to turn Englishmen into instant aristocrats." (*The Illusion of Permanence* 107-8)

The transformation undergone by the British officers in India is treated with remarkable perception by the Indian novelists like Kamala Markandaya, Chaman Nahal, Nayantara Sahgal. Manohar Malgonkar, K.A. Abbas and T.N. Murari. Beneath the apparent metamorphosis of the middleclass Englishman to an aristocrat, they perceive the loss of self-hood and the essential alienation from one's own identity caused by compete identification with the imperial role. In Markandaya's Arthur Copeland (*The Golden Honeycomb*) can be observed the struggle to preserve his identity and essential humanity by refusing to blend completely with the role. In Nahal's Ashby (*The Crown and the Loincloth*) too there is no emotional merging with the role. They remain actors who refuse to jeopardize their real identity in their role as servants of the Empire. But in the typical imperialists we find such total identification with the role which eventually makes them lose their real identity. Nayantara Sahgal's Tom Grange is a good example (*A Time to be Happy*). The author recounts how Tom came to India full of natural curiosity about the new country. In course of time, finer sensibilities dulled and perception grew faint as his conduct came to be governed more and more by his fellow countrymen's dictates about things that were "done" and those that were "not done." Tom gradually became more and more self-important and felt convinced that his very presence in India was accomplishing a mission. The illusion of a noble mission involving sacrifice came to cover the privileges of a colonizer he enjoyed. "This realization altered the tilt of his head and an authoritarian ring crept into his voice."[24] Tom is happily unconscious of the distancing from his own selfhood brought about by the artificial values of the English officialdom in India. Sacrifice of old ideals and acclimatization to the new are especially painful to some. Rogers (*A Bend in the Ganges*), the young British officer who escorts the prisoners to the Silver Jail, becomes guilty and uneasy at Debi Dayal's complaints about the stench from the barrel that serves as latrine for the prisoners. He has to remind himself of the pep talk he had received before joining the service "essential not to let the side down . . . important to back up your official subordinates—always." (118) Once they get over the initial dilemma and transform themselves into "pucca sahibs," the alienation from their own identity is complete.

This entails a blunting of human sentiments, hardening of attitudes towards the Indian and the scrupulous alienation from the native. Henry Winton (*Combat of Shadows*), Firth (*Plans for Departure*), Cyril Weatherby (*A Time to be Happy*) and Patrick Mulligan (*A Bend in the Ganges*) are typical examples. The awareness of one's own racial superiority supported by literature propagating myths of a noble mission and the indispensability of the British presence in India, led to the growth of ethnic feelings among the Englishmen in India. Hence the widespread currency of the term "nigger" which came to be used indiscriminately for Indians or anyone who is not white. The tyranny of officials in power and the brutality of planters and police officers can only be explained by the total rejection of individual selfhood and its attendant values and complete identification with the privileged role of the colonizer. The trampling of the native becomes his prerogative and colonialism is glorified through sugar-coated expressions like "a civilizing mission" or "the whiteman's burden." The Englishman in India at this stage is projected in the Prospero-role of the colonizer that justifies and condones the denigration of the native to "the half-child," "half-savage" image of Caliban.[25] The Prospero complex generates a desire to punish and dominate the native as is evidenced by the oppressive measures employed by the instruments of the Raj—the British police. The attitude of the English sergeant in *The Nowhere Man* is quite representative. He looks down on the human run with "an attitude which annihilated any basis of parity between the two human races, substituting the split levels of vassal and overlord."[26] The Sergeant who goes to Srinivas's (*The Nowhere Man*) house on suspicion of seditious activities is infuriated on finding no evidence and seeks relief in humiliating the young and innocent Vasantha. Ralph Sparrow in T.N. Murari's *The Imperial Agent* gives vent to his terror, frustration and disillusionment by humiliating and harassing him, whose only crime was that he picked up the dead body of the bridegroom shot dead by Sparrow's policemen. Sparrow is the case of a young and ambitious Englishman, feeling cheated and disillusioned when posted in a lonely outpost, without European company, stranded among strangers, as though he had been "shoved out to sea with a boatload of strangers." (247)

The novels dealing with the freedom movement abound in incidents of savage cruelty with which the English police tried to wreck the spirit of the nationalists. Khushwant Singh's Sita (*I shall not Hear the Nightingale*) recounts how a boy volunteer of fourteen or fifteen going to picket an English store, fell at a sergeant's blow and rolled down the steps, bleeding profusely. (143) The innocent Raghubir, a clerk in Silkirk and Lowe, has his head split open when an English sergeant attacks a group of student demonstrators. (*A Time to be Happy* 139) The young Sahdev, walking peacefully along the pavement is killed at one shot because he did not step off it, to give way to a memsahib coming toward him. (*A Time to be Happy* 192) A white sergeant finishes off Kishore because he walks on the special track along which His Excellency the Viceroy's special train is to travel. (*So Many Hungers* 143) The day before the Jallianwallabagh massacre, a young boy Krishan (the fictional guise of Mulk Raj Anand in *Morning Face*) is arrested and flogged for breaking the curfew. Abbas makes Webb Miller, an American journalist his spokesman when he declares to the Viceroy's face that in eighteen years of reporting in two dozen countries he had not witnessed such harrowing scenes as being staged daily by the British armed police as they assault non-violent Indian volunteers (*Inquilab*). In *The World is My Village*, the second part of *Inquilab*, two British military officers whom Anwar and Robert Mills meet on a train to Delhi give animated reports of how they took three planes and sprayed machine-gun bullets from the air on a mob of unarmed, marching Indians. In reply to Anwar's question about the number of casualities, the dehumanized instruments of the imperial regime remark with casual cruelty: "You can never say in such an aerial operation. May be a few dozens . . . may be, more! They fell into ditches and irrigation channels, besides those who fell in the fields, where they tried to hide in the standing crop. So we sprayed the crop also to make sure none escaped."[27]

Orwell, himself a part of the oppressive machinery of the British government in Burma, had diagnosed the root of the cruelty of the English colonizer as the guilt caused by the humbug of the "white man's burden" and the big lie of a noble mission. Flory, a character in *Burmese Days* gives expression to the disgust he experienced "in living a lie," which corrupts them "in ways you can't imagine. There's an everlasting sense of being a sneak and a liar that torments us and drives us to justify ourselves night and day. It's at the bottom of half our beastliness to the natives. We Anglo-Indians could be almost bearable if only we could admit that we're thieves and go on thieving without humbug."[28]

Nirad C. Chaudhuri attributes the degeneration in English conduct and behaviour in India to the effect of the Indian climate and weather on the English character. Chaudhuri writes: "Their sense of proportion broke down, the habit of understatement disappeared, and they became extremists with an incredible stridency in their opinions, which became raw and crude. In many cases they degenerated into outright cads, and the more sensitive or specialized the English organism, the more warped it became."[29] The artificial code to which they conformed in India was, according to him a method employed "to avert this unconscious transformation." (*The Continent of Circe* 136) He points out that Kipling saw this with his intuitive insight and advised his countrymen to give up trying to remain as complex and nuanced as they were born and taught to be, and to become instead clean wolves: "Wash daily from nose-tip to tail tip: drink deeply, but never too deep; And remember the night is for hunting, and forget not the day is for sleep."[30]

According to Nirad C. Chaudhuri, if English life in India was to be kept sane and wholesome, it "had to run, like a train, on rails, and the two rails were patriotism and duty. To allow anybody to slip off that rigid track was to invite disaster as much in public as in private life." (137)

The transmutation of personality brought about by the dispossession of self-hood in the colonial set-up, is perhaps a more valid reason for imperial despotism. The dehumanization of the colonized leads to the colonizer's own dehumanization. That is why Sartre has said: "The engine of colonialism turns in a circle."[31] The segregated mind steeped in illusions of its own glory ceases to view its emotional and physical responses in a detached and critical manner. Charles Dilke's comment that an Englishman visiting India would be horrified by what he saw of his countrymen in India aptly sums up the situation. "England in the East is not the England that we know," says Dilke.[32]

Through Anil Ray, the England-educated Indian youth victimised by the British, T.N. Murari voices his views on the duality of the British character. He says: "You are two people. One I have known well and amongst them I have spent many years of my life. I shall always remember them as friendly, decent, compassionate and open to intellectual debate, believing deeply in the freedom of the individual." (*The Imperial Agent* 128) He likens these Englishmen in England to Jekyll and those who have come to India to Hyde. "They undergo a change in their passage and what arrives on these shores are thousands of Mr. Hydes, tyrants who exile us from our own land on mere whim, imprison us because we want freedom from tyranny, execute us for our rage, suppress our thoughts with impunity." (130) Robert Mills, the American journalist, puts it like this: "That is the contradiction of England's Liberal Imperialism. You can call it—Liberalism at Home and Imperialism abroad!" (*The World is My Village* 446)

The Indian novels project what S.C. Harrex has described as "the morally vacuous insularity of the British community in India"[33] which is one of the main factors responsible for the alienation of the Englishman from the native. Francis G. Hutchins remarks: "The most obvious fact of social life in nineteenth century India was the distance between the two races, distance in every sense of the word." (*The Illusion of Permanence* 101) They tried to plant little Englands in order to segregate themselves from any contact with India. Tc quote Benita Parry, "By the mid nineteenth century racial exclusiveness had become an Anglo-Indian imperative and the community clung tenaciously to the corporate character it had evolved, closing its ranks and attempting to protect its mind against the encroachment of India." (*Delusions and Discoveries* 53)

Kamala Markandaya describes at length the cloistered social life of the English in India in *Some Inner Fury*. English life followed a set pattern in the Presidency with the mofussil-men playing golf or squash in the evenings and women visiting friends in the mornings to play mahjongg. The club was the fulcrum of English social life. The club afforded an exclusive racial aloofness which was ego-gratifying to the British and awe-inspiring to the native. Life in the club on Saturdays was made more colourful by a dance. Membership to the club was exclusively reserved for the English. It was not only a refuge for the lonely and hardworking Englishmen: it was a haven where they could indulge in their English habits without inhibitions. Orwell has described the club as "that remote mysterious temple, that holy of holies for harder of entry than Nirvana!" (*Burmess Days* 147-48). The club is symbolic of "the closed-mind attitude of the ruling class."[34] Kamala Markandaya describes how even when the nationalist movement was raging outside, within the closed walls of the government house, the English community gathered together to enjoy the highlight of the year—the ball at the Government House where the cream of the society gathered. Not to be seen at least at one of these balls meant confinement to a social limbo where one's existence was no longer recognized. Therefore the Government House balls always caused a great deal of tension, heartburning and anxiety. Precise codes and customs prevailed in the charmed society of the English. There was no place in it for those who were ignorant of the rules. If they still presumed to enter, they received no pity: "the walls of the club building were their bastions of freedom behind which they could be as they were, beyond which no Indian could intrude except those who had passed through the fine sieve of selection and whose intrusive powers were therefore minimal."[35] As C.S. Lewis remarked about the refuge of the club in Kipling's stories, it functioned as the "Inner Ring of the Empire."[36]

The close similarity of Nayantara Sahgal's description of the club life in Sharanpur (*A Time to be Happy*) is an indication of the unvaried routine of the artificial life adopted by the British in India. They were so fastidious about the image projected in the presence of the native, that the suppressed self could come out only in the exclusively English atmosphere of the club. Nayantara Sahgal points out how the club provided a fortress for the Granges, Hartleys and other sahibs and memsahibs for self-indulgence and free uninhibited talk. The war and other unpleasant topics were scrupulously avoided in this make-believe world of joy. The historic Quit-India movement was to the ladies just a hindrance to their shopping-sprees. The general reaction it provoked was one of righteous indignation at the ingratitude of Indians and their preposterousness in thinking that they would be able to manage without the British.

A gradual change reluctantly accepted in English circles is apparent in the admission of an educated and accomplished Indian like Sanad (*A Time to be Happy*) into the exclusive world of the English club. The anglicized Indian is occasionally admitted as an exception to the rule—a tendency evident in the 20s and 30s, the decades preceding Independence. In *Some Inner Fury* and *So Many Hungers*, there are references to the parties at the Government Guest House attended by a select few from Indian society. Though this meant a slight increase in racial intercourse, the novelists bring out the ineffectively concealed trace of resentment at the civilized behaviour of the enlightened Indian. John Trent's fury at the impertinence of Sanad in demanding a higher salary as compensation for destroying the Indian monopoly of cloth trade reflects the attitude of the English community (*A Time to be Happy*). Robert Pryor (*Plans for Departure*) too expresses the same sentiment to Nicholas: "They don't see us as morally superior anymore. The war did that, Europeans falling out among themselves. The old imperial magic is gone."[37] One is reminded of the reaction of Ellis, a character in *Burmese Days*, when provoked by the correct English spoken by a native servant. "Have you swallowed a dictionary? . . . We shall have to sack this fellow if he gets to talk English too well. I can't stick servants who talk English." (*Burmese Days* 23) The great days of the Empire had been when they were leading the natives towards the light of civilization. It became distinctly unbearable when the light actually came within the range of vision.

The change that came over the club was equally unpalatable to the Englishman. Nayantara Sahgal exposes the frustration of the Englishman when confronted by the threat of prohibition and the admission of dark-skinned Indians into the charmed circle of the club. A disillusioned Tom Grange comments on the changes in Bombay: "Place [sic] isn't what it used to be. . . . The Willingdon Club's as dead as dodo, used to be as fine a club as I've seen anywhere." (*A Time to be Happy* 238) The disruption of his guarded citadel is perhaps to the Englishman, the greatest tragedy that could have followed the fall of the Empire. Another interesting phenomenon observed and dwelt at length by Kamala Markandaya in *Coffer Dams* is the clannish tendency of the English to form clubs and stick together even after Independence.

Though the illusion of sacrifice boosted the morale of the Englishman in India, the discomforts posed by "the pestiferous vapours of India's least salubrious climate"[38] were an unpleasant reality to be reckoned with. The discovery of the hill-station came as a boon to the English who tried to set up replicas of England in the cool sanctuary of the hills where officials constantly retired and relaxed in the round of typical English amusements. In *Inquilab*, the Viceroy is accused of enjoying the luxuries of Simla, hardly conscious of the fact that the country was fuming like a volcano. Officials like Sir Arthur Copeland (*The Golden Honeycomb*) whose duties prevented them from enjoying the pleasure of life in the hill-station sweated it out alone in official routine, for the family would be packed off to avoid the gruelling on the plains. The loneliness often became more unbearable to the Englishman than the heat. Life at the hill stations is not discussed at length in any of the Indian novels, probably owing to the Indian's unfamiliarity with the life of the English in the hill resorts. Like the clubs, the hill stations also served to widen the rift between the races, closing possibilities for interracial communication and understanding.

Through the subtle use of irony the Indian novelists expose the shallowness of the English amusements at the club and the hill station. Neither institution could boast of any kind of intellectual or artistic diversions. Cyril Weatherby (*A Time to be Happy*) is said to have no problems of adjustment in Sharanpur because it had no pretensions to culture and was purely a commercial city. Weatherby had only to fall into place in the British community life fashioned round the exclusive English club, with its reassuring English pastimes of tennis and golf followed by drinks. Nayantara Sahgal's delicate irony moves in and out of the portrait as she comments: "No awkward nonsense here about the arts, which in some of his other posts had made Weatherby feel out of depth." (165) The attitude reflects that of typical imperialists like Robert Pryor (*Plans for Departure*), the Hon. Buckridge (*The Golden Honeycomb*) and Tom Grange (*A Time to be Happy*). There is a yawning void in their natures that endorses Forster's comment: "Their ignorance of the arts was notable and they lost no opportunity of proclaiming it to one another: it was the Public school attitude; flourishing more vigorously than it can yet hope to do in England." (*A Passage to India* 40) A taste for the arts marred the English concept of the manly, hardworking English official in India, whose favourite pastimes are shooting tigers, playing polo and participating in horse races. The King of Begwad in *The Princes* is depicted as a favourite with the English officials because he could promise a tiger to any aspiring British officer. It was an ego-satisfying game that boosted the morale of the superior Englishman. Riding is the favourite pastime of Sir Arthur Copeland (*The Golden Honeycomb*) when he feels free from the ties of officialdom. The Englishman in India would indulge in only those games that had the attribute of masculinity attached to them so as to preserve their image before the natives.

Rejection of identity and total identification with the aggressive role of the imperialist are prominent features in the planter class portrayed in Indian English fiction. The tea plantations in India lured the imagination of the British and several Englishmen did successful business as tea planters. The planters appearing in the post-Independence novels are the replicas of the tyrannical set portrayed by Mulk Raj Anand (*Two Leaves and a Bud*) and Raja Rao (*Kanthapura*). The plantations in India had been centres of colonial exploitation under the British Raj and the post-Independence novelists also stress this aspect. Whereas Anand and Raja Rao focus their vision on the racial and capitalist exploitation in the estates, Malgonkar's emphasis is on Henry Winton (*Combat of Shadows*) as a case study in the moral disintegration brought about by the failure to live up to the code that forms the strength and glory of the Englishman in India. Though an imperialist to the core, Winton is far from a representative of his class; through his disaster, it is not the fall of a class, but the disintegration of an individual that is depicted. This is brought about more by individual lapses than class prejudices. Winton's fall through neglect of the code is represented through his failure as a planter and a hunter. He fails to win the respect of the labourers in the plantation because of his contemptuous attitude and his moral instability. He sets his dog after a woman seen stealing tea-leaves but falls into a momentary weakness at the sight of her unexpected beauty and fails to deal with her firmly. He exposes his weakness by allowing her to take the stolen property. He appoints Ruby Miranda the attractive Anglo-Indian girl as the headmistress of the school in the plantation, superceding the more qualified Indian teacher already employed there, again exposing himself to the criticism of the natives. With Ruby Miranda he commits the blunder of getting emotionally involved, which according to Sudden Dart would mean "crossing the line" and tarnishing the image of the pucca sahib. As a hunter he not only fails in killing the rogue elephant, but behaves like a coward by deserting his shikari at the moment of danger. M.K. Naik comments that Malgonkar adopts a totally pucca sahib attitude reminiscent of Kipling and John Masters in depicting

Winton's failure through neglect of the sahib's code. His failure is brought home through his own constant mental evaluations of his actions against the standards expected by Sudden Dart, who "represents the British Empire even more than the Viceroy himself." (*Combat of Shadows* 91) Dart gave others "an impression of rugged strength and power, of uncompromising toughness." (30) His artificial code for the English bureaucrat in India, has no bearings on moral values. There is no harm in the planters seeking "discreet ways of finding one's fun on a plantation" with coolie women, but "crossing the line" with an Anglo-Indian was a serious indiscretion. (33) The Empire rested on "hard-core men" (34) like Dart and Winton, but when it came to dealing with crooked politicians like Jugul Kishore, it was not toughness that was needed as Winton supposed, but tact and clever diplomacy. Dart exemplifies the code thus: "We don't grow morals in the tea district, Henry: we grow tea. And whatever is conducive to the growth of tea we foster. . . . There's nothing wrong in the judicious payment of money to keep the right people on our side; indeed it might be called the bedrock of the Empire's frontier strategy." (228)

The vague flutter of Winton's uneasy self is seen at rare moments like when he thinks of owning up his guilt in victimizing his shikari Kistulal and when he becomes violently sick in the privacy of his bathroom after ruthlessly punishing the striking labourers on his plantation. He recognizes that in the effort to conform to the sahib's code, he is dehumanizing himself. The comment throws light on the inner transformation: "His whole being ached to get away from it all, before he was irretrievably sucked in, before he learnt to accept physical violence to passive, unresisting men and women as a part of life, like the dead-eyed Bengali police inspector; or before he broke down altogether." (*Combat of Shadows* 141)

It is Winton's tragedy that he does not attempt to salvage his self; nor does he succeed in living upto the image of the pucca sahib. Lax morals and disregard of all scruples seem to be common features among the planter-class, as portrayed by the Indian novelists. Sudden Dart, the Resident Director of the Tea Estates (*Combat of Shadows*) is a highly pragmatic imperialist, who is interested in growing tea and not morals. Wallach, Winton's predecessor, is spoken of as an Englishman who kept native women as mistresses. Firth (*Plans for Departure*) is the tyrannical bully who believes in settling disputes in his estate by employing toughs to beat them up. As a class the planters seem to have been more tyrannical than even the most authoritative civil officers, threatening local magistrates who tried to interfere on behalf of plantation workers. . . . They stuck together and rampaged together." (41) There were hardly any disputes in Firth's plantations for he knew how to deal with them. Flogging was a usual practice. When Marlowe Croft accosted Firth with the demand for the funeral expenses of a tenant who was beaten to death in the estate, Firth dismissed him with the contemptuous words: "I' ve dealt with the meddlers before, the whole misguided lot from the Viceroy down to the newspapers and daft district magistrates who thought they could tell me how to run my plantation." (41) The planters as a class stood by Firth and took liberal action against Marlowe who had to spend three months in jail. Firth's only failure occurred in the case of his daughter Lulu—his only weakness—who chose Marlowe Croft as her life-long companion. The blow had a shattering effect on Firth who was "glued to the dancing edge of madness for the rest of his life." (42)

The missionaries depicted by the Indian novelists also conform to the imperial code because to the Englishman in India Christianity provided another ground for superiority. The proselytizing mission acquired an aura of a noble and sacrificial endeavour to bring the light of God to the unbelievers groping in darkness. Naturally it entailed a sense of superiority that brought with it an assumption of authority and racial arrogance. Thus Marlowe Croft, the missionary in *Plans for Departure* assumes that the church is a symbol of white solidarity and tries with dogged determination to win over the souls of Indians. Anna, the Danish assistant of the scientist Bose, serves as Nayantara Sahgal's mouthpiece in expressing her indignation at this white invasion of Indian beliefs and traditions.

Croft's dogged determination "to break new spiritual ground" (*Plans for Departure* 48) in a country with its staggeringly old religions takes on the quality of an imperial assault on the village of Himapur. The admission of an untouchable into a class where caste Hindus were given physical training again indicates his aggressive attitude towards native customs. For a person who was disowned by the Christian Church, Marlowe Croft's overzealous determination to spread the Gospel in Himapur and the identification of his role with that of Moses, almost verges on lunacy. Though he professes Christianity so strongly, we find the absolute negation of Christian values in Marlowe Croft's growing aggressiveness. There comes a moment when Marlowe feels that even Lucille's loyalty to his mission was at breaking point and with her lack of faith and blunt talk she seems to be the one enemy that stood in his way. Lucille's timely death by accident affirms Stella's view about Croft as "a sadistic man" who bullied his wife and we are forced to share Anna's suspicions about the man behind the murder. Ironically enough, the Christian missionary is cast into a most un-Christian role where imperial arrogance and doggedness overwhelm finer Christian sentiments.

Kamala Markandaya's Hickey (*Some Inner Fury*) is an over-enthusiastic missionary waging a lonely battle in the alien country. Unlike Marlowe he is able to build a school and coax children into it and even win over the trust and confidence of Premala and secure her assistance. The extremists' attack reduces his life's dreams to ashes and brings to the surface the hard core of the imperialist underneath. In the hour of trial Hickey loudly denounces Govind as though the truth does not matter any longer. In the politically charged atmosphere of the times, the Hickey-Govind conflict assumes the proportions of a racial battle and Hickey becomes the voice of the Empire. As the English rally round the demented Hickey, who appears like a dead man, Mira too recognizes her folly in the choice of an Englishman as life-partner. Thus Hickey becomes instrumental in driving a wedge into the Richard-Mira relationship and igniting the feelings of the Indian mob gathered outside the court. The two portraits are highly prejudiced ones reflecting the resentment of the Indian at the imposition of an alien religion through imperialistic means. At the same time the writers have brought in a touch of pathos into the lives of these men who suffered heavy odds in their endeavour to fulfil what they considered as a holy mission.

Mr. and Mrs. Bridie in *Pleasure City* stand apart from Marlowe Croft and Hickey in that they appear in Independent India, as relics of an Empire that is no more. There is hardly anything imposing about them and their role in the novel is restricted to their love and understanding for Rikki, the fisherboy, whom they lent new aspirations and dreams. They represent the plight of the English who are compelled to stay on in independent India and remind us of the old English couple in Paul Scott's novel *Staying On*. They linger on in India clinging to nostalgic memories of a homeland to which they could never return. Their influence on Rikki symbolizes the impact of western education, cultural values and the sophisticated sensibility of the west on the average Indian who becomes a product of the two entirely different cultures and is doomed to suffer the dilemma of existing in a cultural limbo.

The Indian novelists have succeeded in exposing how the Empire made its presence felt in every aspect of life—civil administration, religion and even education. To the youth of India the Empire manifested itself in its most terrible form through the British inspectors of schools, whose visits were a nightmare to students and teachers. Mulk Raj Anand's Marsden (*Morning Face*) is a typical example. Marsden is a highly coloured portrait of an imperialist deriving sadistic pleasure from kicking innocent children and striking terror into their hearts through his shouting. To the children "the anger of a red-faced sahib seemed to be more terrible than that of a demon like Master Bishan Singh, because no one could guess what further terrors lay behind the master's red face.[41] On the one hand, there is the picture of the stamping, bullying sahib bordering on caricature and on the other there is the more subtle machinery of British education working its way into the minds of the Indian youth, gradually alienating them from their own cultural values and ultimately throwing them into a state of conflict and alienation. As a new brand of anglicized Indians they would be so estranged from their own roots that they would serve as passive instruments of the British government and strengthen the Empire further. The nature of education imparted is based on the system evolved in the English public schools, irrespective of the fact that the public school code has no validity in the Indian atmosphere. Thus we find Mr. Mercado (*Morning Face*), the Headmaster going to the cricket ground to impart the value of games to the children. Anand's novel reveals how the accent was on the recitation of English poems and playing English games; nationalistic activities among students were ruthlessly suppressed. Idealistic involvement in Arya Samajist activities was enough reason for the cutting down of financial grant to schools (*Morning Face*). The fury of Prof. Brown (*Bachelor of Arts*), when a student of the college read a paper in the History Association pillorying the British government, is ample illustration of the parochial attitude of the British.

The British tutors specially imported from England to train the young Indian princes also formed part of the imperial strategy. They gradually alienated the princes from the history and culture of India so that they would take pride in becoming subjects of the Raj. It was a subtle process of enslaving the Indian princes. Mr. Barrington, tutor to Bawajiraj, is described as an Englishman who "has a touching and unshakable belief in the soundness and moral integrity of the Empire and is convinced in all sincerity that India can do no better than to submit to the British presence. This view he is transparently eager to transmit to "his pupil." (*The Golden Honeycomb* 17) Mr. Frederick Moreton, the English tutor to Prince Abhayraj and Mr. Walter Ludlow (*The Princes*), the headmaster of the Chelmsford Princes' College at Agra uphold the public school code that prevailed in Victorian England. With the daily lessons on English customs and manners Mr. Moreton instilled in the war-like Bedar Prince, public school properties like correct dress and manners and typical Victorian concepts like a "ready-knotted tie" indicating bad bringing up. Moreton is a typical colonial instrument steeped in imperial values and one of a class that was responsible for bringing about the alienation of the Indian princes from the country they had to govern and its problems. Mr. Frederick Moreton rises above his role and gives Abhayaraj the warmth of a human friendship and becomes a guide, mentor and life-long companion to his ward. Ludlow's gift to his students is the simplified Victorian public school code which he holds sacred like Gospel truth. The Princes from different Indian states discarded under his guidance their centuries-old culture and religious heritage and learned to accept Kipling's "If" as their guiding principle in life. Ludlow's simple maxims and faith in the public school code took the place of the complexities of Indian religions and the profundities of Indian philosophy. Playing one's cards honourably, settling differences by open fights, excelling in sports, being manly and accepting one's losses with a brave face—were the cardinal virtues according to him. About Barrington's painstaking tutoring of Bawajiraj III, Kamala Markandaya remarks: "He forms a team and coaches him at cricket—not just how to win, but how to lose gracefully. This is excellent practice for the prince, who will have to give ground later on, on grand scale, undertaken in this spirit." (*The Golden Honeycomb* 18) The efficacy of the system represented by these men is best judged by the finished product that emerges from the Military Academy that follows the Chief's college. He turns out to be proficient in the superficial arts of civilized living, but totally ignorant of the requirements of his people and the conditions of his country. He is thoughtless of the need to retrieve what India has lost through years of subservience to the foreign yoke.

The Indian response to the British had always been ambivalent—admiration and respect on the one hand and indignation and hatred on the other. Ashis Nandy speaks of an unbreakable dyadic relationship developing between the ruler and the ruled due to what is diagnosed in psychoanalysis as identification with the aggressor."[42] O. Mannoni in his study of the psychology of colonization goes a step further and points out that a colonized people transfer to the colonizer "the feelings of dependence, the prototype of which is to be found in the affective bond between father and son."[43] These theories explain the ambivalence of the Indian novelist towards the British imperialists. The Indian novelists reiterate the fairness, sense of justice and incorruptibility of English judges and administrators. . . . The English made admirable judges, were fair and impartial though they spoke in a throaty way and were stiff and stand-offish."[44] The sense of justice and incorruptibility of English judges is an oft-repeated theme in Malgonkar's *A Bend in the Ganges*. To quote the character Hari, "we were lucky there was a British judge—no question of bribing him, though the Big House must have done their best. . . . We in India can get justice only at British hands—

never from our own people. They are clean—clean as grains of washed rice." (33) The "fire-eating" Mr. Stewart (*A Bend in the Ganges* 49), the conscientious Mr. Kemble (*Chronicles of Kedaram*) and Mr. Limaye (*Chronicles*) are drawn as gentlemen who inspire respect by their scrupulous adherence to the higher values of truth and justice. Lala Kanshi Ram in Chaman Nahal's *Azadi* even exclaims that "there indeed was no Raj like the Angrez Raj."[45]

The trial of Govind in *Some Inner Fury*, which bears a close resemblance to that of Dr. Aziz in *A Passage to India*, gives room for doubt as to whether the Englishman's impartiality and sense of fairness came out only in cases where both the plaintiff and the defendant were Indians. Racial prejudices became pronounced when one of the parties involved was an Englishman. Kamala Markandaya highlights this parochial aspect of English justice in *Some Inner Fury* when even a Christian missionary fails to adhere to the truth. One needs no better evidence than the exoneration of Dyer after the gross atrocity of the Jallianwallah Bagh massacre. Shamsul Islam comments: "The British can be efficient, fair and impartial administrators as long as they are solving a problem involving Indians alone, but lose their cool as soon as the clash is between themselves and the Indians."[46]

Even justice becomes coloured by ethnocentric attitudes. Commenting on the deterioration in the collective behaviour of the British in India, Nirad C. Chaudhuri writes:

> It is strange that while dealing out justice between Indian and Indian they were outstandingly successful, especially before the nationalism movement queered the pitch of impartiality, in regard to relations between themselves and us, the British in India lost all sense of right and wrong, truth and falsehood, charity and malice, and paraded a racial arrogance whose mildest form was a stony silence or in the case of unavoidable meetings an abrupt, business like termination without even any wishing back to an Indian's wish, and the worst was an obstreperous violence. (*The Continent of Circe* 138)

The British Indian army was the most powerful machinery for imperial administration and expansion. The prominent features of the Army highlighted in Indian fiction are its consciousness of ethnic superiority, its domineering attitude towards the subjugated nation, its exclusive style of living and special code of conduct. The most elaborate pictures of army life are provided by Mulk Raj Anand and Manohar Malgonkar. Both have an intimate knowledge of the British Indian army, lending their accounts an authentic flavour. Malgonkar introduces through *The Devil's Wind* the British soldiers of the pre-mutiny era and their typical colonial response to the unexpected and organized revolt of the Indians. The novel provides evidence for the violence and savagery that racial arrogance and ambition for conquest and domination can lead to. The higher pay and greater privileges enjoyed by the British soldiers in India naturally bred in them feelings of racial arrogance and a sense of superiority which is manifested through the course of the mutiny. The inflexible code of values that governed their attitudes made the white soldiers—popularly referred to as "tommies"—a class apart. Any violation of the code of racial exclusiveness was not condoned, as the experience of Hugh Wheeler clearly indicates. He is victimized and refused promotion, even though he is the most experienced and efficient military officer, because he has committed the unpardonable crime of marrying an Indian lady. The novelist shows how the mutiny brings out the elements of savagery and beastliness in the British.

A slight change in attitude is indicated in the novels depicting the army during the Raj era though it does not imply any thorough transformation. The bitter lessons of the mutiny dictated caution, slightly tempering the tone of authority. Occasional instances of cordiality are recorded though they continue to be exceptions rather than the rule. Mulk Raj Anand in his autobiographical novel *Seven Summers* recollects how Captain Owen condescended to take Krishan in his gig on his way to the maidan. (42) There is an elaborate description of the joyful moments that the entire family shares when Colonel Langden, the Officer commanding the regiment of Krishan's father sends them a box of gifts and a basket of fruit. (118-19) The predominant impression the novel conveys through the experiences of Krishan's father, Ram Chand, Head Clerk of Regiment, is one of constant fear, anxiety and servility which the Indians felt in the service of the English military officers. On the one hand there is the hard effort to please the sahibs, and on the other the constant fear of being suspected of disloyalty. The Indian subordinates are held in perpetual awe of what Mulk Raj Anand calls "the superficial manifestations of Sahibhood."[47] The aloofness and exclusive insularity of the sahibs in the cantonment is described through the childhood impressions of Krishan.

> But the whole atmosphere of the cantonment was dominated by the superior, exalted white sahibs, who lived rich lives in sequestered bungalows curtained off and protected from the dust, flies and natives by tall private hedges, sahibs who occasionally emerged in smart clear-cut clothes, who went about silent and

> mysterious, pink and red blurs, an unknown and unknowable element, except in the gossip of orderlies, bearers and shopkeepers. (*Seven Summers* 96)

The insolence of the class is illustrated through various incidents. Krishan's father reports that the army officers were extremely angry at the indiscipline displayed at the Delhi Durbar, not only by the crowd, but even by one of the Princes, the Maharajah of Baroda, who had turned his back to the "Badshah George Panjam" as he retreated after bowing before his suzerain. (*Seven Summers* 107) Kamala Markandaya records how an Indian cook and a coolie were murdered for petty crimes by the soldiers of the 9th Lancers. (*The Golden Honeycomb* 113) The English community joined to condemn the Viceroy Lord Curzon—whose Christian conscience was deeply disturbed by the incident—for punishing the miscreants. He had committed thereby the unpardonable crime of letting the side down and joining the natives. Captain Cunnigham Sahib (*Seven Summers*) walking with a catapult in hand, was followed eagerly by Krishan only to be sent back shrieking with pain because the irritated Captain actually shot the catapult at him, hurting him in the arm. Debi Dayal's mother, waiting for her son at the entrance of the house was assaulted by a drunken English soldier—an incident that turned Debi Dayal into a bitter rebel against the British government. (*A Bend in the Ganges* 74) The greatest single atrocity that shocked the Indian mind was the Jallianwallah massacre—the cold-blooded butchery of three hundred and seventy nine Indians by Gen. Dyer. (*A Bend in the Ganges, The Crown and the Loincloth, Inquilab*) The incident is discussed by Malgonkar, Nahal and Abbas in their novels exposing the stark cruelty to which racial arrogance can lead. The worst example of ethnic egoism is perhaps the "crawling order" issued by Dyer soon after the massacre so that anyone going down the Kucha Kaurianwala alley had to crawl on his belly. (*The Crown and the Loincloth, A Bend in the Ganges*) The action symbolizes the imperialist's urge to trample on the native, destroying his self-respect and dignity. Mulk Raj Anand recounts how the military officers inspired so much terror among the people that there was a general sense of caution, circumspection and an awe-stricken attitude towards the sahibs. (*Seven Summers* 141)

The ethnic consciousness of the British military officers is exposed by Malgonkar through the discrimination practised against Indians during the British withdrawal from Burma. Though Indian soldiers had been employed in large numbers for the war, during their withdrawal from Burma the British adopted an attitude that revealed their constricted racism. The essential qualification for evacuation was white skin. "Whether you were to be saved or not depended on the colour of your skin. It was not merely a matter of white first' but white only." (*A Bend in the Ganges* 273) Deserving promotions were denied to Indian soldiers. The highest rank that an Indian could aspire to was that of a Major. "The British had never made an Indian a Brigadier yet," reveals Malgonkar in *A Bend in the Ganges.* (270)

Malgonkar celebrates the army code preached and practised by the British military officers and handed over to Indians when they pulled out. His novel *Distant Drum* has been described as "an epitaph for the British Indian army."[48] It is documentation of army life in its serious aspects and depicts the success of an Indian military officer in living upto the mystic code. There is implied irony in the Indian officer's effort to live up to a code moulded to suit British character and ideals. The study of the novel is most significant in that it is an authentic and detailed exposition of a system of values that became a way of life for the military men under the Raj. The three military officers Col. Edward Manners, Ropey Booker and Girgut Jones represent three different attitudes in imperial behaviour. Col. Manners, singularly unfortunate in his career, vents his frustration on the Indian race as a whole, giving rise to open clashes with the officers of his regiment. Ropey Booker is presented as a contrast to Col. Manners, being the ideal officer by English standards. He has a high sense of duty and absolute dedication to the army he served. To the soldiers who served under him, he embodies the army code, being brave and efficient, able to inspire respect in subordinates and command their implicit obedience. He was able to instill in the fresh recruits a high sense of responsibility and the ambition to die in glory as a soldier rather than give up his career and the code. Ironically enough, the same officer turns a "boxwallah" with the fall of the Empire, shaking off the self-imposed responsibilities of a colonialist and handing over the "white man's burden" to the independent Indian.

According to the code that glorifies Ropey Booker and condemns Col. Manners, Col. Jones, the smug and conceited British officer who takes over command of the Satpuras from Col. Booker, appears almost ridiculous. Though kind and without any anti-Indian bias, he is looked down upon by the Regiment because he has never seen active service and therefore cannot satisfy the code. He is thorough in the tactics of war and is able to impress the others by his elaborate tactics. In spite of his failure to live upto the code he gets promoted to Full Colonel and gets appointed as Director of Training at the Army headquarters.

Major Bob Medley (*Distant Drum*) is a tragic instance of the collapse of the code. He could hardly assume the role of the "pucca sahib" steeled to face the show and fulfil the demands of the Empire in the alien land. He is an introvert who cannot share his sorrows with others. When he discovers his wife's infidelity, instead of shooting his rival on the spot like a pucca sahib, he chooses to blow out his own brains. By this act, he makes himself unworthy of sympathy, because the code does not warrant such weakness. It is an Indian who comments on the act as the spokesman of the pucca sahib: "There was a war on; people dying in thousands everywhere. And then some stupid introverted ass who cannot take it, who cannot carry the weight of his own little troubles decides to bump himself off. Who is to blame? What did it matter—one extra dead."[49] His tragedy is that he fails to satisfy Kipling's image of the ideal man who would never have chosen this cowardly path, exhibiting before the public eye the sore spot in his relationship with his wife. It becomes the duty of those around him—the pucca sahibs—to guard the other names from being tarnished. The tragedy of Bob Medley thus becomes a crime from the English perspective not to be sympathized with, but certainly to be condemned. It is Kiran Garud, an Indian, who comes out gloriously as an apostle of the code. Malgonkar seems to endorse Malcolm Muggeridge's epigram that the last true Englishmen are the Indians.[50]

The army code glorified in *Distant Drum,* is put to test in *Bandicoot Run.* If the apostle of the code in *Distant Drum* is an Indian who has accepted the colonial legacy, the black sheep in the army, exposed and condemned in *The Bandicoot Run,* is an Englishman. Brian Gilchrist is a retired military officer who has chosen to make India his permanent home when the British made their retreat. Though acclimatized to India after years of military service, he is still isolated from the Indians as well as from his own countrymen. An imperialist at heart, he could never conform to the image of the incorruptible English officer because he was susceptible to the temptation of bribery. He even manipulates transfers and promotions. He is court-martialled during military service. Even if his service record was unsullied, Kipling would hardly have approved of him because he had violated the code by marrying a Eurasian, what the English called "a country-bred girl." "That was one sure way for a sahib to draw upon himself the fullest censure from others of his caste."[51]

Gilchrist is presented as one who often ponders about Forster's words that if you were called upon to make a choice between betraying one's friend and one's country, one should have the courage to betray one's friend. Perhaps it is on the basis of this criterion that Gilchrist decides to work as a spy for Pakistan, against General Behl, receiving money from the Pakistani chief. As far as Gilchrist is concerned, there is no betrayal of India involved because for the Englishman of his generation India included Pakistan. Gilchrist's muddled loyalties are also an off-shoot of bitterness caused by the prejudice shown by his own community. They punish him severely for marrying a Eurasian girl. The commanding officer, Col. Mosse almost tells him to leave the regiment. Even the wedding gift—which is a parting gift as well—is intended to show their spite. The sahib class never forgives him; nor does he. In spite of this he is shown as acting the pucca sahib on two occasions—once when he declines Jack Pasotti's—the CIA agent's—offer of a lucrative sum and when he refuses outright Behl's bribe to get a transfer from the fighting zone. By failing to live upto the code he has opted to exclude himself from the charmed circle and these occasional acts of sahib-like righteousness could hardly save him. Behl's enmity demands too big a price from Gilchrist. His career that had started as a Major ends as such. The injustice meted out to him in his career and the isolation caused by the lapse to adhere to the code, form the twin forces that lead Gilchrist to his final moral degradation. He steals an important file and sells it to Pakistan.

In spite of the inglorious end of this retired military officer, Gilchrist's lonely and rootless existence in India is representative of the plight of many an official of the Empire. With the fall of the Empire they were deprived of a career and stripped off the glory of the imperial era and their existence in India became a matter of mere day-to-day survival. In Cyril Weatherby, the hardened imperialist (*A Time to be Happy*) one can perceive the dread of retirement and of returning home. Years of exposure to the warmth of the Indian sun make thoughts of home unbearably chill. More disheartening is the idea of finding roots all over again at the fag end of life. The Englishmen who had been playing roles all their lives feel like unhoused beings, alienated from Indian community and unable to find new roots back home. The return from sahibhood to the mediocrity of a mundane existence in England is depressing to many. Over the years they build up an illusory image of the home country that contains only positive values. But the prospect of return reminds them of the unpleasant realities of home and the deprivation involved in a return. Tom Grange and Dora Grange (*A Time to be Happy*) suffer this anguish when Indian independence becomes a reality to be reckoned with. Albert Memmi analyzes the predicament of the colonizer who returns home and says that if the colonizer should go home, it [the mother country] would lose its sublime nature, and he would cease to be a superior man. Although he is everything in the colony, the colonialist knows that in his own country he would be nothing: he would go back to being a medicore man. "Indeed the idea of mother country is relative. Restored to its true self, it would vanish and would at the same time destroy the superhumanity of the colonialist."[52]

The Bridies (*Pleasure City*) on the other hand, stay back because they cannot afford to go back home and start life anew. They survive on nostalgic memories of home and meet with their tragic end in India. The problem of the unhoused English immigrants is dealt with poignantly by Paul Scott in his novel *Staying On*.

Kamala Markandaya takes up the theme of the Englishman visiting the once-occupied country, still clinging to the garb of authority and looking down upon the Indian with contempt. Imperial habits die hard and the Raj lives on in the minds of the rulers and the ruled. Thus we find in Clinton (*The Coffer Dams*)—the English technical expert who comes to India to construct the coffer dams—imperial values asserting themselves once again. *The Coffer Dams* and *Pleasure City* show the British coming to independent India as builders and the dam and the pleasure complex (Shalimar) symbolize the Empire-building process itself. In the typical English way both the building firms start their work by creating "little Englands" in the Indian soil. The tribal settlements are swept away without much ado to build quarters for English technicians and engineers and the experts who have come to construct the dam. As in the colonial days the English prefer to preserve their Englishness and ignore native customs, manners and ways of life. Clinton imposes his authoritarian ways on the tribals, with absolute disregard for the sentiments of the newly independent people and comes to conflict with the Indian engineer Krishnan, the educated tribal Bashiam, and even his wife Helen who sympathizes with the natives. The situation is close to the conflict between the spirit of India and modern civilization symbolized by bridge-building in Kipling's "The Bridge-builders." Whereas Kipling elevates his imperialist to the heroic role of the challenger of the dark powers, Kamala Markandaya presents the conflict from the opposite point of view. Clinton is far from a hero. He has no patience to understand or sympathize with the feelings of the Indians. Work is his sole preoccupation: the dam which is to bear his name is almost an obsession with him. In an accident at the dam site, when forty natives are killed and two bodies are caught under a boulder, Clinton, with absolute indifference to the sentiments of the Indians, decides to incorporate the bodies into the structure. He had behaved differently when two Englishmen were killed because the colour of the skin was the deciding factor in all issues. Clinton's racial arrogance and insolence are shared by Rawlings, Jackson and Smith (*The Coffer Dams*). They evade any contact with the natives. Jackson expresses the exclusive attitude of the English thus: "We like keeping ourselves to ourselves."[53] Whenever anything went wrong, Rawlings puts the blame on the country and "its silly buggers," venting his spleen. Losing face before the Indians is to them the greatest calamity. They regard the Indians with so much contempt that they do not attach any value to their lives and Bashiam's offer to lift the boulder is accepted without revealing the defect of the crane to him and without any testing. Indian lives did not seem as important as his fellowmen's in English eyes. Clinton's attitude is contrasted in the novel with the humane attitude of Mackendrick. It actually wedges a permanent cleavage in his relationship with his wife Helen who identifies completely with the Indian ethos. The final issue that ruptures the surviving links of the martial bond is Clinton's refusal to open the dam and prevent the floods that would swallow the entire tribal settlement. Clinton's racial prejudices are so deep-rooted that he cannot view the Indians on an equal footing at all.

Boyle, the director of AIDCORP (*Pleasure City*) also does not entertain ideas of equality in the treatment of the natives. Without previous notice, the fishermen on the beach are expected to make room for the imposing structure of Shalimar. It lures many fisherfolk from their traditional profession: introduces native lads and girls to the exotic and civilized ways of life. As its immense shadow steals their light—reminding us of the subtlety with which the Empire found room to settle down in India—the fishermen uncomplainingly move their huts to another part of the beach. Boyle's imperial values are disturbed at the levels of familiarity attained by his colleague Tully and the fisherboy Rikky. He feels the need for distances to be kept. He complains that Rikki never seemed to remember that he was a paid servant. On one occasion Boyle is forced to remind Tully "that the sun never set on the British Empire." Tom Grange in *A Time to be Happy* is so embittered by the new sanction of parity to Indians that he grumbles that "the most idiotic thing that the Labour government had done was to give India her freedom." (239) The imperialists found it hard to make the necessary shift in values and emotions in tune with the changed political climate.

Imperialism as an ideology and attitude survives in the anglicized Indian of the post-Independent era. Harish and Sanad in *A Time to be Happy* and Kitsamy in *Some Inner Fury* are Indians who have happily taken over the white man's heritage. The Englishmen returning to India as spiritual searchers or explorers are surprised to find their historic counterparts in the "brown sahibs" in India.

Imperialism as a deep-rooted ideology and a way of life, dictating attitudes and shaping behavioural patterns, is unfolded in Indian English fiction through the wide array of British characters. The English are shown as men driven by the ambitions and dreams for the Empire. The prime motive of their existence is to live up to its code of values. Moral and spiritual concerns lose their significance in this process of deindividuation. The novelists reveal how in such circumstances communication ruptures; perception fails and points of contact between the races fade away. The racial segregation it brings about is manifested in a more intense form in the English women in India, which forms the concern of the next chapter.

NOTES

1. Ralph Ruddock, *Roles and Relationships* (London: Routledge and Kegan Paul, 1969) 23-24.
2. Sir John Strachey, *India: Its Administration and Progress 1888* (London: Macmillan, 1911) 189, 432.
3. Quoted in George Bennett, *The Concept of Empire: Burke to Attlee 1774-1947* (London: Black, 1953) 315.
4. Réne Maunier, *The Sociology of Colonies: An Introduction to the Study of Race Contact*, ed. and trans. from French, E.O. Lorimer (London: Routledge and Kegan Paul, 1949) 31.
5. Benita Parry, *Delusions and Discoveries: Studies on India in the British Imagination 1880-1930* (1972: New Delhi: Orient Longman, 1974) 27.
6. O. Mannoni, *Prospero and Caliban: The Psychology of Colonisation*, trans. Pamela Powesland (1956: London: Methuen, 1960) 97.
7. R.S. Singh, "from Resentment to Social Protest: Mulk Raj Anand," *Indian Novel in English* (Delhi: Arnold-Heinemann, 1977) 38-54.
8. Ashis Nandy, *The Intimate Enemy* (Delhi: Oxford Univ. Press. 1993) 2.
9. Charles Grant, "Observations on the State of Society among the Asiatic Subjects of Great Britain, particularly with respect to Morals: and on the Means of Improving it." Parliamentary Papers (HC). "Report from the Select Committee of the House of Commons on the Affairs of the East-India Company," 16 August 1832, Appendix, 123 Quoted in Francis G. Hutchins, *The Illusion of Permanence: British Imperialism in India* (Princeton: Princeton Univ. Press, 1967) 5.
10. James Mill, *History of British India,* VI (London: Baldwin, Gradock and Joy Paternoster-Row, 1820) 416
11. Kamala Markandaya, "Prologue," *The Golden Honeycomb* (New York: Thomas V. Cromwell Company, 1977) x.
12. S.C. Harrex, "A Sense of Identity: The Novels of Kamala Markandaya," *The Journal of Commonwealth Literatatre,* VI, No. 1. (June 1971) 65-78.
13. Arthur Pollard, "Kamala Markandaya's *The Golden Honeycomb*," *The Journal of Indian Writing in English*, 8, Nos.1 & 2, (Jan.-July 1980) 23-25.
14. Benita Parry, *Delusions and Discoveries* 206.
15. Quoted in Sir John A.R. Marriott, *The English in India* (Oxford:

Clarendon Press, 1932) 191.

16. T.N. Murari, *The Imperial Agent* (Great Britain: New English Library, 1987} 14.
17. E.M. Forster, "Notes on the English Character," *Abinger Harvest* (London: Edward Arnold, 1936} 3-14.
18. Manohar Malgonkar, *A Bend in the Ganges* (1964; rpt. London: Pan Books, 1967) 141.
19. Ethel M. Dell, *The Way of an Eagle* (London: T.Fisher Unwin, 1914) 86.
20. *Ibid.*, "The Safety Curtain," *The Safety Curtain and Other Stories* (London: T. Fisher Unwin, 1917) 49.
21. Allen J. Greenberger, *The British Image of India: A Study in the Literature of Imperialism, 1880-1960* (London: Oxford Univ. Press, 1969) 12.
22. Manohar Malgonkar, *Combat of Shadows* (1962: rpt. Delhi: Orient Paperbacks, 1968) 34.
23. E.M. Forster, *A Passage to India* (London: Arnold, 1994) 50.
24. Nayantara Sahgal. *A Time to be Happy* (Delhi: Sterling, 1975) 102.
25. Terms used by O. Mannoni, *Prospero and Caliban: The Psychology of Colonization* (London: Methuen, 1960).
26. Kamala Markandaya, *The Nowhere Man* (1972; rpt. London: Allen Lane, Penguin Books, 1973) 139.
27. K.A. Abbas, *The World is My Village* (1983; rpt. New Delhi: Ajanta, 1984) 339.
28. George Orwell, *Burmese Days* (London: Secker and Warburg, 1986) 37.
29. Nirad C. Chaudhuri, *The Continent of Circe* (Bombay: Jaico, 1978) 135-36.
30. Rudyard Kipling, "How Fear Came," quoted in *The Continent of Circe* 136.
31. Jean-Paul Sartre, "Introduction," Albert Memmi, *The Colonizer and the Colonized* (New York: Orion Press, 1965) xxvi.
32. Charles Dilke, *Greater Britain,* quoted in *The Illusion of Permanence* 101.
33. S.C. Harrex, *The Fire and the Offering: The English Language Novel of India*, Vol. I 1935-1970 (Calcutta: Writers Workshop, 1977) 98.
34. Kai Nicholson, *A Presentation of Social Problems in the Indo-Anglian and Anglo-Indian Novel* (Bombay: Jaico, 1972) 181.
35. Kamala Markandaya, *Some Inner Fury* (Bombay: Jaico, 1971).
36. C.S. Lewis, "Kipling's World," 90-92. Quoted in Kai Nicholson 179.
37. Nayantara Sahgal, *Plans for Denarture* (London: Heinemann, 1986) 204-5.
38. Francis G. Hutchins, *Illusion of Permanence* 104.
39. Manohar Malgonkar, *Combat of Shadows* 279.
40. M.K. Naik, *A History of Indian English Literature* (Delhi: Sahitya Akademi, 1982) 218.
41. Mulk Raj Anand, *Morning Face* (1968; rpt. India: Arnold-Heinemann, 1976) 110-11.

42. Ashis Nandy, *The Intimate Enemy* (Delhi: Oxford Univ. Press, 1983) 7.
43. O. Mannoni, *Prospero and Caliban: The Psychology of Colonization* 158.
44. K. Nagarajan, *Chronicles of Kedaram* (Bombay: Asia, 1961) 161.
45. Chaman Nahal, *Azadi* (New Delhi: Arnold-Heinemann, 1975) 31.
46. Shamsul lslam, *Chronicles of the Raj* (London: Macmillan, 1979) 36.
47. Mulk Raj Anand, *Seven Summers* (London: Hutchinson' International Authors, 1951) 96.
48. G.S. Amur, *Manohar Malgonkar* (London: Heinemann, 1973) 46.
49. Manohar Malgonkar, *Distant Drum* (Bombay: Asia, 1960) 32.
50. Quoted in G.S. Amur, *Manohar Malgonkar* 47.
51. Manohar Malgonkar, *The Bandicoot Run* (Delhi: Vision Books, 1982) 133.
52. Albert Memmi, *The Colonizer and the Colonized* (New York: The Orion Press, 1965) 58.
53. Kamala Markandaya, *The Coffer Dams* (London: Hamish Hamilton, 1969) 37.
54. Kamala Markandaya, *Pleasure City* (London: Chatto and Windus, 1982) 170.

The Memsahibs

The Englishwoman in India occupies a significant place in Indian English fiction for she formed one of the strongest pillars of the edifice of the British Raj. As the female counterpart of the British imperialist, she came to be labelled "the memsahib"—a hybrid coinage current in British India among the Indians to address a European lady with respect. The term acquired colonial overtones and has come to evoke an image of ethnic arrogance and cold aloofness. Her functional role in Indian English fiction is of a limited and representative quality and is clearly defined by the constricting framework of the colonial set-up. The colonized writer, who had for long been deprived of his dignity, by being reduced to the status of the "native" or the "other" by the colonizer, makes an effort to fictionalize the phenomenon of the white woman as one who had preserved her racial arrogance and struggled to "contain" the Indian in an antagonistic value system.[1]

The impediments to an understanding of the female psyche are many. Apart from the polarities of a contrasting value system, the distinct "otherness" of the Englishwoman's psyche seems to elude the Indian writer. This might account for the reluctance of Indian English novelists—male novelists especially—to portray Englishwomen as protagonists or even to present them in major roles. Of the major Indian English novelists, Mulk Raj Anand and R.K. Narayan have steered clear of this difficult phenomenon. Though the scene of action in Anand's novels is mainly British India, Englishwomen hardly enter his fictional world. The only intruder from the West in R.K. Narayan's novels happens to be an American girl in *The Sweet Vendor*. Raja Rao projects the East-West confrontation by introducing the French wife of Ramaswamy, Madeline, in *The Serpent and the Rope* and the Czech wife of Padmanabha Iyer in *Comrade Kirilliov*: but he too shies away from the depiction of Englishwomen. Of the later novelists, Bhabani Bhattacharya and K.A. Abbas are also no exceptions to this general tendency. Manohar Malgonkar, however, has been bold enough to depict a few among the female species of the colonizer-class and exposes their insularity and racial arrogance in *The Devil's Wind*, *The Combat of Shadows*, *Distant*

Drum and *The Princes*. B. Rajan introduces Cynthia in *The Dark Dancer* as a foil to Kamala and the Indian cultural and spiritual values she embodies. Nahal's Barbara Smiles is a caricature. It is interesting to note that Celia Ashby, Kenneth Ashby's aunt figuring in *The Crown and the Loincloth* is a liberal-minded American lady and his lady-love who is English, remains a memory of the past and never appears in the novel. The only English lady who figures in Khushwant Singh's fiction, happens to be an unconventional person, sympathetic to Indians and above narrow racism (*I Shall Not Hear the Nightingale*). Timeri Murari too has introduced an English lady who rejects the imperial cult in his novel, *The Imperial Agent*. The typical memsahibs figuring in the novel and in the sequel to it (*The Last Victory*) remain marginal figures. Full-length portraits of Englishwomen are almost avoided by the male novelists. The women writers on the other hand, have ventured to probe the alien psyche. They have at least the privilege of a shared feminine sensibility. In spite of that, to a large extent, the Englishwomen in Indian English fiction remain peripheral characters embodying the features of the class they represent.

Englishwomen in India as pictured by Indian English novelists fall into two distinct groups. The typical memsahibs, who are representatives of the ruling class and who seldom attain any individuality within the scope of the novel, form the first group. A few others assume centrality and they are, as a rule, departures from the type. These belong to the second category. They struggle to defy the imperial code that stifles and limits their individuality. The Englishwomen in the postcolonial era—also display both tendencies—there are those who cling on to colonial attitudes and those who are liberated and thoroughly decolonized. The memsahibs in Indian English fiction are often projected as foils to the Indian women. As symbols of western culture and civilization and the socio-political values of the West, they strike a cultural contrast to the Indian female protagonist, and even help the Indian characters to arrive at their own cultural identity. Some are made a tool in the hands of the decolonizing Indian artist to assert the superiority of ideal Indian womanhood.

In the portrayal of the typical memsahibs it is difficult for any Indian writer to reject the fictional image of the Englishwoman in India handed down by Rudyard Kipling as "a frivolous, snobbish and selfish creature who flitted from bridge to tennis parties 'in the hills' while her poor husband slaved on the plains."[2] Mostly the wives who came to India were Victorian women whose emotional and intellectual development had been stunted by the restrictive conventions of Victorian morality. They were hardly prepared for the enormous and continuing cultural shock of India. In the encounter with India, their warped sensibilities forced a retreat into the exclusive English refuges built on the alien soil, away from contact with the native. The wives of most of the bureaucrats appearing in Indian English fiction are modelled on these memsahibs familiarised by Kipling and Mrs. Steele.

Historians and sociologists have been generally harsh on the Englishwomen in India because it was felt with their arrival in India, the Englishmen became more racially aloof and insular. Francis Hutchins points out that the "Englishwomen did not personally cause a narrowing of outlook in English society and widening of the gap between the two races. . . . It seems more correct to say that the British Indian society caused a narrowing of outlook among Englishwomen by refusing them the opportunity of pursuing interests outside its confining limits."[3] The Victorian concept of woman as pure, delicate and unsuited to active life—a perfect contrast to the dominant, vigorous and hard-working man—denied women the opportunity to break free of the restrictions that society had imposed on them. Any attempt to reject the conventions would result in social ostracism which was a grave threat in small stations in British India where five or six English families depended on one another for company and comfort. The women were therefore compelled to lead a life of racial exclusion, their contact with India thinned down to bare everyday exchanges about household affairs with the Indian servants.

Malgonkar's *The Devil's Wind* and Kamala Markandaya's *The Golden Honeycomb* afford cursory glimpses into the attitudes of the Englishwomen in the pre-mutiny era and their experiences during the mutiny. The factors contributing to the deepening cleavage between the races surface in these novels dealing with the first open conflict between Indians and the British. Central to the concept of the Englishwoman's superiority is the myth of the pristine purity of the English race, in which the English in India staunchly believed. As the decolonizing artist, Malgonkar explodes the myth in *The Devil's Wind*. The debunking of colonial myths and the re-instating of native symbols of virtue is a feature common to Third World writers. It is part of the process of emancipation from the clogging deadwood of the colonial era. In *The Devil's Wind*, this is managed through a cleverly contrived half-comic situation which is linked on to the main plot. Mrs. Scobie, the wife of the Resident Magistrate of Kanpur is introduced as the senior lady of the station and the self-appointed guardian of the race. She is shocked when Miss Bolten arrives all the way from a place called Houndsditch carrying a wedding dress of the latest fashion, impatient to marry Aziz—an Indian in the court of Nana Sahib—who had promised marriage when they met in England. The entire British community is shocked at the glaring impropriety of Miss Bolten's action—that a white woman should have come all the way to India to marry a "native"! The British community of Kanpur flocks together to prevent the calamity and a deputation of ladies is sent to Miss Bolten to explain the impropriety of such a union. (*The Devil's Wind* 54) Mrs. Scobie's words to Miss Bolten reveal the racial insolence of the white women: "I never suffer one of them to enter my bungalow from my front gate, but insist on their using the servant's entrance; and then I make them wait in veranda."[4]

In spite of advice, when Miss Bolten remains obdurate in her desire to marry Aziz, the ladies resolve to have her certified insane or to deport her on moral grounds as an "undesirable person." (54) But for the timely interference of Miss Bolten's lawyer, the innocent lady would have been forcibly shipped back to Calcutta under a law instituted to get rid of disease-ridden prostitutes.

Another instance of the racial apartheid practised by the British women is provided in the novel. In spite of her being General Wheeler's wife, Janaki's company was scrupulously avoided by the white ladies of Kanpur. They refused her admission in the exclusive English Doab club because she was an Indian and could hardly tolerate the fact that Janaki danced, went barefoot in the house, wore saris, chewed paan, stained her lips red and the palms of her hands and feet saffron. What was even more unforgivable was that she was very beautiful. "That and also the fact that she was just as proud of being Indian as they were of being British!" (67) Mrs. Scobie voices the attitude of the entire race: "such airs for someone who's only countryborn." (67) The English ladies looked the other way when Janaki passed and never, except in the presence of Gen. Wheeler, addressed her as "Lady Wheeler." Even Wheeler's children, though by English standards, of a higher caste than their mother, were ostracized and were barred from both the army and the civil service by a special directive from London. E.M. Forster has criticised Englishwomen in India as a class for their insensitivity, lack of understanding, and racial arrogance. He says: "She deserves as a class, all that the satirists have said about her, for she has instigated the follies of her male when she might have calmed them and set him on the sane course. There has been an English as well as an Indian purdah and it has done greater harm because it was aggressive. Instead of retiring quietly behind the curtain it flaunted itself as a necessity, and proclaimed racial purity across a live-wire."[5]

The hollowness of the kind of morality practised by ladies like Mrs. Scobie is exposed through an ironic twist in the story. Mr. Scobie himself had the misfortune to discover his hotel in the intimate company of one Michael Palmer and the "self-righteously proper" keeper of Kanpur's conscience had to be hastily taken away to Calcutta by manipulating an urgent transfer for Mr. Scobie, the Resident Magistrate. (*The Devil's Wind* 85) Miss Bolten, whom she wanted to banish as an "undesirable person" got respectably married to a Captain Frazer and returned to Kanpur as a proud military wife—the peer of Mrs. Scobie herself and the moral guardian of the community. Mrs. Scobie is reduced to an object of ridicule and through her the shallow morality of the race is exposed.

The harrowing experiences of the Englishwomen during the Mutiny—the miserable existence for days in the Entrenchment without the basic necessities and with death staring in the face, the Satichaura incident and the massacre of women and children in Bibighar—left an indelible stamp of fear in their minds, deepening racial animosity and distrust and a deep-rooted suspicion about latent savagery in every Indian.

The hoarded experience of the mutiny was handed down from mother to daughter, as precious lessons to be remembered in the course of their Indian tenure. In these lessons the native figured as the Caliban-like savage, out to molest the white lady. This deep-rooted image of the native explains the rude hostility most English ladies displayed in their attitude to the Indians. This is well illustrated by the advice given to her granddaughter by the wife of Colonel Copeland, who was shot in bed during the mutiny by a sepoy of his own regiment (*The Golden Honeycomb*). The Colonel's lady could never understand the forces that led to the event and could be appeased only by witnessing the murder of the sepoy and two of his comrades selected at random. She was hardly conscious of the element of savagery in her own nature that took delight in the cruel murder of the two innocent sepoys. Nor could she understand the national aspirations behind the organized revolt. The only answer she could arrive at was that there was "a savagery latent in the nation." (102) She tells her granddaughter: "Savages, that's all. All of them, every single one. Never trust one. Not one. Ever." (103)

The same insensitiveness to cold-blooded butchery of the native is perceived in Stella Brewster, the wife of the humane and kind District Magistrate of Himapur, Henry Brewster in Nayantara Sahgal's *Plans for Departure*. She sits stoically through the execution of Kudiram, an Indian, who was being punished for killing an English lady and her daughter. When Henry protests against her watching the grim scene among the hostile mob that will crowd to cheer the condemned man, and that too soon after her confinement, she is adamant. She thinks that she owes it to the race and not to go would be a dereliction of duty. "I'd go to the hanging if I were on my deathbed. It's the least I can do. This is the animal who killed Mrs. Kennedy and her daughter. It might have been me or any of us." (70) Stella is steeped in imperial ideology and theories of ethnic superiority. She was bred on stories of the mutiny legend and lore by her soldier-father and had learned to share his belief that the atrocities committed by the British—like the murder of hundred and twenty prisoners—were necessary as deterrents to the atrocities of the natives. Henry's humane concern for the Indian is a sentiment that she cannot comprehend and the rift in political attitudes finally leads to the breaking of the marital bond.

The hardening of hostilities in the post-mutiny era is depicted by Indian writers as manifesting itself in the tendency of the English ladies to shrink into their own *English cloisters*, away from the contaminating *presence* (emphasis mine) of India. Corollary to this is the need to relegate the native to the position of a slave, to brand him as an uncultured, untrustworthy and wild creature. Kamala Markandaya diagnoses the English tendency to identify the non-white to the "ape-just-off the-trees"[6] image. From the image evolves a nebulous feeling that "to speak in evolutionary terms, non-whites are slightly less advanced than whites. The sinister corollary is that when the chips are down, as the saying goes, they are slightly more expendable." ("On Images" 6) In the Englishwomen this tendency to treat the average Indian as an expendable and insignificant being, leading to the total negation of the validity of his existence, is more pronounced than in men. This has already been perceived in the attitude of Lady Copeland and Stella Brewster. Ravi the protagonist in Kamala Markandaya's *A Handful of Rice* is shocked at the absolute indifference of the memsahib to the death of his father-in-law, Apu, who had served them throughout his life. What she is concerned about is only the delay in delivering her clothes and the unpleasantness of wearing the same flowery frock worn many times before for the Saturday reception. The snuffed-out human life dwindles into insignificance before her narrow racist vision. She shares the snobbery of her class that never bothered to think about the existence of the Indian menials in between the periods when they appeared. Ravi often feels that the memsahib sees him not as a man, but as an inanimate object. She would stand before him and Apu, wearing next to nothing, admiring herself in the long looking glass. They are to her "cardbourd figures that she found strange to think of as human beings, with lives of their own, and continuity, with children."[7]

Lady Copeland's (*The Golden Honeycomb*) distrust of the entire Indian species is representative. Her grandmother's warning that all Indians are savages, pursues her and she does not let any Indian pierce the crust of her carefully-built English nest. Even when she plays the charming hostess to the warm and effusive Bawajiraj, she holds herself aloof and withdrawn. She brushes aside a sobbing Janaki—a helpless servant girl—pleading for help, as an encumbrance to be hastily rid of. (175) Rabi and Bharathi, the native Raja's children, are unpleasant guests to be avoided at all costs. The rigidity of her code hardens Lady Copeland to such an extent that even the other English ladies of the cantonment hold no warmth towards her. They diagnose the reason to be her "air," which the author defines thus: "An invisible diadem, or core of ice, that made you remember distances and keep them." (308)

"The truth of India" as handed down by Lady Copeland to her daughter Sophie nullifies the growing emotional rapport between Rabi and Sophie in the exciting atmosphere of the Holi celebrations. The accumulated colour prejudice of centuries surfaces at the crucial moment, making Sophie withdraw and interpret Rabi's urge as a deliberate scheme to rape her. Kamala Markandaya establishes beyond doubt that the concealed undercurrents of hatred between the races would not let such a union take place. Sophie's return in the company of Cicily Ramsden and Lieutenant Aspinall—both of her own race—is symbolic of her withdrawal into the exclusive world of the white. Millie Rawlings expresses the same attitude when she says, "Never trust the blacks. That's my motto and I stick to it."[8] Mannoni's remarks about the racism of the European women in Madagaskar hold good for their counterparts in India: "The colonial woman is, as it were, the feminine counterpart of Prospero, but—it is an astonishing fact—[in Madagaskar] the European women are far more racialist than the men. Sometimes their racialism attains preposterous proportions."[9]

In the Indian situation, the extreme racism of the Englishwomen manifests itself in the clannish grouping of the community in clubs and hill-resorts. The shallowness of life led by the memsahibs in India at these resorts is exposed by every Indian novelist. Their life in India, rendered luxurious and wasteful by the undreamt-of privileges of a colonial set-up, left them with enormous leisure which they spent in the meaningless and tedious social round of mahjong, bridge, parties, and gossip. They withdrew into the clubs because they "wanted to create for themselves and their menfolk an island in the vast sea of India—and to a large extent they were successful."[10] The intrusion of Indians into these self-made islands is hardly forgiven. Lady Copeland (*The Golden Honeycomb*) neither understands nor forgives Arthur Copeland's thoughtless act of inviting Bawajiraj in the sacred nest of their English home. (96) In *A Handful of Rice*, Ravi wonders at the cushioned quietness of the inner rooms of the sahibs' houses of which he had occasional glimpses as they climbed up the sweepers' staircase with the bundles of new clothes for the memsahibs. (159) The sudden hike in social position and financial status afforded by a career in British India made the memsahibs indulge in all kinds of whims about dresses. Kamala Markandaya says how the memsahib ordered "a whole host of things—housecoats, dresses, slacks, flowered shirts to wear over them—far more than she needed," because she very well knew that "she would never be able to afford so many clothes once she left India." (*A Handful of Rice* 159) Sarah Rushton's remark, "I do enjoy being a memsahib" is a frank confession of the pleasure they derived from their newly acquired status in India.[11] She is the frivolous, vainglorious type who draws her friend Elizabeth also in to the memsahibs' world of dalliance and vanity.

The Englishwomen who came to India, were largely from the middle classes and India meant to them a sudden elevation to unexpected opulence and power. Even an English girl, Elizabeth, returning to India after education at home is depicted by T.N. Murari (*The Imperial Agent*) as becoming conscious of the transformation wrought on her character by life in India. The author remarks about her: "India aroused mysterious passions in her, long unrecognised in an English climate, an English civilisation. The veneer was paper thin, tearing already." (117)

In her case, the newly acquired sense of overweening confidence bestowed by her status in India, makes Elizabeth defy long-cherished moral rectitudes and enter into a scandalous laison with a romantic young man of dubious character. India seems to let loose hidden urges suppressed by the unrelaxing ethic code of Victorian England. In *A Time to be Happy*, Nayantara Sahgal tells the story of a middle-class English wife, Dora Grange, who was transformed into the leading memsahib in the English circles of Sharanpur. Her husband, Tom Grange had not been able to afford the membership of a single club in England. Tom Grange reflects on the fact that "in England, his wife Dora, would probably have had to do her own cooking and cleaning while here she had untold leisure and servants to wait on her." (10) In Sharanpur she reigns over the club—her durbar—with queenly airs and people vie with one another to win her favour. Her birthdays are remembered and people come from offices to pay respects.

English novelists have also recognized Englishwoman's infatuation for India because of the power and the glory the country invests on her ordinary middle-class personality. Rodney in John Master's *Nightrunners of Bengal* is desirous of making some money and returning to England, but knows only too well that nothing would induce his wife Joanna "to give up this life and return to middle-class non-entity in England."[12]

The club provided a fortress for the memsahibs where they could indulge in free, uninhibited talk. Conversation flowed smoothly, carefully avoiding the stumbles of the war, or the national movement raging outside the bastion of the club. The Quit India movement is to the ladies only a hindrance to their shopping sprees. (*A Time to be Happy* 118) In this charmed circle, a newcomer like Meredith Cornell's daughter could create quite a sensation by disclosing that the Vicereine recognized her and invited her for lunch on her second day in Delhi. (118)

Glimpses of British social life that formed the major attraction of the "golden honeycomb" of the Empire are afforded by Kamala Markandaya in *Some Inner Fury* and Malgonkar in *Combat of Shadows*. Saturdays are the highlights of the week when life is made colorful by a dance in the club. On Sunday mornings the English group together in houses. Women arrange to meet their friends three or four mornings a week to play mahjong and another two or three mornings to roll bandages for the Red Cross as part of war effort. The Government House balls are major events that occur twice a year. Not to be seen at one of the balls is enough to consign a lady to that social limbo where none recognizes her existence anymore, and no further invitations come her way; and so there is some anxiety and heart-burning regarding these. (*Some Inner Fury*)

Malgonkar records the amusements in the town of Chinnar where the English in *Combat of Shadows* come together to participate in the Chinnar week 1938 "which always promises days of clean English fun." (6) There will be "tea and tennis afternoons and bridge parties with the burra sahibs, memsahibs and sedate, decorous lunch parties and chamber music and once-a-week dances, and perfumed, bare shouldered, civil, acquiescent, middle-aging women outnumbered three to one by the men and living in a permanent haze of male adoration." (*Combat of Shadows* 19) In the heart of Chinnar was the Highlands Club—part hotel, part sports club—a generously, even extravagantly subsidized institution maintained for the planters so that they should not be deprived of what were regarded as "the normal relaxations of an English way of life." (20-21)

Dennis Kincaid remarks about the life of the Anglo-Indian women: "Save for arranging a wealth of cut flowers, laid to her hand by the faithful Mali, an Anglo-Indian girl's domestic duties are practically nil. Intellectual pastimes are not within her reach and religion is left to those who have given up their lives to it. Small wonder that . . . even the more seriously inclined succumb for a while to the irresistible charm, the lightness and brightness of Anglo-Indian social life."[13]

In the unrelieved monotony of their carefully segregated lives, the club became the very centre of the Englishwoman's existence in India.

The unvaried round of social entertainments created for them a make-believe world of illusory happiness where life consisted in shallow talk, idle gossip and superficial pleasures. Stella Brewster (*Plans for Departure*) is lured away from home by the amusements of Lucknow because Himapur doesn't have a club to boast of. The club actively contributed to the emotional petrification towards the native for it alienated the women successfully from the Indian surroundings. According to Shamsul Islam, "The world of the sahibs, particularly that of the memsahib, has no place for the Indian except in the role of a servant."[14] India forms just a picturesque background to their activities. The image of India they form in their minds is one "reflected through a prism of cultural convictions which distorted the subjects in view."[15] Dora Grange's regrets about India reveal how little the Englishwomen gain from their stay there. Her exposure to India is so meagre that the country dwindles in her memories in to the twice-a-week-dinners with the Carstairs, Saturday nights and Sunday lunches at the club, sports and shikar and an occasional trip to Delhi. She recollects: "I just can't talk to them [Indian women]. They smile and simper. We have nothing in common." (*The Imperial Agent* 52) She is fully aware of the Englishwomen's inability for cultural assimilation and the narrow hide-bound water-tight nature of their existence. "Theirs is a different India. We don't belong. We are not welcome either," says she. (52) She compares their life in India to existence in a prison where they belong to each other and not to India. One is reminded of Mrs. Burton's warning to Mrs. Moore in *A Passage to India:* "You're superior to them, anyway. Don't forget that. You're superior to everyone in India except one or two of the Ranis, and they're on an equality."[16] The refusal to reach out, the racial arrogance and total ignorance of the native language shut out all communication making it impossible for the Englishwomen to attain even a glimpse of the rich and alien culture of India. The spirit remained unscathed and starved by the artificial barriers that blocked all contact with the Indian ethos.

Nayantara Sahgal presents in her novels a common phenomenon of British India—the unmarried English girl sent out to India to look for prospects for marriage. Neeta Gupta has commented on the batches of "husband-hunters for whom India was no more than a marriage market."[17] They set off to Bombay with "minds and caps made up" and armed with "a special license in the chest"[18] as Thomas Hood satirically describes it. Marcella, the sophisticated artistocratic lady in *Rich Like Us* and Marion Finch in *A Time to be Happy* are typical examples. Sharanpur hardly satisfies Marion Finch because her hostess, Gwen Hartley, though well-meaning, is a bore and could not provide Marion an interesting escort. The one escort, Ronald Sharpe—appointed to squire her at the various social functions—does not seem attractive in spite of his tempting bank balance. Though Marion wants to get married, she does not want to commit herself to the first individual who comes her way. She would rather weigh other prospects first and while she is weighing them, she sees no harm in enjoying herself. So she picks Sanad, the young Indian subordinate to Cyril Weatherby, much younger than herself and quite an attractive prospect for a temporary flirtation. Marion is exposed as a frivolous woman, all set to enjoy life in India and ready to employ her feminine charms uninhibitedly to achieve her purpose. She makes Sanad feel, by her way of talk and behaviour, that he is to her like a coveted trophy. Sanad, himself an anglicized and sophisticated Indian, could see through the shallowness of Marion Finch and he realises that "Marion collected trophies of this kind the way shikaries came to India to bag tigers" (124).

Whereas the imperialist Caroline Bell (*Possession*) takes possession of the body and soul of Valmiki, Marion finds herself confronted by an alert Indian mind that resists possession by the colonizer and plays the game without getting emotionally involved and hurt. Still the image of the colonized as "the savage native" persists and Marion is said to get out of the affair with Sanad, "the tingling sensation of the barbarian ancestor all over again." (*A Time to be Happy* 124)

Marcella (*Rich Like Us*) is also depicted as a frivolous woman, whose shifting loyalties are contrasted with the intense emotional commitment of her Indian lover. While Marion Finch (*A Time to be Happy*) is presented through Sanad's perspective, Marcella is viewed through the eyes of another Englishwoman in India—Rose. Rose's perceptions have never been sharpened or polished by education and her tongue and manners have never been chastened by the elegances of upper class living. Marcella shares Marion's light-hearted attitude towards life and "walked into the lives of Ram and Rose with the effortless, guiltless ease of the ruling class and occupied it. She and Ram behaved like rightful lovers, making Rose an outsider."[19] After a tempestuous love affair, Marcella leaves Ram and goes back to England with the same effortless ease with which she had entered their lives. Ram is left an emotional wreck—desolate, forsaken and old—and Marcella returns four years later with her husband Brian, happily blooming in her marital state.

The shallowness and insincerity of the Englishwoman as exposed in these characters, might be the consequence of her emotionally impoverished state. E.M. Forster has spoken of "the undeveloped heart"[20] of the Englishman: the English ladies seem to suffer from a *closed heart* (emphasis mine) that shows a dearth of genuine human warmth and an incapacity to generate sincere emotional response to situations and complete, life-long devotion in love. Emotional stringency that refuses to let the feelings flow unchecked is the root cause of their petrified relationship with the Indians as well.

The typical colonial wives like Ginger Barnes (*The Crown and the Loincloth*), Minnie and Mrs. Timmons (*Rich Like Us*), Mrs. Dart (*Combat of Shadows*), Mrs. Gibson (*The Princes*), Mrs. Hartely (*A Time to be Happy*), Mrs. Burdett (*Some Inner Fury*) and Mrs. Mary Pryor (*Plans for Departure*) are "mummified identities"[21] caught in the colonial world: they act out their roles as "memsahibs," carefully guarding their spirits from being touched by the reality of India. They are mostly passive acquiescents in the imperial game being played out by their male partners. In the colonial set-up where values are strictly arranged according to priorities like social classes, they are never called upon to make any moral or emotional commitments.

Thus Mrs. Firth and Lucille Croft (*Plans for Departure*) are pictured as silent accomplices of Mr. Firth for they hardly ever think of the injustice and racial arrogance behind the routine thrashings administered by Firth to the workers in the plantations. Lucille even comes to believe in the moral righteousness of his actions because he always tells her that he would never have got any indigo planted if he had pampered his workers and waited for pen pushers to decide rights and wrongs. Ideological leanings which had been simple and clear-cut with her father become muddled after her marriage to Marlowe, which turns out to be a disastrous union. Even before her death she realizes that her love for Marlowe and the life with him are over. There was nothing in common between them and the sharp tongue and rude manners of the planter's daughter stand in the way of the missionary's advancement towards his goal. The pathetic end and loveless funeral of Lucille Croft ultimately save her from becoming a thoroughly undignified character.

In the Englishwoman's perspective, shaped and moulded by the imperial value-system, any violation of the code on the part of her male partner or the failure to live up to the code, is an unpardonable sin. It can even cause a rift between partners and lead to a rupture of marital relationship. Jean Walters (*Combat of Shadows*) and Margot Medley (*Distant Drum*) are typical examples. Henry Winton is corrupt and morally degenerate and fails on all fronts—at the personal, official and public—by his personal infidelity to his wife, his corrupt and racially arrogant ways as a planter and his failure to live upto the rules of the game as a hunter. Jean Walters, the "all-white girl from his own country" is compelled to reject him. (*Combat of Shadows* 151) She shakes herself free from the inhibited and jealous relationship with Winton by committing the act of adultery with Eddy. It is Winton's moral depravity and his infidelity to her that drive her to take revenge on him by the daring act.

The privations of the code are brought to focus by the tragic death of Bob Medley. (*Distant Drum*) It is Bob Medley's innate goodness and deep loyalty to his wife that turn out to be his bane. His nobility is his flaw: he cannot act the pucca sahib and accept his wife's occasional flirtations in his stride—which is treated by Margot and the adherents to the code as a sign of unpardonable weakness in the colonial officer. Margot does not hold herself responsible for even his tragic end. She tells Kiran Garud: "No, no one can help these things . . . they, they just happen to one." (*Distant Drum* 29) The tragedy leaves Margot unruffled for she might never have had anything in common with her introvert husband and from her perspective it is Bob who had acted silly by giving way to despair. Kipling's ideal Englishman would never have succumbed to failure in such a cowardly manner. Thus the tragedy of Bob Medley becomes a crime even from Margot's perspective—not to be sympathized with, but certainly to be condemned.

Placing the British women in the context of post-Independent India, Kamala Markandaya and Nayantara Sahgal assert the continued prevalence of colonial attitudes even after Independence. Caroline Bell in *Possession*—conceived as a parable on imperialism—is the most powerful symbol of the craving for possession that manifests in all colonial operations. Years after Independence Caroline's intrusion into the tranquillity of an Indian village and the aggressive possession of Valmiki, an unknown rustic prodigy, are conceived as an analogy for the imperialistic appropriation of the orient with total disregard for his individual selfhood leading to depersonalization of the individual entity and cultural asphyxia. It is a unique re-enactment of the colonial process of conquest, subjugation and occupation, at the level of personal relationships. To quote Mannoni,

> In short then, what I want the reader to realise is that a colonial situation is created, so to speak, the very instant a white man, even if he alone, appears in the midst of a tribe, even if it is independent, so long as he is thought to be rich or powerful, or merely immune to the local forces of magic, and so long as he derives from his position, even though only in his most secret self, a feeling of his own superiority.[22]

In Caroline's appropriation of Valmiki, the political and economic motives of the colonial situation alone are missing. She arrives in the Indian village, discovers the budding painter in the God-forsaken place, and weans him away with all the arrogance of the colonizer to the seductive sophistication of the west. Caroline moulds the possessed identity with total disregard for the alien cultural and spiritual values, attempting a westernization—as brought about in India through English education—that would deprive the individual of his moral and spiritual props and lead to deindividuation. As Margaret Joseph has commented, allegory is carried to extreme limits as though the author is eager to rub the meaning in.[23] Caroline is depicted as wealthy, beautiful, arrogant, voracious and egoistic, belonging to the lines of British officers who once ruled India. She was the daughter of a former Governor of an Indian state "descended from a long line of men who had ruled India in the days of the British Raj."[24] To quote Margaret Joseph, "Caroline is obviously England queening it over her colonies, possessor of India, its benefactor and despoiler in one." (*Kamala Markandaya* 50) Her imperious efficiency in managing her affairs in the Indian village and her absolute indifference to Valmiki's feelings in asking him to walk away from the life he had known serve as painful reminders of the bitterness of British occupation to the colonized psyche of the narrator, Anasuya, as well as to the reader. Whereas Valmiki is innocently unconscious of her virtual possession of his soul and body achieved with the matter-of-factness of a business transaction, the pain and suffering wrought by her action and the memories of colonial subjection evoked by it, are experienced acutely by the central consciousness, Anasuya. Caroline has no fears or doubts about the justice of her action or its outcome. "She was supremely confident, born and brought up to be so, with as little thought of infallibility as a colonial in the first flush of empire, as a missionary in the full armour of his mission, dogged by none of the hesitancies that handicap lesser breeds." (15)

Once the process of occupation is complete, Caroline sets her heart on bringing out the artistic talents in Valmiki, gives him all the equipments necessary for his vocation: exposes him to the best works in Switzerland, France, Italy and Greece and even moves to a drab little district to provide the boy a milieu that does not overawe him. However, the creative springs that flowed unchecked in the confusion, squalor and agglomeration of colour that India is, seem to dry up in the comforts and luxury of the west. The anguish and emptiness he feels is symbolized by the one picture that he draws—The Desert. The Caroline-Valmiki relationship at this phase can be called a love-hate relationship, symbolic of the historic relationship between Britain and India. Caroline has tightened her hold on Valmiki through physical intimacy. Yet Valmiki tells Anasuya: "She does not care for me. She cares only for what I can do, and if I do it well it is like one more diamond she can put on the necklace round her throat for her friends to admire: but when I do nothing, I am nothing to her, no more than a small insect in a small crack in the ground." (55)

Elena J. Kalinikova has pointed out the analogy between Caroline's role in converting the illiterate goatherd into a famous painter and that of Prof. Higgins in transforming the flower-girl from the London streets into a fine lady.[25] But whereas Higgins' love is tender and solicitous, Caroline's passion for Valmiki is the selfish, proprietorial craving for authority and possession. Haydn Moore Williams has described her as "a master of possessiveness."[26] She is purblindly ruthless and demanding and callously brushes aside the two girls—Ellie, the emotional wreck from a Nazi concentration camp and Annabel, the young and blooming English girl—who stand in the way of Valmiki's development. The frustrated attempt to break away from the clutches of Caroline makes Valmiki realize the tenacity of the chains that bind him. Her possessive arms have reached out to every part of his being. Anasuya remarks: "Caroline thinks Valmiki belongs to her and in a way she's right. She won't let go. People don't easily give up what they think are their possessions. The English never have." (198)

Mannoni has analyzed the nature of the colonial who is not spurred on by political or economic motives, but is greedy after psychological satisfactions and declares that he is more dangerous. (*Prospero and Caliban: The Psychology of Colonization*) The possessor, in the inordinate lust for possession, becomes the victim of the passion for possession. S.K. Aithal perceives half-hearted attempts on the part of Caroline to show that she is aware of the need to discard colonial attitudes, as when she places the faintest emphasis on London "as if it were a little parochial to think that everything sprang from there." (*Possession* 68) But the colonial attitude is so deeply entrenched in Caroline's nature that in spite of her consciousness of the political changes that have put India on the map, it is "obviously not deep enough to induce radical self-analysis and lead her to model a behaviour ingrained in her."[27]

By projecting the Swamy as the real adversary of Caroline, Kamala Markandaya gives the colonial paradigm the added dimension of an east-west conflict. Though Caroline has succeeded to a great extent in alienating Valmiki from his cultural and spiritual moorings, she has not been able to fulfil his need for the spiritual meaning of India. Caroline's pragmatic wisdom and "sophisticated instinct for possession" finally crumble before the "Swamy's nonchalant philosophy of ascetic detachment."[28] Valmiki's liberation from the clutches of Caroline becomes symbolic of India's struggle for independence. As one who came "of a breed that never admitted defeat" (233) Caroline has the last word in the word-duel with the Swamy. She refuses to accept the evidence of the superior quality of Valmiki's work which itself affirms the artist's need for independence and the higher excellence of art which is man's self-expression of the communication with the divine. She cannot let go of the illusion of her own power and turns away with the optimistic words that there will come the day when he would crave to return to her. The imperial ego cannot deign to admit that the sun would set in the British Empire.

Millie Rawling in *The Coffer Dams* is another typical memsahib clinging to illusions of power and racial superiority in the exclusive English island she strives to build up in an independent India. She has come to India as the wife of a technical expert collaborating in the Clinton-Mackendrick project. Her sensibility has been moulded by a pre-war Africa and she has no hesitation regarding the stance to be adopted in postcolonial India. The author remarks: "With no leeway either side there were no strains imposed. She was spared the bewilderment of Lefevre, the conscientious embarrassments of Mackendrick, the self-assertive exertions which Jackson in his off-moments confessed, exhausted him." (37)

Rekha Jha attributes Millie's attitude to the "past experience of a colonial life" that made her perceive the possibllity of "only one relationship between colonists and natives—that of overseer and serf.'"[29] Millie is proud of the exclusive cult of the English memsahib and strives to keep it pure. There were few left and she feels it necessary that they should meet occasionally for parties and picnics, keeping up the English spirit in the Indian wilderness. She guards her Englishness from being contaminated by contact with the alien environment. In the struggle to preserve her national and racial identity, she goes to extremes—organizes feverish activities like coffee-parties, shooting, jaunts to the nearest town that boasted a civilized club with a dance band and a bar and shopping in the big city emporiums—in order to prevent them all from being engulfed in eastern inertia. Helen (*The Coffer Dams*) contemptuously describes her efforts as "stiff little fences erected by silly old women afraid of the rape of their minds." (38) Oblivious of the changed values in the postcolonial set-up, she hardly comprehends the concealed contempt in the suave faces of the Indian shopkeepers as she persists in the self-assigned role of the imperial memsahib. Words like "blacks" and "niggers" pour out of her tongue with hardly any inhibition. Helen's empathy with the alien culture shocks her because in her perspective the worst calamity that could befall an Englishwoman in India was "to go native." (40)

Millle's pathetic struggle to escape the influence of India ends tragically as she loses her hold over the fragile props that sustained her mental balance. The odds projected by India are too much for her. The situation closely resembles the plight of the pioneering, colonial woman in Katherine Mansfield's story "Millie,"[30] brought to the edge of sanity by the harshness and loneliness of the colonial background. Millie Rawlings has too many odds to struggle against—the drink invariably runs out when the evening is still young: the Indian countenances hardly try to conceal the contempt, hurt and insult as they encounter the white: prohibition denies the comfort of getting drunk when the drag and dissatisfaction of colonial years pull her down: and finally comes the death of Bailey, the one devoted friend with whom she had started a desultory affair to escape the stress and strain of life in India. The slow disintegration of Millie's bearings is portrayed convincingly by Kamala Markandaya. But she withholds her sympathy from the victim of an out-dated ideology that should have been buried with the Empire. Pat Barr's analysis of the impact of India on Victorian women holds good in Millie's case: "For the average memsahib, whose own full personal and intellectual development had invariably been stunted by the restrictive conventions that Victorian England imposed on its womanhood, India was one enormous and continuing cultural shock."[31]

The problems of adjustment faced by the memsahibs in the period of transfer of power and the first years of Independence are brought out by Nayantara Sahgal through the portrait of Dora Grange (*Time to be Happy*). Dora, who had virtually reigned over the Sharanpur Club, feels her domain slowly slipping away from her grasp, with the dawn of Independence. The club, which had been the exclusive sanctuary of the English, is "polluted" by the bare brown bodies splashing in the swimming pool beside the white ones. Dora Grange was used to the sight of bare-bodied Indians; she had seen more naked than clothed Indians in the twenty-odd years she spent in India, but those were working people, labourers on the roads and beggars. But it irks her to watch the Indians of her own class, whom she customarily meets, and who were always well-clothed, jumping in and out of the water with the whites in a non-chalant fashion. Dora does not hesitate to reveal her feelings openly. She says that there is no need to throw open the membership to Indians, because no one prevented them from having their own club. Adopting the condescending tone of racial superiority, she says: "They just want to make themselves felt, that's all. It's so childish." (214) With her class she shares the characteristic colonizer mentality and believes that the Indians, as a race, were too immature to govern themselves. "You can't hand independence over to people as a gift. They simply don't know what to do with it," says Dora. (*A Time be Happy* 214) It is difficult for a person like Dora, who had basked in the glory of being "the burra memsahib of Sharanpur" to shed the plumes and descend to the monotony of being an ordinary person. To live on in India without the chivalrous attention, exaggerated courtesy and flirtatious glances of her social subordinates—"marionettes prancing to a jolly tune" (211)—would be like a living death. Unlike Dora, her husband Tom had always been aware of the transitoriness of the splendour of a sahib's life in India. He had kept himself mentally prepared for the day on which he would again become an ordinary British subject. But he knew that the adjustment would be harder for his wife, that too at an age when adjustments are not easy.

The Indian novelist achieves greater empathy with those Englishwomen who are departures from the typical memsahibs who have a liberal and humanistic attitude towards the Indians and break free from the rigid mould of the imperial role. Though rare, such women are closer to the Indian psyche and as those who guard their own selfhood, they attain greater individuality within the fictional framework. Mrs. Traylor in *I Shall Not Hear the Nightingale*[32] is a typical example. She shares her husband's liberal views and reflects the changing trends of thought in many Englishmen and women of the last decade preceding Independence. Taylor declares the Indian's right to freedom openly: Mrs. Joyce Tailor persuades her husband to extend the cup of mercy to Bhuta Singh and his sick wife, by releasing their son—suspect in a murder case—as a Christman gift. This essentially Christian act of goodwill raises her far above the fossilized Anglo-Indian community. Her genuine concern about Sabhrai's deteriorating condition, her daring in violating the protocol to meet an Indian subordinate's wife at the station, her extreme humanity unchecked by ethnic prejudices and her total withdrawal from the artificial glamour of her position as Deputy Commissioner's wife—are qualities that bear witness to a distinct individuality and nobility of mind. Unlike the shadowy memsahibs—Mrs. Hartley, Mrs. Barnes and others—she doesn't merge into the angularities of the class; nor does her individuality and abstinence from the code pose a crisis in marital relationship as in the case of Helen Clinton (*The Coffer Dams*) and Jean Walters (*Combat of Shadows*). It is her good fortune that her husband shares the same liberal attitude.

Jean Walters, who comes from an Indian army background, could be expected to conform strictly to the imperial code which was extolled like the Gospel in the military circles. Though a natural heir to colonial values, as the daughter of a former British Indian officer, she hardly acknowledges the colonial value system Kai Nicholson remarks: "Jean as a character represents an aggressive version of Mrs. Moore and a more-to-the-point Sara Layton."[33] She shows a frankness of expression and an openness of mind that come to open conflict with the "closed minds" of the English community in India. She shrewdly fathoms Sudden Dart's cunning in tactfully persuading Winton to take up the task of kllling the rogue elephant, creating the impression of singling him out for a special honour. When Henry Winton refuses to accept the truth and feels flattered about Sudden Dart's faith in him, Jean tells him frankly: "Some day, . . . some day you will stop being a boy scout, Henry Winton, and grow up, I mean really grow up. And then, mister Winton, you are golng to get a nasty shock." (44) The truth of her words strikes Winton rather too late, in moments of shocking self-realization.

Jean's friendly reference to "our Indian boys" guarding the Channel, pricks the race-proud Henry. (171) With the same openness she accepts the friendship of Eddie, the Anglo-Indian and later commits the unpardonable crime of falling in love with the Eurasian. Her infidelity with Eddie is her revenge on her corrupt and disloyal husband who has failed in giving her love and loyalty. It is as though her free and spontaneous nature finds the desired liberation from the inhibiting bond of marriage in the relationship with Eddie. In Helen Clinton (*The Coffer Dams*), there is a similar urge to establish intimacy with Bashiam: as though intimacy with him would mean an escape from the bonds of her position within the suffocating limits of the English community. The sexual act becomes svmbolic of spiritual liberty for both the women.

The women who are brought into perspective in the context of post-colonial Indo-British relations, show a greater range and variety, precisely because they are not part of the colonial regime. Colonial attitudes and memories linger; but these women, unlike Millie Rawlings (*The Coffer Dams*) do not cling on to the false assumptions and dead values of an erstwhile empire. Mrs. Bridie (*Pleasure City*) who came to India with her missionary-husband in the days of the Raj, stays on after Independence, clinging to nostalgic memories of a "home" to which she could never return. The Bridies are viewed through the adolescent eyes of Rikki, who is fascinated by the unexplored regions of knowledge they open before him and is repelled to a certain extent by the distinct "otherness" of Mrs. Bridie that makes her so different from Indian women. In spite of her puritanical restraints, Mrs. Bridie warms to Rikki, almost accepts him as her unborn son and initiates him into the world of books, sharpening his sensibilities and giving him a finer perception that alientates him even from his own fishing community. Her influence of Rikki thus symbolizes the impact of western education, western values and the more sophisticated sensibility of the west on the average Indian who becomes a product of two entirely different cultures and is forced to exist in a limbo. In a moment of man-to-man intimacy with Bridie, Rikki comes to know that the Bridies were childless because of prim Rosie's puritanical frigidity. in spite of that Bridie called her "Primrose" and sometimes under his breath "God's Bridie." (13) Often Mrs. Bridie's puritanism places barriers in Rikki's exploring, adolescent, curiosity. Rikki acknowledges his debt to her: "She gave me a lot. More than I knew. I wish I had known, at the time." (*Pleasure City* 227) Tully consoles him saying that it was not one way. Rikki's stepfather had also remarked about the satisfaction she might have derived from Rikki's innocent affection. "She knew what she took, and what she gave. She was not a child. You were." (227) The gaping emotional void in her childless existence was almost filled by Rikkie, the only consolation in her pathetic life in foreign soil where she always dreamt about the "home" she could never reach. She is devoid of all those racial complexes that give Englishwomen in India arrogant airs and create emotional barriers with Indians. Mrs. Bridie's situation becomes pathetic as she nostalgically revives memories of frost in England in the gruelling heat of a tropical May and as she suggests going to the hills, to Lovedale or Wellington—the unfashionable places where the missionaries and tommies go—even when she knows that she cannot afford it. She shares with Rikkie her cherished recollections of English flowers and English pastries, arousing in him a curiosity to know and fascination for the unknown land beyond the sea. Unlike Lucille Croft whose imperial upbringing made her extremely unpleasant to everyone and led to an unmourned death in a foreign soil, Mrs. Bridie's tragic end by botulism is regretted and mourned by Rikkie. Years later he acknowledges her gifts to him and takes Tully to the graves of Mr. and Mrs. Bridie—an indication of loyalties aroused and maintained, in spite of racial barriers.

Indo-British relations in postcolonial India forms the thematic concern of Kamala Markandaya's *The Coffer Dams* and *Pleasure City*. Nayantara Sahgal's *Rich Like Us* covers a long span of time starting with the days of the nationalist movement and stretching on to the period of the Emergency (1975). Both *The Coffer Dams* and *Pleasure City* depict the English coming to independent India as builders. In *The Coffer Dams* Kamala Markandaya presents Helen Clinton—the new Englishwoman, devoid of colonial prejudices and racial complexes, and contrasts her with Millie Rawlings in whom the memsahib mentality still prevails. An interesting assortment of Englishwomen is presented through *Pleasure City*. There is Corinna, the ravishingly beautiful and restless wife of Tully who comes to India with the spirit of a tourist in search of new attractions; there is Mrs. Pearl who falls in love with India and breaks her bonds with England to stay on in India with her adopted Indian child (dealt with in the next chapter) and there is the searcher, Mrs. Lovat who undertakes the exploratory journey to the East in search of new answers. Nayantara Sahgal's Marcella (*Rich Like Us*) too is a neocolonialist coming to discover the hitherto hidden spiritual and cultural wealth of India, hitherto unexplored by the colonial rulers. But it is not Marcella—the sophisticated English lady—but the cockney-speaking daughter of the English shopkeeper, Rose, who occupies the central status in *Rich Like Us*. Different facets of feminine experience are unravelled through these women and their encounters with India. Corinna, the smart independent English lady, is projected almost as a rival to Rikki, the Indian fisher boy who develops a possessive love for Tully. She is presented through Rikki's consciousness and we view her as an intruder into the haven of Rikki's blissful companionship with Tully. The colonial drama of conquest and subjugation operates in the Corinna-Rikki relationship when she succeeds in winning his admiration for her superb skill in the art of surfing and he becomes her radiant pupil. In spite of this, Corinna cannot establish the same emotional rapport with Rikki as Tully does, because she is inescapably English and cannot let India enter her spirit as Tully can. It is India that drives a wedge into the Corinna-Tully relationship. Corinna could not comprehend Tully's total involvement with India; nor could she adopt the traditional loyalty of Tully's Copeland grandmother whose guiding principle was that "one's place was by the side of one's husband," (*Pleasure City* 133) making choices simple. Corinna feels no such sense of duty binding her to Tully and hers is an honest relationship where there is no place for pretensions. She realizes that she cannot combat the invisible walls of India that alienate Tully from her—a woman would have been an easier rival. "She wouldn't have minded a woman, flesh and blood . . . unlike this citadel that evaporated before her when she would have challenged its bastions." (264) She takes her revenge by letting herself into Ranji's charms. Her final defiance of the elemental powers in taking part in the last run to decide the winner, against Rikki's warnings, causes Rikki almost his life In his attempt to save her. Subdued and humbled by what her impetuous arrogance has caused a young fisherboy who meant so much to Tully, Corinna apologizes to him. We perceive in Corinna a new humility that India through Rikki has taught her. She achieves an inner growth through the humble recognition of forces beyond human control and depths of loyalty and love that she could never fathom. But she fails to comprehend what Rikki, or the country to which he was inextricably bound, meant to Tully. India remains as elusive as ever to

Corrina's alien psyche but it does not bring about a break in the Corinna-Tully relationship. Mrs. Pearl, on the other hand, attains a complete identification with the alien country and makes India her home.

Through Mrs. Adeline Lovat, Kamala Markandaya introduces the eager tourist, a typical neo-colonial phenomenon, who wants to exploit the experiences of India and write a book about them. Her excessive curiosity and eager guestioning repels Rikki who feels she is prying into the fisherfolks' private life. Unlike Mrs. Lockwood, another tourist who comes just for the pleasure of visiting the place and stays only for a week, she makes herself unpleasant by her perpetual questioning. Rikki is amazed and irritated at the absolute lack of imagination that arouses her disbelief in legends that had been part of traditional Indian lore, handed down from generation to generation. The cultural barrier makes comprehension difficult, creating voids in communication. The probing and doubting western intellect seems strange to the emotional and intuitive apprehension of the fisherboy. Rikki almost becomes hostile: "Could she not imagine? How then did she get to her truths? He began to wonder about the books she wrote." (155) The dichotomy between the eastern and western approach to life is brought home by Kamala Markandaya, through the situation. The intellectual exploration conducted by the West, which has to arrive at the truth through logical reasoning and deduction, is here sharply contrasted with the emotional and intuitive awareness of it by the East. Kamala Markandaya has a dig at the preposterous tourist who irreverently probes the mystery of India, when she remarks with subtle irony that Mrs. Lovat's books about India were popular everywhere except in India. She could never make out why it had to be so. Markandaya hints that the elusive spirit of India evaded these tourists who were not even aware of it when they wrote books about the apparent surface reality of India.

Marcella, who comes back to India on a second visit, is a woman of greater depth and larger vision for she is the product of a civilization which is "matchless in the Western world for its unbroken continuity." (*Rich Like Us* 233) Her visit to India with her husband, was to be an explorative adventure into the decorative arts and cultural history of the mid-seventeenth century to mid-eighteenth century. Unlike Mrs. Lovat, her interest in India is not superficial and she is all set to bring out the hidden diamonds from an ever-fascinating cultural mine.

Chaman Nahal's *English Queens* is a satirical exposition of the blind admiration for the English language, ways of life, English literature, dress and customs that have become India's bane. The tendency has been recognized by Memmi (*The Colonizer and the Colonized*) as a typical feature of a newly independent nation to be tethered culturally and emotionally to the apron-strings of the erstwhile ruler even after the attainment of political independence. In his humorous satire Nahal pictures this Anglophilism as a predominant feature among Indian ladies, whose weakness is exploited very cleverly by Lord Mountbatten to secure India's cultural and emotional subjection to Britain. He chose six ladies to create a new Order—of the English Queens—who would be handed over a charter assigning to them the exclusive gift of the English language, which would not be used by the English people any longer. Barbara Smiles, an English lady who has taken up permanent residence in India, is one of the Queens. Even as the solemn oath is being administered to the Queens, Lord Mountbatten winks at her, sharing with her the big joke he was playing on the Indian ladies. Barbara Smiles is depicted as a thorough hypocrite who makes profit out of the educated Indian's Anglophilism. She makes a fortune by presenting an Indian image to her admirers, quite in harmony with the Indian atmosphere and the Indian situations that she creates in her novels. The English teachers in India praise her as an Indian Thackeray. Retaining all her English likes and dislikes, Barbara cleverly dupes her Indian readers, by appearing before them clad in an Indian sari, with the incense burning in her room and images of Durga and the Buddha adorning it by their serene presence. She exploits the gullibility of the Indians and establishes a reputation as a great novelist. Nahal's satire sparkles when he recounts Barbara Smiles' brilliant contributions to India—like introducing romantic love to India through her novels but toning it down to Indian platitudes like "true love comes after marriage" and inventing the convenient device of the middle man, indispensable in an Indian situation. A crisis arises when a girl of her own circle goes against the fictional situation and makes direct advances to Pradeep. Barbara Smiles is forced to make a pathetic confession: "The go-between is my bread and butter. Just as Eliot's Wasteland won't sell without his notes my novels won't sell if the go-between is withdrawn. Please don't take him away from me."[34] The shallowness of her fiction and the platitudes that make up popular cheap journalism are exposed here. She assembles the factors that appeal to Indian and western readers alike, in the correct proportions—a road accident, a hospital scene, a police scene, a jail scene and a court scene for the Indian: and an India full of cockroaches and flies to satisfy the expectations of English readers. Nahal's portrait of Barbara Smiles is intended to reveal the shallow Anglophilism that makes Indians still admire hypocrites like her—an indication of the continuing moral and cultural subjection to the whites.

The feminine sensibllity makes inroads to better understanding of the Englishwoman's psyche, as evident in the portraits provided by

Kamala Markandaya and Nayantara Sahgal. In Markandaya's case, her placement as an expatriate writer living in the ex-colonizer's country affords a sharper perspective and a deeper insight. Nayantara Sahgal resides in India, but is westernized enough to be close to the Englishwoman and to be able to depict the peculiar emotional and psychological problems of the Englishwoman in India. In *Rich Like Us*, her full-length portrait of Rose—an English lady married to an Indian and making India her home—brings into focus not only the conflict of eastern and western cultures incipient in an interracial marriage, but also the cultural void between the cockney-speaking English lady and the aristocratic Indian, refined and polished in the subtle art of sophisticated liking. The racially superior Englishwoman is relegated to the position of a culturally backward class and is effectively contrasted with another aristocratic and snobbish English lady, Marcella, who becomes a rival in love as well. Rose, however, is a character who has transcended the prejudices of race and class and is hence grouped with the other humane characters alienated from their own as well as the Indian ethos.

The deconstruction of ethnocentrism undertaken by a decolonizing artist is often carried out through a reversal of values and a re-assertion of the superiority of national culture. Thus, in post-Independence novels, we find the Indian woman continually pitted against her English counterpart almost always leading to an exposure of the shallowness of western culture. Orientalist discourse celebrating the Englishwoman is counteracted effectively by deliberately projecting western women as foils to Indian women. Sometimes they assume a significant functional role in the novel, helping the Indian protagonist to a re-discovery of his own self and repossession of his own identity. Many Englishwomen already discussed can be viewed in this light. Cynthia (*The Dark Dancer*), Caroline Bell (*Possession*) and Sophie (*The Golden Honeycomb*) have a prominent catalytic function in propelling the Indian protagonist's quest for wholeness.

Cynthia is the less convincing of the three women characters, mainly because the author views her as a projection of Krishnan's ideas about the west and not as an individual in her own right. Dieter Riemenschneider comments: "Rajan, it seems to me, is not really interested in Cynthia as a person in her own right, but only in his hero's morbid preoccupation with himself."[35]

Cynthia figures in the novel at first as the disturbing, conscientious westerner, reminding him of his own country and even prodding him to a guilty awareness of his ignorance about the happenings in his country. The same Cynthia becomes the symbol of the materialistic, progressive and seductive west, when she comes to India, for here she is pitted against the passive, traditional and tranquil Indian wife, Kamala. Krishnan lets himself in to Cynthia's charms only to realize during the short period of his life with her, that she, who wants to possess him wholly, can never help him to acquire wholeness. Kamala's stoic endurance, infinite patience with his vagaries and her undemanding acceptance symbolize the traditional aspects of ideal Indian womanhood and contrast glaringly with Cynthia's overtly independent, impetuous and demanding nature. Kamala finally succeeds in reforming her truant husband, creating a better person out of him. Cynthia, by making him realize the hollowness of western cultural mores—which he had been blindly pursuing—fulfils her function as a catalyst, driving him back to Kamala and leading to the rediscovery of lost identity. The contrast between Kamala and Cynthia is driven too hard, thus making them symbols projecting abstract ideas, rather than real persons. While Cynthia is the "body beautiful," Kamala is rooted deep in her soil and culture; Cynthia angrily rejects Krishnan when she cannot have him whole; Kamala accepts him without a harsh word when he comes back to her. Rajan writes about Cynthia: "At no time had she even thought of compromise. She had made him reach and she had let herself be given, the green of her country when he was ready for it, its loneliness, the cascade of its vigour. But the price of her dedication could not fall short of his complete acceptance, his readliness to live in her world entirely, and in her happiness, to its island limits."[36] Kamala, on the other hand, is ready to accept without thinking of reward, almost as a "dispassionate Karma" as dictated by the Gita. Uma Parameswaran called the novel "an intense story of the self-division and maturation of an individual,"[37] brought about through his contrasting experiences with the two women representing eastern and western values.

In *Possession* Kamala Markandaya uses Caroline to initiate Valmiki into the sophistication and rank materialism of western culture, thus arousing in him an awareness of the contrast between her possessiveness and the detachment of the Swami. Caroline's craving for possession is inspired by the neo-colonialist's enthusiastic adoration for an alien culture and art. She reduces Valmiki to the status of an inanimate object of adoration and denies him his human dimensions. Caroline's love has thus a destructive quality that transforms a person into the level of a "thing," a "non-human entity," whereas the Swami elevates him to the status of an artist communing with God translating art into a medium for self-expression. The religious and spiritual quality of art is lost on Caroline who is a product of a limiting materialistic culture. The aggressive seduction practised by Caroline, makes Valmiki realize the implied negation of his own identity and he tells Anasuya that her regard for him is dictated by his output as a creative artist; as a person, he is of no value to her. (55) With this realization comes an awareness of the Swami's sublime vision of art and the artist's vocation. Valmiki's struggle is resolved and he returns to India with an absolute sense of identification with the wilderness that is India: "a wilderness [that] is mine, . . . no longer terrible as it used to be; it is nothing." (220)

The Sophie-Rabi alliance in *The Golden Honeycomb* is effectively employed by Kamala Markandaya to bring out all "the rancour and sadness of the British-Indian relationship."[38] An intimacy that has sprung up naturally through shared interest and mutual attraction, ruptures on the verge of union, because of the pent-up prejudices of centuries, welling up in Sophie and projecting invisible barriers. However, unlike Mira (*Some Inner Fury*) who got deeply involved in the affair with Richard, Rabi is on his guard because he knows that Sophie is sure to be influenced in the course of time by people like her mother. Margaret Joseph has commented on the evolution of thought perceptible in Kamala Markandaya's treatment of the Sophie-Rabi affair from the earlier tragic Richard-Mira episode. Here Rabi guards himself from wrecking his heart for he knows that his future is not with a race "seduced by an arrogant philosophy and tainted by pride." (*The Golden Honeycomb* 407) Sophie's rejection of him confirms his fears and he is driven to Usha, the Dewan's daughter and to an awareness that in the union with her alone can he achieve wholeness.

The narrowness of outlook and the emotional starvation of the feminine psyche are identified and analyzed as typical English weaknesses and are constantly projected against the broader and more liberal attitudes of Indian women as well as women of other nationalities. The emotionally impoverished Angela Davis, who rejects Kenneth Ashby (*The Crown and the Loincloth*)[39] because of her nervous fear of taking the plunge into life, is juxtaposed in Ashby's thoughts with the young sensuous women of the Punjab who swing in the mango grove and sing to their heart's content, songs—literally, mating calls—that celebrate the life of the senses, of love, of springtime happiness and a rejuvenation of spirit. Celia Ashby, Kenneth Ashby's American aunt, figures as a frank critic of British imperialism and narrow racism. She describes the death of thousands of Indians through the annual phenomena of the famines as deliberate genocide. She attacks in her will the hypocrisy of the English who provide all luxuries to the officers in India, but let the tommies live in deplorable conditions—a reminder of the class system of the English at home. She is refreshingly different from the narrow-minded Englishwomen who deliberately close their eyes to the reality around them.

Anna in *Plans for Departure* is the Danish narrator whose consciousness acts as the medium of perception for the reader. Her broader vision and unprejudiced outlook afford a clear perspective of the Stella-Henry relationship and the invisible walls that rose and pulled them apart. Anna, the Danish assistant to the Indian scientist Nitin Bose, refuses to conform to the rigid formalities of a memsahib's life. Her informal ways and humane attitude, freshness of mind and openness of outlook provide a sharp contrast to Stella and suggests a might-have-been partner for Henry.

A prominent feature that reveals itself in the portrayal of the Englishwomen in Indian English fiction is the technique of depersonalization employed by the Indian novelists to reduce the colonial women to types displaying class-behaviour and even a clannish consciousness. It is a recognized characteristic of Third World literature that it feels compelled to rewrite its distorted history, restate its values and renovate its culture and tradition—in short, to displace the western vision of the "orient" or the "other" propagated by the colonizers, by the eastern or oriental vision of the west. Using cultural parameters the Indian novelists proclaim the superiority of Indian culture and womanhood to the western. The English women characters mainly serve as instruments employed to expose the inadequacy and weakness of the system they represent and project the superiority of their eastern counterparts.

Kamala Markandaya and Nayantara Sahgal come closest to the comprehension of the alien feminine psyche. None of these writers have attempted to use the first-person narrative technique in the depiction of Englishwomen. This reluctance to attempt an inside-portrayal of the Englishwoman's consciousness, speaks for the intellectual honesty of the writers. The challenge of colonialism, resting on widely propagated ideas of ethnic and cultural superiority, is encountered on its own terms through a total reversal of the colonial paradigm and the projection of the Indian woman as the culturally superior being. Anita Desai, who has made the feminine psyche her forte has not bothered to solve the enigma of the Englishwoman in India, though the cultural differences surfacing in an Indian-English marriage and the ethnic hostility the Indian has to combat against in England, form the thematic concern of *Bye-Bye, Blackbird.*[40] Sarah, the English girl wedded to an Indian, does not hold any deep-rooted prejudice against the Indians as a race, but Anil's Bengali music jars on her English sensibility and their tastes in food prove fatally uncompromising. However, she struggles to sustain her marriage and resents the racial hostility that makes life in England difficult for them (dealt with in a later chapter).

The racial exclusiveness of the Englishwomen in British India and the hangover of colonial prejudices have placed obstacles in the Indian novelists' approach to Englishwomen. Hence the stereotyped portrayal of the typical English memsahibs. With the women of the post-independent era, the Indian English novelists are more successful for the writers as well as the Englishwomen have attained a greater degree of liberation from the levelling influence of the imperial ethos. The Indian novelists' imagination is stirred by the white women who strove to attain empathy with India, alienating themselves from their community in the process and still failing to achieve total identification with India. Their struggle in a cultural limbo poised between two worlds and their failure to belong to either, become thematic concerns in many Indian English novels. By refusing to accept orientalism and the constricting codes of the female English community in India, these liberated women earn a place along with the sensitive British men who seek spiritual empathy with India. These English men and women, who are doomed to suffer as nowheremen, form the subject of the next chapter.

NOTES

1. The terms in quotation are from Jameson, *The Political Unconscious: Narrative as a Socially Symbolic Act* (Ithaca: Cornell Univ. Press, 1981).
2. Quoted in Pat Barr, *The Memsahibs: The Women of Victorian India* (London: Martin Secker and Warburgh, 1976) 1.
3. Francis Hutchins, quoted in Peggy Woodford, *The Rise of the Raj* (Kent: Midas Books, 1978) 85.
4. Manohar Malgonkar, *The Devil's Wind* (London: Hamish Hamilton, 1972) 54.
5. E.M. Forster, "Reflections in India: 1—Too Late?" *The Nation and the Athenaeum*, 30 (21 January 1922) 615.
6. Kamala Markandaya, "On Images," Paper read at the Seminar on Socio-literature at the East-West Centre for Cultural Interchange, Honolulu, August 1973, 5.
7. Kamala Markandaya, *A Handful of Rice* (Delhi: Orient Paperbacks, 1985) 160.
8. Kamala Markandaya, *The Coffer Dams* 37.
9. Mannoni, *Prospero and Caliban: The Psychology of Colonization* 114.
10. Michael Edwardes, *Raj* (London: Pan Books, 1969) 48-50.
11. T.N. Murari, *The Imperial Agent* 102.
12. John Masters, *Nightrunners of Bengal* (1951: London: Michael Joseph, 1962) 25.
13. Dennis Kincaid, *British Social Life in India, 1608-1937* (1938; London and

Boston: Routledge and Kegan Paul, 1973) 272.
14. Shamsul Islam, *Chronicles of the Raj* (London: Macmillan, 1979) 94. ·
15. Benita Parry, *Delusions of Discoveries* 105-6.
16. E.M. Forster, *A Passage to India* (London: Penguin, 1974) 42.
17. Neeta Gupta, "The Memsahibs of Anglo-Indian Fiction," *The Literary Half-Yearly*, XXIX, 1 (Jan. 1988) 55.
18. Quoted by Dennis Kincaid, 164.
19. Nayantara Sahgal, *Rich Like Us* (London: Heinemann, 1985) 90
20. E.M. Forster, "Notes on the English Character," *Abinger Harvest*, 5.
21. S.C. Harrex, "A Sense of Identity: The Novels of Kamala Markandaya," *The Journal of Commonwealth Literature*, VI.
22. O. Mannoni 18.
23. Margaret Joseph, *Kamala Markandaya* (New Delhi: Arnold Heinemann, 1980).
24. Kamala Markandaya, *Possession* (Bombay: Jaico, 1963) 3.
25. Elena J. Kalinikova, *Indian English Literature: A Perspective*, ed. K.K. Sharma (Ghaziabad: Vimal, 1982) 156.
26. Haydn Moore Williams, "Victims and Virgins: Some Characters in Kamala Markandaya's Novels," *Galaxy of Indian Writings in English* (Delhi: Akshat, 1987) 111-21.
27. S.K. Aithal, "Indo-British Encounter in Kamala Markandaya's Novels," *Journal of South Asian Literature*, 22, 2 (Summer Fall 1987) 52.
28. S.C. Harrex, *The Fire and the Offering: The English Language Novel of India, 1935-70* (Calcutta: Writers' Workshop, 1977) 252.
29. Rekha Jha, *The Novels of Kamala Markandaya and Ruth Jhabvala: A Study in East-West Encounter* (New Delhi: Prestige, 1990) 35.
30. Ian Gordon, ed., *Undiscovered Country: The New Zealand Stories of Katherine Mansfield* (London: Longmans, 1974).
31. Pat Barr, *The Memsahibs: The Women of Victorian India* 143.
32. Khushwant Singh, *I Shall Not Hear the Nightingale* (1959; rpt. Bombay: IBH, 1970)
33. Kai Nicholson, *A Presentation of Social Problems in the Indo-Anglian and the Anglo-Indian Novel* (Bombay: Jaico, 1972) 208.
34. Chaman Nahal, *The English Queens* (New Delhi: Vision Books, 1979) 73.
35. Dieter Riemenschneider, "British Characters in Indo-English Fiction," *Aspects of Indian Writing in English*, ed. M.K. Naik (Delhi: Macmillan, 1979) 147.
36. B. Rajan, *The Dark Dancer* (New York: Simon and Schuster, 1958) 180.
37. Uma Parameswaran, *A Study of Representative Indo-English Novelists* (New Delhi: Vikas, 1976) 125.
38. Arthur Pollard, "Kamala Markandaya's *The Golden Honeycomb*," *Journal of Indian Writing in English*, 8, 1 & 2 (Jan.-July 1980) 25.
39. Chaman Nahal, *The Crown and the Loincloth* (Delhi: Vikas, 1981).
40. Anita Desai, *Bye-Bye, Blackbird* (Delhi: Pocket Books, 1970).

Between Two Worlds

Albert Memmi, in his famous work, *The Colonizer and the Colonized*, distinguishes between the colonizer who willingly adopts the role of usurper and the one who rejects the colonial ideology. To quote Memmi, "If every colonial immediately assumes the role of colonizer, every colonizer does not necessarily become a colonialist."[1] The colonizer who refuses to conform to the rigid mould of the imperial value system, either withdraws silently or remains to fight and change the conditions around him. By deliberately choosing the difficult path, he alienates himself from his own fellowmen. He invites their antagonism either by open rebellion against their mode of life or implied criticism of their code of values. The kind of humanitarian romanticism he displays, is looked upon in the colonies as a serious illness or the worst of all dangers.

The conscientious rejector of colonialism thus becomes a criminal in the eyes of his community. He is one who has moved over to the side of the enemy. In imperial nomenclature, his crime is that of letting the side down—the worst crime a colonizer can commit. However, ethnic identity with the ruling community turns out to be too strong a barrier to overcome. Internally he is forced to segregate himself from both communities and remains poised between two worlds. As an isolated being, his lone voice of protest becomes the feeble cry of an ineffectual angel beating its luminous wings against the pillars of the Empire. As a dissenter, he invites the rancour and contempt of his fellowmen. As a foreigner and a member of the ruling community, who takes sides with the native and champions the cause of their freedom, he wins sympathy and tolerance from the occupied people, but not love or complete emotional rapport. He remains an outsider in both cultures. If his own kind, the colonizers are chased out of the country, the colonized may not make any exception for him. He thus leads a lonely and painful existence, torn between personal loyalties and ideals on the one side, and the shared collective responsibility to the oppressor group on the other.

Englishmen harbouring such unhoused sensibilities occupy significant roles in Indian English fiction. They are grouped in this chapter and as the title indicates, their mental conflicts and their precarious placement in the colonial set-up form the subject of inquiry here. They are the outsider-insiders in the Indian cultural ethos, striving for complete rapport, but destined to remain the heroes between two worlds and the polarities of the different value systems that govern them. The process of decolonization goes on in them and can be recognized in the steady denial of "the tyranny of externality"[2] and the assertion of an authentic emotional life. Absence of racial arrogance and ethnic prejudices in them help the Indian novelists to establish greater emotional identification with the characters, thus attaining a deeper insight into their psychic problems. The implied value system operating in the writings of the Indian English novelists naturally projects these rejectors of colonialism as the noble and virtuous men in contrast with the die-hard colonialists. Ethics of virtue and essential goodness are redefined to suit these Englishmen of essential humanity, extreme sensitivity and liberal-mindedness. They are men who have transcended national and ethnic barriers and are able to perceive the undercurrents of love, humanity and truth in all races. As men who guard their conscience and retain their essential nobility against the temptations of colonial privileges they command respect.

On the basis of the difference in their response to the colonial set-up, it is possible to discern three distinct categories emerging from the anti-imperialists in Indian English fiction.

1. Those who passively accept their roles in the imperial regime, even when they are mentally hostile to the ideology of the colonizer.
2. Those who reject the system outright, loudly denounce the scandalous exploitation of the native and openly side with the occupied nation's efforts to resist colonial oppression.
3. The "decolonized"[3] white men who totally reject western culture and enter into an emotional and spiritual communion with the east. Some of them even choose India as their permanent home.

Alienation from one's own community is a natural consequence in all cases. It is found that this does not guarantee total identification with the Indian ethos nor total acceptance by the native community. The resulting alienation from both English and Indian communities leaves these Englishmen unhoused beings, caught in the existential angst of the modern man, dangerously poised between two worlds and without roots or a sense of belonging in either. Apart from the problem of alienation, their condemnation of the colonial system, sympathy for the national movement, desire to relate to the Indian through promising friendships are issues that form the concern of the novelists. The decolonized white men who have succeeded in emancipating themselves from the emotional burden of white destiny, but fail to find permanent anchorage in India, the host country, present a more interesting area of study. One of the side issues arising from the novelists' scrutiny of their rootless existence in the adopted country is the disharmony in martial relationship caused by the conflict of ideology between partners.

A phenomenon of the post-Independence era, recognized and dealt with by the Indian novelists, is the white man's journey to the east, in search of spiritual answers, leading on to an affirmation of eastern values and even a return to nature and primitive roots, as against the attraction of the glossy civilizations of the west. The case of the decolonized white men is explored by the Indian novelists with great insight and it is stated in unambiguous terms that India cannot be a permanent home for these "nowheremen." In the entire range of the Indian English novel, there are only stray instances of Englishmen who have found permanent roots in India—in itself a clear illustration of the above statement. To quote Helen Tiffin, "Only by the rejection of material possession, and of the attitudes of white destiny can colonizer or conqueror spiritually possess the new land."[4]

The dissenting colonials who are passive rejectors and who continue to be part of the established pattern form the first category brought under purview in this chapter. They do not adopt any effective measures to change the moral situation they denounce. They even enjoy most of the privileges that they want to reject. They just manage to prevent themselves from falling into the hardened stance of the usurper and preserve the capacity to understand and sympathize with the native. Hugh Wheeler, Charles Hillersdon, John Lang (*The Devil's Wind*), Kenneth Ashby (*The Crown and the Loincloth*), Sergeant William Davidson (*Azadi*), Platt (*The Nowhere Man*), Richard (*Some Inner Fury*), Donovan (*Chronicles of Kedaram*), Cole (*Chronicles*), Wilson (*Silence of Desire*), Taylor (*I Shall Not Hear the Nightingale*), Henry Brewster (*Plans for Departure*), Arthur Copeland (*The Golden Honeycomb*) and Mark McIvor (*A Time to be Happy*) fall into this category. Their predicament can be aptly described by quoting Meenakshi Mukherjee as she deals with Sarah Sen's plight in Anita Desai's *Bye-Bye, Blackbird,* for like Sarah, they undergo "the suffering of daily duality—for having to inhabit two incompatible worlds."[5]

The historical figures, Sir Hugh Wheeler and Sir Charles Hillersdon in Manohar Malgonkar's *The Devil's Wind*, embody the agonizing pull between divergent loyalties. Wheeler's marriage to an Indian lady and his thorough acclimatization to the subject people and their culture become his bane. He is totally alienated from the English community of

Kanpur and is virtually ostracized from English society and humiliated in official career. The English condemn him for having gone "native"; the natives murder him for being "English." His tragic fate fully endorses Memmi's premise about "the leftist colonizer" who, he says, "is part of the oppressing group and will be forced to share its destiny, as he shared its good fortune. If his own kind, the colonizers should one day be chased out of the colony, the colonized would probably not make any exception for him."[6] Charles Hillersdon too suffers a similar fate, though he was a romantic who responded to the lure of Sanskrit literature and developed, like Wheeler, a warm friendship with Nana Sahib. Nana Sahib came to consider him "a cultivated English Brahmin," an "exact opposite number" of his (117) whereas he became suspect in the eyes of his compatriots who branded him "orientalist." In the hour of crisis, as ethnic feelings over-ruled all other considerations, Hillersdon was shot dead in the Entrenchment where the English had sought refuge during the Sepoy Mutiny.

John Lang, a lawyer from England (*The Devil's Wind*), however, has a moment of triumph when, by a bold act of defiance he could declare his allegiance to his friend Nana Sahib and express his animosity to the power-mad, self-righteous English officials in India. He plays a prank on the East India Company's officials by certifying Ayodhya Prasad's portrait to be Nana Sahib's, thus finding a means to express his dislike of the pompous and power-corrupt officials of the Company.

Kamala Markandaya has depicted poignantly the crisis of identity suffered by a humane person cast in the imperial role, through her portrait of Sir Arthur Copeland (*The Golden Honeycomb*), the Second Political Agent of Devapur State. The pomp and glory invested by the post of "the Honourable the Resident," makes heavy demands on his self and he is often compelled to stifle his natural humanity and liberal vision to appease the imperial code. The restraints imposed are many and his essential self struggles to escape being submerged beneath the rigid formalities of officialdom and the careful guarding of British interests. His artificially imposed rigidity is exposed by Kamala Markandaya through his encounters with the emotional exuberance of the Indian prince and the spiritual depths of the Brahmin minister Tirumal Rao, son of the former Narasimha Rao.

Sir Arthur Copeland's unmistakable imperial leanings are revealed in his sincere efforts to subject Rabi to the British system of education, in order to produce "an ideal prince' like Bawajiraj III. In spite of this, his essential humanity is stressed throughout. Arthur Pollard remarks that even his name Copeland is deliberately chosen, in the sense of "managing."[7] If he does ill, it is because of what he calls "defects of imagination." So he escapes being a hardened imperialist and lends himself to sympathy and understanding.

He feels genuinely guilty about the lines drawn in the relationship with the native and is painfully conscious of the rigorous curb on his emotions when Waji visits his home and exudes a spontaneous warmth towards his children. He feels ashamed of the sham performance put up by his wife and himself and at such moments enters into a search of his soul only to become aware of the alienation from his real self brought about by the privations of the role. Impulsive stirrings of good will have to be hastily stifled, by reminding himself of judicious pieces of advice like "princely participation in the British scheme is too important to be the subject of parley while in the grip of wayward emotion." (125)

The approaches to personal relationships made by Sir Arthur go a long way in winning him popularity and adoration. Moreover, he had always been cautious in the exercise of authority for "to have applied more than a touch of the rein would have branded him in his own eyes as a failure." (326) Persuasion was the weapon in his armour that helped him to bring the Maharajah to his point of view.

Sir Arthur shows the willingness to change with the times as the national movement gathers strength in Devapur. In him Kamala Markandaya shows the development of awareness, described by Leonard Woolf in his autobiography, "from an innocent, unconscious imperialist"[8] disconcerted by the atmosphere surrounding a ruling caste in a strange Asiatic country, to a full knowledge of what his position as ruler over subject peoples entailed. He tries to make compromises and invites Indians to tea-parties at the Residency for the first time. In the British encounter with the Gandhian non-violent protest against the imposition of salt-tax, staged by Rabi, Sir Arthur yields gracefully to public pressure, thus preventing an awkward confrontation with the masses. By his graceful yielding he sets an example for all the British officials of the Empire and the Crown itself. The results of his action are extremely gratifying to Sir Arthur, who has experienced the burden of goodwill the people bore him. "Indians asked for so little, he felt, and if you give that little, the response was out of all proportion." (379) His action which prevents an open confrontation with a crowd of non-violent people led by the prince himself, provides a fitting finale to his career in India. He sets an example to the English community of essential humanity triumphing over staunch imperialism and narrow racism.

Many liberal-minded Englishmen, having an anathema to the colonial system are found entangled in the bureaucratic set-up of the regime, torn between the demands of an authoritative job and personal leanings. Mostly they struggle to safeguard their humanitarian sentiments from being crushed by the self-righteous value-system of the ruling community. Characteristics that differentiate them from the ruling community can be identified. Unlike the imperialists who segregate themselves into the exclusively English cloisters of the clubs and the hill-resorts, these broad-minded individuals are seen to be liberated selves, whose spirits are not bound by narrow racism. They overcome the ethnic barriers that separate man from man; refuse to be satisfied by the monotonous, clannish life of the club and from beautiful friendships with the Indians. They retain a freshness of mind free from the clogging prejudices of colonialism and evince a live curiosity to explore the untasted glories of the Indian classics. They are frank in the loud denunciation of imperialism and openly express their sympathy for the Indian liberation movement.

The bitter indictment of the ruling community is evident in their acts and deeds. Cole, the Manager and Headmaster of a Mission High School (*Chronicles of Kedaram*) is portrayed by K. Nagarajan as a confirmed democrat and an anti-imperialist endowed with a breadth of mind and largeness of vision which the narrow-minded colonialists could never possess. In the thirties as he watches the activities of the Indian National Congress, he comments to his friends that the Congress was moving in the right direction and compliments its achievements in the socio-political fields. He declares to their utter disbelief: "I would much rather be ruled by Congress than by I.C.S." (159) But Sastri knows that 'one swallow doesn't make a summer' and it needs several Englishmen like Cole to bring about a change in the attitude of the English race.

Khushwant Singh's John Taylor, the Deputy Commissioner of Punjab, retains a liberal mind within the strait-jacket of official authority. When he openly declares his allegiance to the Indian national movement, his subordinate, Buta Singh is puzzled about the authenticity of this Englishman and comes to the conclusion that was "an oddity—an oddity to be respected and liked." (*I Shall Not Hear the Nightingale* 24) Taylor, though sincere in his condemnation of imperialism, is wary of fascist powers wresting authority. He remarks to Buta Singh: "You know we are anxious to get out of India and hand over the reins of power to you people as soon as the war is over. But we will not leave the country to the Japanese or the Germans. (159)

Nahal has also brought out the feeling of bitterness that troubles the conscientious Englishman through his portrait of Sergeant Bill Davidson in *Azadi*. Bill Davidson had been eye-witness to the ruthless destruction of the local cultures of Malaya and Africa by the British and he is painfully conscious of the injustice of meting out the same fate to India which has a long history and rich cultural heritage. Bill had grown to love India and smarts under the injustice of continued British rule. He shows unusual maturity and an earnest regard for the welfare of India as he warns his Indian friends against undue haste in speeding up the transfer of power: "Don't get me wrong. I'm not advocating continued British rule. What I mean is haste will lead to fragmentation. In the interest of a united India the delay of a month or year won't hurt, it would rather strengthen the nation, if the Indian leaders were not too rash." (119)

Both the Indian and English leaders seem to lack the foresight of Bill who always maintains that "there's something of a panic in the way they [Indians] behave, and this will result in tragedy." (121) When at last partition becomes a hard reality to be reckoned with, Bill asserts that it was "the most stupid, most damaging, most negative development in the history of the freedom struggle here." (122) Bill is pained by the fact that English are speeding the issue. He feels that the British should have stood by the Cabinet Mission Plan, even though there were protests from Indians because it would have granted partition avoiding at the same time its evil effects. Bill speaks like a man who is hurt inside, whose dreams have been miscarried because what happens in India with the partition strikes him as a personal tragedy.

Sympathy for India and her cause enable these English men to attain an emotional rapport with the Indian ethos, which in itself explains the satisfactory and rounded portraiture achieved by the Indian novelist in these cases. Free from the dehumanizing colonial code, these characters lend themselves to individualization. They emerge from Indian fiction as more convincing characters.

Henry Brewster, the District Magistrate of Himapur (*Plans for Departure*) is a portrait done with great sympathy and understanding by Nayantara Sahgal. This is specially so, because for the most part, we are made to view Henry through the loving and admiring eyes of the Danish lady Anna who is in love with him. Henry is projected as an idealist who shares the awareness of Taylor and Bill Davidson about the unjustified continuation of British presence in India. Henry often visualizes the departure of the British from India with bag and baggage in twenty or thirty year's time. He thinks that the Government should have been "planning to phase itself out, and passing acts of conviviality meanwhile, instead of riot acts." (36) He wants to announce to his English friends that their days in India are numbered. He has a veritable abhorrence of imperial measures like public executions of native wrong-doers and finds it extremely difficult to satisfy the demands of his job. The duality within himself torments him as he stands as silent witness to the execution of Khudiram, himself "a symbol of authority, questioning the authority he was exercising." (70) Anna's assessment of Henry Brewster is quite expressive of his attitude: "Henry Brewster . . . is a mold-breaking man, but as the imperial mold [sicl is not likely to break, I should call him a mold-cracker instead. Quite some cracks he has made, mainly by being informal and friendly." (87)

Henry is portrayed in contrast to the hardened imperialist Robert Pryor and the missionary Croft who looks like an empire-builder. It is Henry's dream to resign his post and return to England because he knows "there is another England, one that doesn't preside over executions on soil where it has no right to be in the first place. There is a new world in the making at home! I wanted to be present at its birth." (281) Henry's dreams are not fulfilled and it is war and later death that provide him the longed-for release from the suffocating imperial machinery. His dreams could hardly flower in the clogging system of which he was a part because his ideas and thoughts were totally incompatible with its values. When he wrote cautious creeds recommending policy changes, suggesting that whole populations could not be treated with suspicion and championing an equal relationship which could only be developed by mixing of the two communities, the top-brass started viewing him with suspicion and branded him a person of "flawed" reasoning, mentally unsound. Pryor's epitaph for Henry sums up the views of the Imperial system regarding such misfits: "A capable man, one of our best, but he never did understand the ideology of rule." (206)

The ideology of rule becomes equally unpalatable to Kenneth Ashby (*The Crown and the Loincloth*) who feels his mission in India is a mission of love. Though the responsibility of office, as the Deputy Commissioner of Amritsar, is heavy on him he feels the pull of conflicting loyalties as he comes to love India and its people and considers it his duty to help India win her freedom through the goodwill of England. Ashby's Ideology and humanitarian sentiments are contrasted with the die-hard imperialism of Dyer. Dyer cannot understand why Ashby should intervene when he is punishing Sunil on seditious charges. However, years of schooling in non-involvement and avoiding alliances makes it difficult for Ashby to take up cudgels on behalf of the Indian nationalist movement. His sympathies lay with the nationalists, but he couldn't desert the Raj, of which he was an integral part. Ashby's ambivalent stance towards the Indian and the conflict with the Empire, do not become major issues in the novel. Nahal saves his Englishman from taking the crucial decision and committing the unpardonable crime of deserting his own side.

Passive and silent acquiescence in the working out of the imperial machinery takes a more pronounced form in Richard (*Some Inner Fury*) who just lets himself be overpowered by the force of circumstance. The honest, sincere, warm and friendly Richard Marlowe is said to be refreshingly different from the cold, aloof and insular English community "who had forgotten the decencies of England amid the authoritarianism of empire." (124) Kamala Markandaya has made Richard pleasing and likeable with his curiosity to know India, his dislike for the rigid formality of English behaviour and his informal and almost involuntary custom-flouting. Even after assuming office, he does not let his individuality pale into the rigid formality of officialdom. He fulfils the requirements of his post with the punctiliousness of an English officer, but seems to be more his normal self when he discards the formal mask and goes off with Mira to unfrequented Indian restaurants in by-lanes and holiday resorts where the spirit leads him. He sits cross-legged on the floor of Brahmin restaurants, shows the courage of mind to break away from the traditional rut and to enjoy life in one's own original manner. It is a remarkable feature in a member of the ruling class in the occupied country and it is a quality that compels one to admire him. Richard shows a sympathetic understanding and consideration for the Indian ethical values that bind Mira and imposes a restraint on his passions. He is even ready to comply with her mother's wish and wait till Mira is twenty one, to get married. In spite of such genuine and sincere efforts to identify himself completely with the Indian ethos, at the hour of crisis Richard finds it difficult to make a choice. Throughout the novel, Richard is presented through Mira's perspective which itself does not guarantee a detached and objective portrayal of character. At the end when passions run high in the court where Govind is being tried, and Mira's word is pitted against that of Hickey—the English missionary—and consideration of "my people" and "your people" have created grooves in every relationship, and Mira too is carried away by the overwhelming surge of national feeling, Richard is left the victim of political and racial allegiances that override personal loyalties. We are left to wonder about his passive submission to fate and to piece together a tragic tale of mob violence from a blood-stained piece of shirt and Mira's memories. Mira's viewpoint becomes a restraining factor to Richard's growth and denies the possibility of insights into any internal conflicts that he might have experienced.

Nayantara Sahgal presents through Mark McIvor (*A Time to be Happy*) a perfect contrast to the authoritative imperialist Cyril Weatherby. Whereas Weatherby fumes and blusters with the power invested in him, McIvor is quiet, unassuming and friendly. He dispenses with the formalities of the colonial bureaucrat and treats his subordinates as equals, insisting on abandoning even the "Sir" when they come to discuss official matters with him. He exercises authority in a quiet way, unlike Weatherby who bursts into fits of temper. He is friendly with his Indian subordinates and even attends social functions to which they invite him. Unlike Taylor (*I Shall Not Hear the Nightingale*) and Cole (*Chronicles of Kedaram*), he does not openly side with the Indians and does not envisage the possibility of immediate independence for India. He has little faith in the national leaders, but feels that the administration would be safe in the hands of western-educated Indians like Sanad. He tells Sanad: "You must remember that when, eventually, India becomes a self-governing dominion, we will have left her a trained army and a trained civil service. These are the elements that will run the new regime." (150)

McIvor transcends racial and national barriers and envisages the evolution of a universal culture—its members being men of a civilized, educated breed who cannot be confined within national or racial boundaries. He thinks that the world is in need of such a universal culture. He views Sanad as a typical representative of this new brand of men, because he could move with ease in the Indian and English circles, assimilating the best of both worlds. Because of his broader vision that engulfs the entire world, he cannot understand why Sanad should feel alienated from this countrymen. McIvor could accept Independence and the rejection of British rule with philosophic equanimity because of his higher perception and understanding of the alien country and its culture. He is an example of an Englishman who could take pride in the achievements of the Empire without imbibing the arrogant imperialistic sentiments of the ruling community. His approach to the colonized is that of a curious friend, eager to know and understand the culture and values they represent. Racial and cultural barriers melt away before his humanitarian sympathies.

Rejection of imperial cult resulted in the alienation of these Englishmen from their community. For the imperialists who believed in their ethnic superiority, the club was a symbol of racial segregation in British India. As a natural corollary to this, those who rejected the imperial value-system displayed an aversion to the club and its snobbish and artificial life. These officers who refused to go to the club, were taking upon themselves a voluntary exile from the English community—a crime for which they could be branded outcastes or rebels. They found themselves excluded from the ruling class leading the life of exiles in a self-created island of lonelinness.

Wheeler (*The Devll's Wind*) for instance, is rejected by the entire English community for having committed the unpardonable crime of marrying an Indian lady. The Doab club and other British clubs are closed to Wheeler's "country-born" wife Janaki. She, in turn, closes the

Flagstaff House against the English community, making Wheeler's alienation from the community total. Taylor (*I Shall Not Hear the Nightingale*), as Deputy Commissioner, is elected President of the exclusive European club. But he never visits the club. So the Taylors soon find themselves exiles in a lonely island with just one another for company. They have to resort to their own pastimes like riding, taking long walks and watching birds—thus finding more than adequate compensation for the tall talk and pomposity of club-life. Loneliness owing to ideological differences with the English community is coupled with that caused by his wife's desertion in Henry Brewster (*Plans for Departure*). Solitude descends on him like a pall, which cannot be shaken off. The occasional efforts to establish points of contact with the society outside turn out to be miserable failures. Most of the liberal-minded Britishers are lonely men, outcastes from their own community, groping for an emotional anchorage in India.

The love for the host land, the curiosity about its culture and values and the desire to establish contact with the natives are the initial steps that lead to the "decolonization" of these Englishmen. Recognition of native culture and the validity of the occupied people as human beings are crucial factors in the breaking up of the colonizer-mentality and the creation of "decolonized" men. Memmi describes the process thus: "Since he has discovered the colonized and their existential character, since the colonized have suddenly become living and suffering humanity, the colonizer refuses to participate in their suppression and decides to come to their assistance. At the same time, he has understood that he has only changed his province, he has another civilisation before him, customs differing from his own, men whose reactions often surprise him, with whom he does not feel deep affinity."[9]

Ashis Nandy has pointed out how the "discovery" of the "Orient" by the colonizer, described elegantly by Edward Said,[10] "was designed to expel the other Orient which had once been a part of medieval European consciousness as an archetype and a potentiality."[11] It is the rediscovery of the oriental archetype and the reawakening of interest in the culture he represents, that constitutes the process of decolonizing. Colonial images of the Prospero-Caliban nature are toppled. We find these white men reaching across the barriers of culture to establish enduring relationships with Indians. This is made possible by an enrichment of mind achieved through eager curiosity to explore Indian culture, literature and religion.

In each one of these Englishmen, who have made the difficult choice of rejecting the inherited culture, we can find the pull towards Indian culture, religion and literature. India exercises a fascination over them which they can hardly resist. In Wheeler (*The Devil's Wind*) it manifests as a superficial preference for Indian Kurta, pyjamas, and hookah, for Indian food and the habit of speaking Hindi to his family. In Hillerdson (*The Devil's Wind*) on the other hand, the interest is deeper and more scholarly. He is essentially a romantic who responds to the call of India, not out of infatuation for wealth or power, but out of eagerness to plunge into the untasted glories of Sanskrit literature. He makes a study of Kalidasa as a dramatist. His friendship with Nana Sahib is the affinity between two cultured minds drawing nourishment from one another. It is Hillerdson's "unnatural" aptitude for eastern literature and culture that makes him suspect in the eyes of his compatriots and earns him the nickname "orientalist" as dubious a term in imperial nomenclature as "native." Cole's (*Chronicles of Kedaram*) love for India is inspired by the vagaries of its climate and the rich landscape that offers abundant scope for a naturalist. On a holiday he would disappear with knapsack and staff into the recesses of the forest or the top of some unscalable mountain and return home laden with botanical specimens or fossils or pieces of stones—landmarks in his pursuit of knowledge. Cole too is a classical scholar, proficient in Sanskrit and Russian. Donovan (*Chronicles of Kedaram*), the Irish collector of Kedaram, comes to India with working knowledge of India and her antiquities. Refreshingly free from the influence of *Kim* and *The Plain Tales*—the Gospel of the British imperialists in India—he develops a fondness for Tamil language and literature which earns him in English circles the reputation of being a crank.

Lewis D. Wurgaft in his work The Imperial Imagination[12] analyzes the imaginative element in the British involvement in India and points out that beneath the hard and taciturn surface of British rule there was a greater depth, a pathos, responsive in part to a universal restiveness in man, in part to the vast landscape of India that heightened the sense of isolation and melancholy and to the grandiosity of her past that afflicted its alien rulers. According to him the mysterious and unknown in Indian life remained as central to the British experience in India as the tactile and familiar. Wilson, a character in Kamala Markandaya's *A Silence of Desire* responds thus to the fascination of the "great glittering saphire of night that arched above them": "These splendid Indian skies . . . they make up for almost everything else. They're out of fairystory books, those stars, too big and bright to be true . . . strange, isn't it, to think that they might be worlds like ours, filled with pompous little performers like us."[13]

Kenneth Ashby (*The Crown and the Loincloth*) who comes to India nursing a broken heart finds "abundant recompense" in the glories of the Punjab. To the Englishman brought up within the puritanical frame work of Christian morality with its underpinnings of sin and guilt, the sheer abundance of the joy of living symbolized by Basant—a festival of rejuvenation of life celebrated in the Punjab—becomes an enriching experience. The festival gave expression to the sense of joy of immediate living, and the sheer pleasure and delight of being flesh. Whereas giving in to delight and even talking of delight was anathema to western minds, the haunting love-songs of the young girls swinging in the mangogrove provided a sharp contrast in attitude, for they were outpourings of the passion of love and frank yearning for the beloved. Ashby's broken heart receives the kiss of renewed life in the exotic land and what started as "a voyage of escape soon turned into a voyage of renewal." (24)

India, the adopted land, becomes a life-giving, spiritually enervating experience to each one of these self-exiled Englishmen. In the effort to establish contact they form individual ties with Indians, making enduring bonds of affection possible in spite of racial and political animosity. The friendship between Wheeler and Nana Sahib is a remarkable instance of human ties surviving the test of circumstances and triumphing over the limitations of a colonizer-colonized relationship. Hillersdon and Lang also show a preference for Nana Sahib's company and the deep loyalties aroused by the relationship. The colonial construct of the deceptive Indian leader is revised and recast by Malgonkar and the tragic ends of Wheeler and Hillersdon are projected in the right perspective—as the victimization of the innocent in the inexorable course of history.

Sir Arthur Copeland's relationship with Bawajiraj (*The Golden Honeycomb*), Platt's friendship with his Indian subordinate Narayan (*The Nowhere Man*), Davidson's brotherly warmth towards the Indian college students Arun and Munir (*Azadi*), Ashby's moments of enlightening communion with Sunil (*The Crown and the Loincloth*), Kenny's unusual friendship with Rukmani (*Nectar in a Sieve*) and Mark McIvor's intimacy with the narrator-cum-actor in *A Time to be Happy* are instances of the emotional rapport achieved in the Indo-British relationship. Sir Arthur's relationship with Bawajiraj III is more than cordial and deepens onto a personal friendship beyond the requirements of official cordiality. As a Political Agent, Sir Arthur can never let himself forget the obligations and inhibitions imposed by the elevated post he adorns. So he strives to maintain the status quo, scrupulously addressing the Maharaja as "Highness," but during certain moments of intimacy, as when they are out on a tigershoot, he lets himself lapse into an involuntary show of affection calling him "Waji," a dimunitive that Bawajiraj cherishes. Naturally the constraints imposed by this official post as well as his rigid culture make him suffer from severe emotional restrictions that defined the limits of personal relationships. On one occasion Sir Arthur lets himself be carried away by sentiments of sympathy and fellow-feeling for Waji whom he invites home to dinner. Intuitive apprehension of Bawajiraj's agony strikes a cord of sympathy in Sir Arthur, who is reminded of his own forlornness during the annual separations from the family. He, therefore, overlooks racial barriers and commits what is even in his wife's eyes an act of sacrilege. He actually invites the native and brings him into the nest of inner harmonies that his wife has so carefully constructed in the torrid Indian soil and preserved from defilement through native encroachment. Colonial compulsions force Sir Arthur to suppress his real self. This is brought home powerfully through the genuine abandon and warmth with which he welcomes Waji when he visits him at his home in England. Sir Arthur remains extremely sensitive even in the imperial role and suffers a great sense of guilt about the limits to personal relationships with the natives. He often enters into a search of his soul only to become aware of the alienation from his real self wrought by the privations of his role. The friendship between Sir Arthur and Bawajiraj III almost approximates to the Aziz-Fielding relationship in Forster. To quote Shamsul Islam, "the greatest strain on their friendship is the strain of imperialism." (*Chronicles of the Raj* 39)

Platt, the deputy Principal goes out of the way to befriend his Indian subordinate Narayan (*The Nowhere Man*). He takes upon himself the guilt of the entire community that brands Narayan as a lunatic for defying the British Raj by reciting an Indian hymn at a public meeting. He feels he has to atone for the sins of the community to which he belonged by virtue of skin-colour alone and carries luscious fruits and cordials to the asylum, calling the gifts his "conscience fodder." Whatever power he could wield and whatever influence he could exercise on the imperial machinery, he uses for this Indian friend of his and makes arrangements for his son Sreenivas to go to England.

Cole's friendship with the Indian lawyer Vasudeva Suri (*Chronicles of Kedaram*) and his friendly, jovial and fun-loving nature save him from merging into the stereotyped figures of the sahibs in Indian English fiction. Suri, being himself educated and westernized, responds with equal openness whereas Buta Singh, the Indian subordinate of John Taylor—the Deputy Commissioner of Punjab (*I Shall Not Hear the Nightingale*)—feels hesitant about entering into a relationship with his English superior, a relationship that permits familiarity. His is the typical Indian reaction because Indians are mostly reluctant to accept offers of friendship from the ruling community, finding it difficult to overcome the inhibitions imposed by a ruler-ruled relationship. The best Taylor could achieve is the befriending of Buta Singh's family in an hour of crisis. Buta Singh himself is puzzled about the authenticity of an English officer who declares his allegiance to the Indian national movement. The dependence complex recognized by Mannoni in the colonized psyche,[14] is predominant in Buta Singh's responses. His tendency is to refer to the British government as "Mah-Bap" which is a common Indian feature in dependents' behaviour towards the master. Gomathi Narayanan cites this to illustrate the pattern of dependence in the Indo-British connection.[15] It is difficult for the Indian to shake off the tone of servility issuing from the dependence-complex and developed through years of imperial domination. In spite of the limitations of their friendship, Taylor becomes the moral anchor of the family in its hour of crisis. The release of Sher Singh as a Christmas gift to the ailing wife of Buta Singh is the crowning glory of Taylor's humanity—a magnanimous gesture on the part of the Englishman towards the Indian. However, the friendship between Taylor and Buta Singh never rises above the level of officer-subordinate relationship or at the most between noble benefactor and humble recipient.

The shackles of officialdom scarcely prevent Sergeant Bill Davidson—a loner in the military quarters—from striking a warm friendship with Arun and Munir, two angry young college students seething with protest against the British occupation of India (*Azadi*). What begins as a chance acquaintance deepens into a warm friendship because of Bill's deliberate efforts to surmount the deep-rooted prejudice in their minds against the ruling class. Gradually they are made to realize that he is different from the white sahibs they had known. When his dreams for a liberated India are miscarried by the speedy transfer of power and the resulting holocaust, he directs his efforts to whatever assistance he can lend to his Indian friends. He provides two army trucks to enable Lala Kanshi Ram and his family to evacuate to the refugee camp. The last comforting word of kindness to Lala Kanshi Ram comes from this Englishman. To the frustrated man whose life lay in shambles around him, he says: "Perhaps, you will come back here." (148) Bill Davidson has to leave India when the wounds in his sensitive heart are still raw. Through Ashby and Bill Davidson, Nahal suggests the possibility of forming human ties beyond the political, racial, and cultural boundaries. What Lala Kanshi Ram tells his wife after the harrowing experiences of communal barbarism holds good for these Englishmen endowed with finer sensibilities. He says he has "ceased to hate." (338) The colonial experience seems to have given these Englishmen a similar release from hatred, a broader perspective and an awareness of a larger reality.

In *The Crown and the Loincloth*, Nahal lends broader dimensions to the friendship between Sunil and Kenneth Ashby. The friendship that springs up between the British officer and the Indian nationalist overcomes the intricacies of an oppressor-oppressed relationship and its choking limitations and reaches a moment of absolute emotional rapport, of perfect communication between spirits. Sunil's confession about the way in which he has mismanaged his personal life by falling in love with Rehana, a friend's wife, who had a tragic end in the earthquake, makes Ashby aware of common grounds tread on, and passionate experiences that can be shared by all men irrespective of colour, race and culture. Sunil's regret that he did not raise his passionate love for Rehana to the sublimity of an ethereal experience by writing a poem, a novel or even making a painting about it, wrenches from the reserved Englishman a similar confession. The Indian heightens his perspective so that he realizes for the first time the immense and enduring value of the love-experience of the past. Sunil's disclosure that what is important is the experience itself and not fulfilment, comes as a revelation to Ashby who had been nursing his grief so long. Sunil tells him that writing the poem was what mattered—even if it was only in one's own mind—because the experience would then be elevated above mere physical passion. To Ashby this revelation gives relief from pain and peace within himself.

The new point of contact established between the two tortured souls elicits from Sunil a depth of loyalty that triumphs over racial, historical and political hostilities. It calls for the sacrifice of his own life to protect the Prince of Wales, the living emblem of the regime he opposed. Sunil's sacrifice is inspired by loyalty to his friend who had invited him to attend the fair and that too dressed in his own English clothes so that he would be admitted to the special enclosure. The trust he places in Sunil and the gesture of friendship he extends to him, brings in its stead greater rewards than he has bargained for.

The Iove affair between Richard and Mira in *Some Inner Fury* is an instance of a relationship that transcends ethnic barriers and reaches the level of intimacy. Though Richard and Mira hardly feel the stress of racial and cultural distinctions, they become the victims of the political hostility of the times. The short-lived love affair is conceived as a beautiful relationship bringing out all the tenderness and passion in Richard. But he has from the beginning a philosophic awareness of the world and its forces waiting outside. He says: "But you know, I don't think one can keep the world at bay for a long time." (191) In spite of Richard's devotion to Mira and his total emotional involvement in the affair with her, Kamala Markandaya categorically denies the possibility of a union between them, especially at the time of the massive Quit India movement that roused the whole of India as one force against the British. Mira's love for Richard proves ineffective to resist currents of hatred that swept off everything alien. Richard who tried to identify himself with India and her people has to be rejected even by Mira, the woman for whom he had reserved his noblest and most tender emotions.

The tragic finale of the Richard-Mira affair projects in magnified form the problem of cultural alienation that prevents the unhoused sensibilities of the anti-imperialists from attaining a sense of belonging to the adopted land and its culture. They drift away from their own community, only to realize that they never can totally empathize with the alien culture. Nor does the Indian community show the willingness to accept them. The resulting conflict and sense of rootlessness leave them drifting between two worlds, unable to occupy either. The conflict and agony of not belonging lend dignity to the characters.

The most poignant expression of the identity crisis resulting from alienation is found in Dr. Kennington, in Kamala Markandaya's *Nectar in a Sieve.*[16] Kenny strikes an unusual friendship with a native peasant woman, rooted in traditions and endowed with the infinite fortitude of the Indian woman that helps her endure all the sufferings of life with stoic calm. Kenny, by offering her medical assistance and thus helping her to overcome the curse of infertility, helps to strengthen her marriage. The extraordinary friendship between the English doctor and the Indian village woman provokes insidious comments from the villagers and the novelist herself has left its definite nature undefined. Throughout the novel, we are reminded of the limits to understanding imposed by cultural and racial barriers in such a relationship. Emphasizing the narrow, compartmentalized nature of the experience like a precious treasure hidden away in a box. Ann Lowry Weir remarks: "Rukmani does not intend to spend her every waking moment in his presence, devoted to his cause, he is an important person in her life, but she does not let his influence extend beyond a certain well-defined realm in her emotions."[17] Though Kenny is an alienated soul who has uprooted himself not only from his country but even from his family, he suffers from an acute identity crisis because of his inability to empathize with Rukmani and her people. He is exasperated at Rukmani's attitude to suffering and poverty. He urges her to protest against suffering, but she meekly submits to calamities. He calls Indians "acquiescent imbeciles" (114) and vehemently protests when Rukmani accepts suffering saying that fasting and suffering cleanse the soul. The walls between them are many and insurmountable. Kenny wanders between the two worlds, a lost and dispossessed self, unable to find his place in either. He remarks to Rukmani: "I have the usual encumbrances that men have—wife, children, home—that would have put chains about me, but I resisted and so I am alone. . . . I work among you when my spirit wills it. . . . I go when I am tired of your follies and stupidities, your eternal, shameful poverty. I can only take you people in small doses." (71) His predicament can be best expressed by the powerful words of the West African poetess Mable Segun:

> Here we stand,
> infants overblown
> poised between two civilizations,
> finding the balance irksome.[18]

The process of acculturation, voluntarily undertaken by the unhoused Kenny does not make him acceptable to the Indian society because from the perspective of the colonized, he is no different from the rest of the community. Even Rukmani, who has recieved rare glimpses of his tormented psyche, remarks: "this is not your country and we are not your people. If you lived here your whole life, it still would not be." (109) This is perhaps the most emphatic pronouncement made by the colonized, of its total rejection of the members of the ruling community, in spite of their spiritual empathy with Indian culture and nationality. Alienation from both cultures intensifies Kenny's sense of lost identity. His desperate need for selfhood and a spiritual anchor sounds almost pathetic: "Sometimes I do not know which is my country. Until today I had thought perhaps it was this." (109)

The dilemma posed by cultural duality and the loss of identity is experienced by Henry Brewster (*Plans for Departure*) and Kenneth Ashby (*The Crown and the Loincloth*) as well. But since they choose to remain within the bureaucratic framework, they can shift the responsibility for their imperial ties to the system. Their suffering does not have the intensity of Kenny's agony. The pull between divided loyalties is singularly absent in a few Englishmen who choose to rebel outright against the imperial system. They have broken their allegiance to the Empire, by severing all ties with it and openly siding with the Indian national movement. The absence of a clearly defined role liberates them from the conflict of ideological polarities.

These open rebels form the second category chosen for scrutiny in this chapter. They are mostly intellectuals who consider the Empire to be the emblem of Britain's ideological failure in human relationships. Their liberal views are voiced openly and they take sides with the revolutionaries in an unhesitating manner. They suffer no dilemma about their allegiance. In *Inquilab*, Abbas introduces two English revolutionaries—Spratt and Bradley. In the twenties when a surge of protest rises against the Simon Commission and reaches a high temperature, and hartals, strikes and black flags become the order of the day, Abbas's protagonist Anwar meets two Englishmen—"the lean and lanky Spratt with his Charlie Chaplin moustache and the bulky Bradely"[19]—who are members of the Aligarh University Marxist study circle. Anwar is dumb-founded to find them shouting anti-imperialist slogans like "Down, down with imperialism and up, up with Revolution." (198) In the novel, their roles are limited to this one incident, suggesting their function as sources of inspiration to Anwar to study the Marxist ideology by which the members of the ruling class found emotional identification with the Indian struggle against the British. If Spratt and Bradley are young revolutionaries of the Marxist group, Reginald Reynolds, another young Englishman, turns out to be a disciple of Mahatma Gandhi and an inmate of the Sabarmati Ashram. He is an English Quaker, transformed into a Khaddar-clad, Gandhi-capped supporter of Indian nationalism. Anwar meets him by accident and learns from the newspapers that he has come as Gandhiji's special envoy to deliver his letter—a historic ultimatum—to the Viceroy. Anwar feels that there is an un-English tenderness in Reynold's blue eyes, as though his pro-Indian mission has invested him with a pleasing and spiritual expression. In conversation Anwar finds that he has none of the brusque hauteur of the "burra sahib." When asked whether it was not strange for an Englishman like him to be taking the Indian side against his own people, he replies: "Yes, my friend, unfortunately it is strange. That is why it is necessary. Some of us at least must expiate for the sins of the Empire which have been committed in our name." (250) The thumb-nail sketch of Reynolds, created through the impressions of Anwar, gives us an inkling into the guilt-complex that was tormenting liberal-minded and conscientious Englishmen who took upon themselves the sins of the race. In his journalistic style Abbas sketches these figures with a few strokes and they have only peripheral roles in the novel, set in the period of the historic struggle for Independence.

In his post-Independence novels, Mulk Raj Anand shows a tendency to present British intellectuals who are absolutely devoid of colonial prejudices. They are depicted as championing the ideals of Independence and self-rule. They are thoroughly decolonized white men, but they fail to develop into credible individuals unlike the flesh-and-blood figures created by Anand in the white heat of indignation in the pre-Independence era. Dieter Riemenschneider has pointed out that the British intellectuals reflect "the author's preoccupation with the intellectual's role in capitalist society."[20] The intellectuals introduced in *Morning Face*—second in Anand's autobiographical series—appear also in the third novel of the series, *Confession of a Lover*. But they fail to grow within the fictional framework. They remain the author's mouthpieces, expressing his liberal views. As Saros Cowasjee remarks, the English characters, "Reverend Thomas Williams, Mr.B.G. Horniman and Mr. Marmaduke Pickthall speak in a lofty manner and what any one of them says can be assigned to another with no injury to their respective personalities."[21] Prof. Henry of *Confession of a Lover* is no exception to this. He is portrayed as one who has discarded the superficial finery of western clvilization and opted to explore the wisdom of the Rishis, of the Vedas and the Upanishads. The spokesman's function becomes undisguised when he says, "I am against Imperialism, the Whiteman's Burden stuff and Western civilisation, which has staged a great world war. I see wisdom in your ancient tales. I believe Gandhi is right."[22] He thinks that to be forced to go back to England, to his previous occupation as a Don at Cambridge, is a very small price to pay for his belief in India's right to freedom and to the revival of her old glory.

Whereas the imperialists sing the gory of the public school, Henry thinks that public school education has dulled his body and he is dying of the effects of civilisation. Like Platt in *The Nowhere Man*, he is so conscientious that he feels he must pay for his British karma. Like Annie Besant, he too has discovered the profound wisdom of the Upanishads. He says: "You see the answers given to such questions in the Upanishads by the ancient Indian sages are far more profound than those given by Christianity in the West." (68) It is after meeting Mrs. Annie Besant that he gains new insights into the wisdom of the East.

Krishan is impressed by the fact that Prof. Henry has neither the arrogance of the British imperialists nor the pride of omniscience that the Brahmins displayed. The most remarkable feature about him is his strange humility. Ironically enough, it is from Prof. Henry that Krishan, the Hindu, learns the Hindu philosophic truths like the immortality of the spirit and the relevance of romantic love as a stage in the evolution of man and his growth towards divine love. Commenting on love, he says: "It is the only permanent reality of love which helps one to destroy sex desires and leads one to the highest consciousness. Love resolves all conflicts." (234)

Prof. Henry sounds like a Hindu religious philosopher when he advises detachment to Krishan. He asks him to be free of experience. "The experience of pleasure and pain consigns one to the dreary world. One must attain silence." (238)

Anand uses Prof. Henry to make the blind Anglophiles conscious of the political and economic aspects of imperialism. At the meeting of the "Minerva"—a society modelled on the Freeman's Lodge of the English—Prof. Syed Hassan sings the panegyric of the British in India and in reply Prof. Henry reminds the Indians gathered there of the clever diplomacy with which Britain had been systematically destroying the political and economic structure of India—destroying the Indian panchayat system, Indian industries—and even undermining Indian culture and tradition. An ardent spirit of revolution invigorates his words as he tells Krishan: "Bharat is the land of wisdom. The truth and non-violence of Gandhi will flourish because the peasants are seized of it. The one thing before us today is the struggle for freedom!" (248)

Prof. Henry's suspension from the college triggers off a student strike which lands Krishan in prison. The British Professor's role in the novel is mainly that of a guiding light to Krishan in his exploratory journey through life. In spite of the spacc allotted to Prof. Henry in the novel, he fails to come to life because there is hardly any inwardness in the portrait. He is presented through the admiring eyes of Krishan, who cannot meet him on a level of parity, making it impossible to get insights into the working of his psyche. It is a portrait done from the exterior and hardly rises above a propagandist mouthpiece; nor does it succeed in touching the heart like that of Ashby (*The Crown and the Loincloth*) or Tully (*Pleasure City*).

The rejection of Christianity and the embracing of oriental religions—Hinduism by Prof. Henry and Islam by Marmaduke Pickthall, is extremely significant as a feature of the process of decolonization working itself out in the Englishman. Christianity gets equated with the oppressive system of colonialism and the rejection of Christianity becomes essential in the revolution towards total emancipation. Charles Zwingmann has recognized this aspect of Christianity: "Perhaps no religious infrastructure of a microcosmos in recorded history has been equally efficient in torturing, manipulating, suppressing and destroying directly and indirectly human relations over as long a time and on such a (global) scale as the Christian system."[23]

Prof. Henry extols the wisdom of the Upanishads and aspires to attain "the highest consciousness" celebrated by the Theosophites. Marmaduke Pickthall proves himself to be an ardent convert saying his prayers five times a day and translating the Koran. Apparently Mr. Pickthall values the belief in Islam much more than the teachings of Christianity. The sins of his community lie heavy on his conscience and he wants to apologize for the atrocities of Dyer. He equates Gandhi with Allah and considers him as one who could change even the mind of God and as one who loves all human beings.

The guilt of the entire race seems to rest on these two Englishmen. Horniman, a journalist and writer, apologizes to Krishan for British bad behaviour because he had been beaten for breaking the curfew. Like Pickthall he too is anxious to assure his Indian friends that not all Englishmen are like Dyer. Horniman blames the British for teaching the armymen wife-beating and strongly disapproves of Gandhi's attitude to his wife, about which he remarks that Gandhi was treating Kasturba "as a doormat." (221) Horniman becomes a great source of encouragement to Krishan in his writing and warns him of his exuberance. The relationship with Krishan defines and limits the roles of these Englishmen.

Unlike Prof. Henry and Mr. Pickthall, Rev. Williams does not feel the need to discard his faith to be true to his political ideology. He remains the kindly padre and gives Krishan a taste of Christian charity by befriending him in the hour of need. In the white heat of indignation he bursts out: "I tell you, the white sahibs have done nothing. Only imposed the machine civilisation on the people with the sword. Money is the whiteman's God. Exploitation is his religion!" (186) There is a warm human touch and a spontaneous generosity in the man, which are quite redeeming. Unfortunately, the character is not developed any further and we are just told about his kindness to Krishan, in paying his fare and guiding him to the security of Horniman's patronage. At Krishan's remark that he has not met an Englishman like him, he says: "Let me prove to you on my return from leave, that I am what you think. . . . As a padre, I am interested not in the fall of man but in his redemption. . . . As a human being I am obsessed with the need for our recovery." (184)

Annie Besant herself appears in the novel, as an English lady who speaks at the Khalsa College and exhorts the Indian students to join the struggle for Independence. The excited response of the students leads to the suspension of Prof. Henry.

One is forced to agree with Saros Cowasjee who has commented on the contrast between the confirmed imperialists and exploiters that represent the English community in Anand's pre-Independence novels and the sympathetic intellectuals ready to fight for the Indian cause in his post-Independence works. "We cannot help suspecting that Anand is building up a case against Britain by showing that every thinking Englishman was against British rule in India."[24]

It is significant that such outright rebels are conspicuously absent in the works of other novelists. They remain pencil sketches done by the journalist or mere devices that function as media for expressing the writer's anti-imperialistic views.

The third category of emancipated or "decolonized" British characters (applying the term in the sense in which Frantz Fannon has used it) has only moved a step farther from those who have rejected colonialism in spirit, while still conforming to their imperial roles. Categorization cannot be very clear-cut in such cases and it is possible that some of the rejectors of colonial ideals already dealt with, might seem qualified to be included here. The shades of difference are rather too subtle to enable classification into water-tight compartments. The characters included in this category are the British who came to India after the attainment of Independence and a few who have made India their home after the fall of the Empire. Unlike the rebels who preach their ideals and openly resist the imperial system, these men seldom preach. It is through their mode of life that they strike a contrast to the imperial attitude and ideology. They have emancipated themselves from the prejudices of the colonial period and show an openness of mind, and even a craving to know, to explore and to embrace Indian culture and spiritual values. Since they are no longer a part of the ruling regime, the pull of loyalties is absent in them. In most cases the Indian experience acquires the dimensions of a spiritual search. Decolonization means to them not merely the rejection of an ideology and attitude of the colonial past, but a return to the land their mother country has lost materially, in order to unearth her hidden spiritual wealth left unexplored till now and to possess her spiritually. This is made possible by the complete rejection of material possessions and the attributes of white destiny. The exploratory journey to India ends differently for different people. In a few cases the erstwhile colonizer accepts India as his permanent abode, reaching his journey's end here.

The journey pattern is commonly observed in post-Independence Indian English fiction. Helen Tiffin has identified it as a typical "decolonization pattern" in Commonwealth literature. The journey is undertaken by the "colonial man, former agent of white European destiny," who finds that "the colonial situation had foisted on him a two-fold necessity—to reject what of his old tradition was inapplicable in the new environment, and secondly, to arrive at some spiritual understanding of his new world by imaginative surrender to it."[25] He has to cover "vast spiritual and imaginative distance" before his new land could be spiritually his "place." (147) The pattern can be observed in the "decolonization"—virtually a spiritual and emotional purging undergone by Helen and Mackendrick (*The Coffer Dams*), Tully (*Pleasure City*), Michael Calvert (*A Situation in New Delhi*), Rose (*Rich Like Us*), Alice Soames and Kim (*The Imperial Agent* and *Last Victory*). With Helen who comes to the Indian villages as the "burra memsahib" of the Clinton-Mackendrick group of builders, India becomes an enlightening experience (*The*

Coffer Dams). Contact with the tribals of the village and their educated representative Bashiam marks for her the beginning of a journey into the world of the orient and even a return to nature and to the primitive world of instincts. At every stage of the journey she discards the ties of western civilization and white racism. She adopts the language of the tribals, severs even the marital bond, takes to living with Bashiam and feels for the first time, a oneness with nature, a sense of true belonging. Her frequent journeys into the jungle symbolize her return to nature and the primitive roots. On the initial excursion into the jungle itself she strikes points of contact with the villagers because she has alredy rejected the inhibitions of her class and the arrogance of her race. Bashiam, the hillman soon becomes her linkman, providing the information she seeks of a country and a people who intrigued her, whetting a curiosity with which she had always been liberally endowed. By learning the language of the village tribals she overcomes the one barrier to communication. When she finds herself mentally distinguishing between "these people" and "my people," she struggles to get the colonial-racial distinction out of her system. She tells herself: "So it's getting me too, that old indestructible Indian bug, she thought with icy dismay. But these people aren't different clay, they're like me, like people like me. What is for me, is for them, there's no other kind of yardstick that's worth anything." (48) Through Bashiam's impression we are made aware of her uniqueness.

> She was not like the other memsahibs, even these latter-day-ones, whose outlook barred them from allowing their interest to be sparked by anything; nor was she like those others, the recorders, the authors and researchers who alarmed him by taking down everything he said for use in the books they were going to write, attaching an importance to every trivial detail in a way that first bewildered and then tired him out. (81)

The spirit of rebellion shared by Bashiam, as a tribal-turned technician and Helen as a memsahib who refuses to bear the memsahib's load, brings them together. Helen voices it quite clearly: "We're alike, we're freaks only to the caste we come from, not to each other." (136) She laments that her senses have been blunted by the concrete and mortar that flattens down everything in her world. Even from animals they cannot learn for "we're Christians you know, an arrogant people, as we deprive them of their rights." (138) In the artificial world of western civilization, they have moved so far away from nature that even animals have lost the power of instinctive knowledge. The journey she has undertaken is a demanding one, one that demands a rejection of all that her class and race represents. With rejection comes a sense of belonging—a sense of "place." "But here—now—I don't feel that [the sense of being lostl anymore. I belong, I'm not alone. Everything is a part of one, and I am a part of everything—not just a pop-up cardboard figure." (139) The transformation in her is perceived by the philosophic and omniscient headman of the tribe. "You see, you have changed" said the headman. "Between then, and now, you are a woman." (145)

In Helen we find every stage of the regressive journey from civlliza-tion, which in itself is a journey of progression towards complete de-colonization. Every stage of the journey pattern envisaged by Helen Tif-fin can be identified in Helen's gradual transformation.

> In the course of the journey the historical colonial pattern of destruction and division is usually reversed. The white parent or overlord is led like a child through the harshness and danger of the new environment, to gain no economic advantage whatsoever, to sometimes lose his own language and adopt that of his native companion, and to dispense with his own narrower Christian concepts in favour of those of the native companion (whose relationship to his gods is appropriately connected to this specific land) or an amalgam of all religions.[26]

Through the systematic destruction of what is axiomatic to the concept of white destiny—racial superiority, right to land and people, imposition of language and religion—Helen comes to spiritual terms with "place". Dr. Haydn Moore Williams remarks: "The most interesting character is not Helen but the brooding Scotsman Mackendrick whose second-sight mysticism creates a strong bond with the tirbals that is much more interesting than Helen's sexual and cultural 'slumming.'"[27] Though Haydn Moore Williams draws a distinction between Helen and Mackendrick, and finds Mackendrick more authentic, it can be noticed that Mackendrick is still caught in the pull between opposing loyalties at the beginning of the story and it is only towards the end that he acquires the courage to plunge into the journey of decolonization which Helen has already undertaken. He is free from colonial sentiments, has an essentially humanitarian vision that manifests itself in his attitude to the Indian labourers and is thus endowed with the mental framework to undertake the journey. Mackendrick possesses "that odd quirk of vision that enables him to look at two worlds." (36) He shares the moral and social commitments of Helen, whereas Helen is the total idealist as contrasted with the realist Clinton. Mackendrick, like Bashiam, is able to see both sides of a dilemma and is therefore disturbed by choices made or actions taken, especially when the unpleasant task of execution falls on his shoulders. Mackendrick has the painful role of the moral conscience of the Clinton-Mackendrick team. Clinton's oppressive mass punishments—like cutting a week's pay for all the labourers—make him feel guilty and hurt. He could only grieve for the blunting of humanity and finer sensibilities in the Englishmen when they came to another country, especially a country once occupied by them. Unlike Helen who couldn't give in to Clinton, Mackendrick, even as he pleads for the overworked labourers who badly needed a pause to reflate, submits to the stronger will of Clinton. He himself attributes this submissive attitude to the years of experience "during which a callousing took place." (122) Mackendrick's tragedy is that he could see Clinton's point of view as well. He has already discarded the illusion of white supremacy and adjusts to his role in the new Independent India where there is no reserved place for the Englishman. He quietly accepts the fact that he has no authority over the tribals except when they laboured for him. He is, therefore, incredulous when Rawlings reveals his frigid stance by still gloating over "the white man's burden." "In this day and age, one did not know, one held beliefs from which such words could spring?" (166) His complete rejection of ideas of white supremacy is indicated through his protest against the ostentatious practices still followed by the Rawlings, and his regard for the common man who is supreme in the new setup. The distinctions between "your people" and "our people" are conspicuously absent in his mind and he partakes in the shame, sorrow and indignation experienced by the tribals at every oppressive act on the part of the white builders. When Clinton refuses to breach the dam to save the villagers from drowning, it is Mackendrick who reminds him that he is playing with the lives of others over whom he has no authority. "It is not we who take the risk. We make the calculations, it is they who run the risk." (216) It is in desperation at the unrelenting prejudice of the white supremacy that Mackendrick finally seeks the way of the East—of the spiritual as opposed to reason or intellect. With Helen he too makes the journey to the village to meet the tribal chief, who is the symbol of oriental wisdom in the novel. The journey to the tribal chief is indicative of the denial of the accessories of western civilization and of the acceptance of the primitive, the instinctive and the spiritual. It is he who gets the final answer of the tribal chief as he lay on his deathbed. Like Helen, Mackendrick too sees into the ultimate values and the meaning of life at levels beyond the practical and the scientific. The discovery of place does not mean the end of the journey for Mackendrick or Helen. India becomes for them a spiritual abode; but they would return home indicated in the novel. Fannon has stressed the importance of "process" rather than arrival in the politics of decolonization.

Tully, the central figure in Markandaya's *Pleasure City* comes to India with an open mind that is full of eager curiosity about a land that has housed his imperial ancestors.Through the AIDCORP Markandaya provides a colonial framework within which Tully and the British characters are placed. Their relations with the fishing folk of the village exposes the deliberate distancing and patterns of behaviour common to the colonizer-colonized relationship. Tully is alienated from the other Englishmen because of his liberated view and it is this separateness that draws him close to Rikki, a fisherboy who serves as the native-interpreter guide in his journey of spiritual quest. Tully grants Rikki perfect freedom in the AIDCORP, establishes contact on a level of equality, seeks his friendship and receives what he can teach him of the sea and the fishing folk and the Bridies, thus developing a relationship that is mutually enriching. Moments of communion become possible because he had transcended the corrupting influence of race, nation and culture and attained "a quality of simply being that washed over them like water or light and merged them into one landscape." (147) In such moments of total belonging Tully discards even his national identity and becomes one with the place. Corinna, his wife, becomes painfully aware of this, as soon as she comes to India. Corinna feels that she is excluded from Tully's world for the place has "wrapped itself round" (246) Tully. What Galliard in John Buchan's last novel *Sick Heart River* remarks about the north could very well be applied to Tully's identification with India. Galliard says: "It has become part of me, as close to me as my skin. I love it. It is myself."[28] Tully, like Galliard, feels perfectly at home in India. He visibly blooms in the Indian surroundings. Often Rikki and India are in his mind, one and the same. Tully's discovery of his spiritual homeland and the profound peace it brings to him, do not sanction adopting it as his permanent home. Tully's trust in Rikki is more than rewarded by the latter's noble sacrifice—of risking his own life—for the sake of his wife. India has built invisible barricades between Tully and Corinna, but they become aware of residues of tenderness that remain. They could be pieced together and a new life built on them. The possibility of Tully's coming back and staying on in India is not totally denied in the novel. Tully is charmed at Rikki's question whether he would stay on in India. He replies that he might stay on, but not like the Bridies—as the last relics of an Empire that was gone—but would rather stay on his own right, for the sake of the love he bore towards India. Here too, the quest and the discovery of a place to belong to—of a spiritual home—is given greater prominence than the end of the quest. In the course of the quest we find the destructive and divisive barriers of colonial-conquest legacy between the native and the English breaking down. In the place of the primitive tribal triumphing over the technically qualified western man in *The Coffer Dams*, here we see the triumph of child over man, of instinctive and unself-conscious knowledge over the self-conscious and of the spiritual over the material.

Nayantara Sahgal's novel *A Situation in New Delhi* begins with Michael Calvert's decision to journey back to India after ten long years of futile struggle to belong to England. Through Michael Calvert, Nayantara Sahgal exposes the unhappy predicament of an Englishman who had emotionally adopted India as home, going back to England after Independence, only to find himself rootless, alienated from the motherland. The unhoused sensibility could not even strike contact with his own countrymen; both his marriages fail. The author remarks: "Except for his writing, he had lived a half-life for ten years."[29] His life had been a series of exiles from the adopted country. He was born in India, but at the age of eight he was sent to school in England, to return only for a short period during the war. After the war, he came to India as the representative of a British newspaper, only to depart unwept, like the rest of the British though he was more of an Indian than an Englishman. For ten years he searched for moorings in England and at the news of Shivraj's death, decided to return to India, to write the biography of his admired leader. During the journeys to India, he had discarded, one by one, the accessories of his white destiny. The first glimpse of the great national leader Shivraj was, to Michael like coming under a spell. He came completely under his influence during his life as reporter in India in the pre-Independence period. As he reported on the political developments in India and rang the curtain down over the Empire (even before those at the Whitehall did) he was letting himself be engulfed by the spirit and elusive charm of India. The charm of India became inseparable for him, from the charm of Devi, Shivraj's sister. Almost unawares, he was becoming decolonized and addicted to the spirit of India. He started wearing Indian clothes. He came to know more people then than ever afterward. Then he allowed Devi to take over his life. But there could not be any fulfilment or permanency in the relationship because Devi's devotion to her great brother and her sense of duty to him obliterated everything else in her life. Michael, the Englishman, could not understand this devotion to a brother, and smarting under the pain of rejection he felt a bitterness against the country itself that took everything from him. But when he reached England he had the feeling that "he had left home." (52) In spite of his rebelling and fuming English spirit, he had entered so deep into the spirit of India that "he had understood Devi after all, wretched and unwilling though he had been." (56) In the ten years' sojourn in England before he finally comes to India, he experimented three times with marriage only to realize that his "violent indelible past" in India would not let him begin anew. (56) He could not feel a sense of belonging in England, "he could not in the beginning think of them [the English people] as his own." (9) "He felt connected with the people around him less through blood than pleasant mutual exchange and goodwill." (9) He had to relearn what the English said, did and thought and birds, flowers and leaves seemed as good a place as any to begin. Once he comes back to India after the ten years' drifting in England like an anchorless vessel, the change is quite obvious. A sense of place, of belonging, develops almost unawares and the embers of human relationships kept at bay for ten years, suddenly catch fire and sparkle. The author says how "within minutes after Michael's arrival, ten years vanished trace unseen between them." (77) When their friend Usman arrived, Michael and he "embraced like long-lost brothers and started a string of questions and incomplete answers." (77) It is as though he has reached the end of his journey. The journey's end brings in its wake the tragic sense of a loss of values in Indian politics caused by Shivraj's death and the horrible end of Rishad. When Devi resigns her job and leaves for Kashmir, Michael stands alone in Devi's house and realizes that whatever foreignness it had for him had now become too much of a part of him to seem so. It combines his biggest as well as his most trivial experiences and much of his conscious growth and yet ultimately all of this boiled down again to "the friends he had made and what they had taught each other." (163-64) The enlightening knowledge that the strongest thing in human life was influence brings the comforting thought that Shivraj is not dead after all. The process of decolonization here leads not only to a sense of place, but a knowledge of the depth and meaning of life as well.

Alice Soames (*The Imperial Agent*) is caught in the conflict between her husband's imperial attitudes and her own identification with India. Like Helen (*The Coffer Dams*), she develops a genuine interest in the Indians and resents the British presence in the country. She writes to her daughter that as soon as she came to India, she fell in love with the country. She felt "she had come home." (266) It was her passion for India that led to her downfall. The emotional incompatibility resulting from ideological conflict involves in her case the loss of her family. She is expelled from home by her husband, the Colonel; her lover is killed by his men and the fact of her existence is deliberately concealed from the children by the colonel, who makes them believe that she is dead. This total denial of her identity as wife and mother creates an emotional void in Alice's life, partly filled by Romesh's love and intellectual companionship. Her ire against the callous system that victimized her finds expression through the articles she writes for Romesh's journal. She is so thoroughbred an enemy of colonialism that she actively participates in Romesh's nationalistic work, craves to meet Gandhi in South Africa and virulently attacks the Viceroy for his flambuoyant style of living in India. When Romesh is arrested and she is not, because of the colour of her skin, she realizes that she will never be permitted to attain complete identification with India. Even Romesh feels bitter and thinks that they will have to separate because he has to prove his loyalty to the nation before his people. The Indian accuses her of her "otherness"; the English harass her for betraying her community. Alice, the decolonized being is caught in the conflict between these forces and is forced to leave India, her spiritual "place." The journey pattern is discernible from her first venture out of the secluded cloister of imperial eminence to independence and empathy with the Indians. The journey leads on to active involvement in anti-imperialistic activities, identification with the problems of the millworkers and finally to a meeting with Gandhi, which is the culmination of the process of decolonization. But as in the case of Helen and Mackendrick, India can provide only a temporary abode for the decolonized white woman.

T.N. Murari has chosen the popular hero of Imperial Britain as the chief protagonist of his novels, *The Imperial Agent* and *Last Victory*. The author strikes back at the Empire by portraying Kim's growth to an awareness of the hollowness of imperial values and his rejection of them and identification with the Indian national movement. As an imperial agent, Kim is initiated into the dubious morality and exploiting ideology that sustained the British Empire in India. Kim becomes a useful tool to his fosterfather, Col. Creighton, because of his intimacy with the people of India and his knowledge of Indian languages. The unjust arrest of Anil Ray and the murder of his uncle by Captain Goode, the murder of a young and innocent Indian bridegroom by Ralph Sparrow, Kim's arrest for taking the dead body, and the Colonel's efforts to make use of Kim as a spy on fellow-prisoners, are events that develop in Kim an aversion for the oppressive and crooked machinery of the Raj. His decision not to be a part of it any longer unleashes the forces of the Empire against him. His last illusions are dispelled as the Colonel's own men try to kill him. He is shocked to realize that from the favoured position of a son he has been reduced to that of a pawn in "the great game of ruling an Empire."[30] He realizes that men of such duplicity cannot rule the country and he decides to play the Great Game against the Colonel, the man he had loved as a father. Here the process of decolonization is indirectly effected by the imperial machinery itself. By choosing India, Kim loses his foster father as well as his calling. His identification with India becomes complete when he fights along with the Indian sepoys in the world war and finds himself grouped with the other Indians during convalescence in England, and spoken of contemptuously as these "damned bogs." (326) Kim's death at Jallianwallahbagh as a victim of imperial oppression absolves him of all his earlier values and he stands purged as a thoroughly decolonized being. The journey pattern is a dominant feature of these two novels and Kim's journey through India from village to village assumes the nature of a spiritual quest.

Marital incompatibility resulting from ideological polarities is a recurring theme in all the novels depicting decolonized Britishers. Dr. Kenny (*Nectar in a Sieve*) is one who severed family ties because he cannot wrench himself away from the adopted land, in spite of the exasperation caused by the passive endurance of the Indians. In the Helen-Clinton relationship (*The Coffer Dams*), the partners drift apart due to sharply divergent attitudes: "It was as if they were walking on different levels: he on the floor, she on the underpass. He had, as he said, an overall vision. She saw the detail: Das, and the birds, and the passions below. We go our different ways, she thought, and may be his as valid as mine; but could not drum up much conviction and it remained an intellectual exercise." (100) Helen's ignited emotions and Clinton's callous indifference clash at every point. The absolute lack of sympathy on his part creates for her an island of loneliness from where she cries out: "Can't you care? Don't human beings matter anything to you? Do they have to be a special kind of flesh before they do?" (105)

Finally, Helen is driven to Bashiam with whom she shares the common ground of loneliness and alienation from their fellow men. Clinton's involvement in later events like Bashiam's accident and mutilation, and the threat of floods only widen the gulf between the two. But Helen does not think that India will offer her a permanent home. It seems imperative that she has to return.

India cleaves a wedge in the Tully-Corinna relationship (*Pleasure City*). Corinna actually feels the invisible presence of the barrier that keeps Tully away from her. She comes under the spell of the admiration of the Indian youth—Ranji—only to return and pick up the broken fragments of a tender relationship with Tully. Though Corinna does not take any hardened colonial stance like Clinton, she too fails to understand Tully's preoccupation with India and his spiritual identification with the country. It is significant that the emotional gulf between couples in all these cases seems to cause infertility. Voids of communication and failure to attain empathy with the mate are symbolized in all these cases by physical sterility.

The rift between Col. Creighton and Alice occurs due to Alice's interest in the natives and her tendency to identify herself with their cause. The gulf between husband and wife widens as Alice grows tired of her husband's distance from India and from every human passion and she seeks relief in the company of John Woodruff. However she is denied liberation through love and has to seek it on her own, at the risk of sacrificing the children she loves. Later she finds an ideal companion in Romesh, but the question of marriage hardly arises and finally the harsh fact of racial difference becomes the barrier between them.

Alienation from the adopted country dries up the very springs of emotion in Michael Calvert whose dispossessed self seeks anchorage through two marriages. Both fail because Michael cannot get emotionally involved with the women who come into his life. His second wife Nell attributes it to the hold of his Indian past. It is as though India has absorbed all the best elements in his nature and once out of India, he is a veritable shell of his former being—devoid of the very springs of emotion and hence, sterile and ineffective. This is made obvious in the novel by the miraculous transformation in the dried-up, prosaic, emotionally spent Michael when he comes to India. Almost overnight he blossoms into an effusive, charming, talkative and romantic personality, as though the magic wand of India had brought to life the springs of pent-up emotions.

The symbol of sterility is employed by Nayantara Sahgal in the story of Rose in *Rich Like Us* to convey the sense of loneliness and alienation. A novel written with a lot of bitterness against the political dictatorship during the Emergency period, it exposes the corruption, malpractices and cruelty that went on at the time in the corridors of power. Against this background is unfolded the story of an unusual English lady, cockney-speaking, lower middle-class, and full of the joy of living, whose journey to India in the first flush of love, takes her through a wide range of experiences during a crucial phase of Indian history, extending from the pre-Independence to the Emergency period.

The meeting between Ram and Rose takes place in a chocolate shop in London, and from the first moment it is a case of romantic infatuation for both. Thoughts of deserting her parents and even the forbiddingly unpleasant idea of being the second wife and all the unknown fears about an alien culture, melt away from Rose's mind, because of her consuming love for Ram. Despite Rose's irresistible good looks, her exuberance, shrewd practical sense and loving nature, her passage to Ram's life is not smooth. The family—Ram's father and his wife Mona—wages a relentless cold war against her. Rose withdraws into her cloister while Mona reigns over the house. Rose survives the shock of the first weeks of adjustment and tries to reconcile herself to her undignified status in the house because Ram refuses to divorce his legally wedded wife. But in the life with Ram there are compensations too. She leads a life of idle luxury at Ram's house which often brings to her mind the struggle of her parents and she wonders if she had even seen them looking at each other, "and not at kitchen sinks and washing tubes and dirt shovels?" (56)

As the political movement for Independence rages outside, Rose feels exposed to danger because she belongs to neither side. "How can anyone live two lives, be on two sides, without going mad?" (59) What Keshav, an active supporter of civil disobedience movement and a candidate for the I.C.S. tells her of his own predicament aptly describes Rose's state "as two people, at home and in exile, ecstatic and wretched, Indian and British, saved and doomed." (60) Mona's child Dev makes her predicament worse because she realizes that without a child of her own, she would never be mistress of the house, not even her half of it. "She would pass through this family, this frightening unshakable permanence leaving not the shadowiest imprint of her own on it." (64) These ominous forebodings come true in Mona's case because even though she succeeds in winning over Mona by saving her from suicide and her father-in-law Lalaji by saving Ram's declining business, Dev's animosity and bitterness assume terrible proportions and finally destroy her. Being an outspoken, frank and innocent person, it is difficult for Rose not to blurt out the things that go on in the house behind closed doors. Dev's loose sense of morals, his dishonesty and cruel disregard for the sentiments of Ram and Rose seem to receive moral sanction in the peculiar political climate of the Emergency period. He is close to the power echelons of the central government and malpractices like forging Ram's cheques—against which Rose raises her feeble voice—prove to be part of the established order of the day. Through all these demoralizing experiences Rose emerges as one who positively affirms the worth of humanitarian sentiments. The climate of the imperial era does not change her even on the surface. As the wife of an Indian, she hardly fits the role of the typical English memsahib. The usual airs of arrogance adopted by Englishwomen once they land in India, remain unknown to her. She is singularly free from racist feelings of white superiority. Her heart goes out to the Indian servant Kumar and the handicapped beggar. Though she feels a sense of freedom and release in the company of Dick and Minnie—her only English friends—and is almost excited when her old boyfriend Freddie comes to India, her loneliness does not arise from racial separateness. Her innate sympathy and understanding help her to establish contacts with Indians and in Sonali she wins a true friend. Her aloneness has a poignant intensity because it is emotional and moral. She is an agonized soul struggling to preserve her cherished human values in a corrupt world where forcibly sterilizing old servants or handicapped beggars and manufacturing cars in a bottle factory pass for social reform and industrial advancement.

Rose is a thoroughly decolonized personality. Whereas Ram fills his shop with foreign goods, it is Rose who discovers the beauty of Indian shawls and handicrafts and fills the shop with such things. When Ram's father starts conducting prayer meetings at the house, she too starts participating in them. She feels a sense of belonging to Ram's family once Lalaji and Mona take her into the fold of their warm affection. They give her moral strength to bear the loss of her parents in the war. She watches the political scene in India and with her shrewd and practical knowledge of British character, comes to her own conclusion. She says: "The British don't leave their homes even when the skies are black with bombers and they certainly wouldn't stroll away one summer day from their empire without good reason." (143) She is certain that the British wouldn't leave until "they were decided the game was up, and it would never be up until they saw doom spelled out in a language they understood. When it was, nothing would induce them to stay. An island race needed no second warning of danger." (143) She reacts to the events following Independence and partition, with sympathy and perception. She is so noble at heart, that she can take upon herself the sorrows of humanity and grieve for an armless beggar and offer him shelter and food.

It is interesting to note that the emotional alienation between Rose and Ram is not brought about by ideological differences or the cultural and racial disparity between the East and the West, but the finer and unbridgeable voids between the anglicized, highly educated, refined and cultured upper class Indian and the cockney-speaking, lower middle class, and crude English woman. Nayantara Sahgal has stressed the identical nature of the cultured aristocracy all over the world in *A Time to be Happy* also. This is brought out quite clearly through the instant rapport and perfect understanding between Marcella and Ram. Marcella who belongs to the cultured aristocracy is all that Rose is not. Whereas Rose drops her 'h's, Marcella matches Ram perfectly in talk, manners and sophisticated arts. With Rose joining them, "the atmosphere was transposed to a different key, to accommodate the wife Rose, the child Rose, pretty common little Rose." (90) For the first time she realizes that "a manner of speaking was an unscalable wall of steel and concrete between half the world and the other half." (91) The sense of being an outsider in the charmed circle of the sophisticated elite haunts her when Ram grows prosperous and his contacts increase. She feels she is the wrong wife for Ram who needs someone with a proper vocabulary and a better accent. Ram's fussy manner and overflowing social life exasperate her and she longs for Lalaji's business at floor level in the bazaar. She has to suffer further humiliation when Ram asks her to stay apart so that he could cultivate his intellectual companionship with Marcella. She seems to be so acculturised to Indian values that she displays the passive endurance of an Indian wife when she declares that what she "couldn't bear in any circumstances would be a divorce." (192) With the five years' rupture of all contact with Ram, when he comes back with the house-building euphoria enveloping him and Dev and Nishi, Rose finds it hard to shake off the sense of being an outsider. Ram's stroke becomes the climactic event that finally leaves her stranded and alone in a world where she is not wanted. Under Dev's roof, she lives with the ever-mounting fear of being killed. The secrecy about the activities in the house, more than anything, tells her "how much she had irretrievably lost, how alone she was." (215)

The drunken outspokenness of Rose in the company of Nishi's friends finally decides her destiny. Just as she has feared, she is finished off and thrown into the well, to be laid to rest, unmourned and unregretted. Sonali who has arranged artifical hands for the beggar at Rose's request, the beggar and Kumar—the servant—are the only mourners. The author's own words form the best epitaph for a person like Rose. "But Rose had transcended those things, blood, race, distance. . . . There had to be a special grace and favour reserved for people like her who loved and cherished strangers." (228)

Rose is a character who grows and develops in the novel. Stripped of racial and colonial prejudices, her experiences in India lead to her spiritual growth. Her life in India can be viewed as a journey of decolonization during which she gradually comes to identify herself with Ram's family, achieves an emotional rapport with Ram's father and even with Mona. Her sympathies soon extend to the masses outside and reaches even the anonymous destitute, the beggar. Her visits to the thirteenth century relic—the tomb—in the garden thus takes on the significance of a spiritual journey, for there in the company of the beggar—whose mutilated body reminds us of Caliban—she has moments of enlightenment. The animal-like native here actually becomes the interpreter of life in the journey towards spiritual fulfilment. Even in moments of loneliness, in the tomb, we find her at peace with herself and arriving at insights about life and time. "Now she knew time didn't pass. It was present, all of it, all the time." (194) The journey pattern as described by Helen Tiffin is too obvious here, to be ignored, and we find Rose growing to philosophical wisdom towards the end of her journey.

The return of the ex-colonizer to the former land of occupation as tourist, writer or spiritual searcher is a fequent feature in Independent India, not neglected by the post-Independence Indian English novelists. Disillusionment with western civilization in the post-war period leading to a renewed interest in the spiritual wealth of the East, has been the root cause of such exploratory journeys. A typical example for the inquisitive neo-colonialist is provided by Kamala Markandaya in *Pleasure City*. Lovat who comes to India to write a book about the previously occupied country has more than a superficial interest and evinces a desire to probe and dissect the alien country, its customs and traditions. It is this cold, anatomical dissection of the country for display that the natives dislike. Rikki displays the natives' abhorrence for such foreigners.

Unlike Mr. Lovat, Anand's Ashley Gibson (*Private Life of an Indian Prince*) takes a deeper interest in India. Ashley Gibson is a rich young English writer, who is engaged in some archaeological research in India. He happened to be travelling back to Bombay after holiday in the U.K. when he met the mad Prince Victor and Dr. Shankar in the plane. Realizing the plight of the Prince, he offers Dr. Shankar his car and takes them to the aerodrome so that he could take the Maharaja to Poona straight-away. When he comes to know that Captain Pratap Singh has been arrested by the police at the airport, he insists on accompanying Dr. Shankar on the journey. Gibson tells him of his fascination for the Indian fatalistic attitude of mind. He is "one of those rootless cosmopolitan young English intellectuals who had been reacting like Maugham, Huxley and Heard and the Quakers to the impact of science and believed . . . in the 'Spiritualism of the East' against the 'materialism of the West.'"[31]

Marcella and her husband (*Rich Like Us*) come back to India after Independence to explore Indian history and to conduct an exhibition of Indian art of the seventeenth century in London. Marcella tries to initiate Sonali into the rediscovery of Indian history of that particular era. Here the searcher is a refined, cultured and sophisticated person, who can discover the elegance of Indian art and culture.

Tully (*Pleasure City*) and Helen (*The Coffer Dams*) also are souls groping for spiritual moorings, though they come to India under different obligations. The rare occurrence of an Englishman or woman making India his or her permanent home is cited in R.K. Narayan's Mathieson (*Waiting for the Mahatma*) and Kamala Markandaya's Mrs. Pearl

(*Pleasure City*). Mathieson, whom Sriram—R.K. Narayan's weak and wavering Gandhian—accosts, turn out to be an Englishman who has made India his home. He had come to India in his twenties and had stayed on through the political turmoils till he is sixty-two. He is of great service to India because he employs five thousand field labourers and about two hundred factory hands and office workers. The demand to quit India seems strange to him and he tells Sriram, though he was not born in India, "It is just possible I am as much attached to this country as you are."[32] He has become so acclimatised to India that uprooting is an agonizing thought. Unfortunately R.K. Narayan does not develop this interesting British character and we are provided only a glimpse into this phenomenon of an Englishman who has taken up permanent residence in India. However, Sreenivas's meeting with Mathieson occurs before the dawn of Independence and how Independence and the transfer of power affect Mathieson is hardly mentioned in the novel.

Markandaya's Mrs. Pearl (*Pleasure City*) is a more satisfying portrait. Her innate kindness and nobility of mind, are reminiscent of Mrs. Moore in Forster's *A Passage to India*. She has hardly any airs, absolutely no pretensions of superiority—racial or national. Her humane warmth encompasses the alien country and its people. The courage she shows in becoming foster-mother to an Indian waif springs from the essential nobility of her nature that overcomes racial and cultural barriers in the pursuit of kindness and love. Compared to Mrs. Moore, she is more down-to-earth and can never aspire to the spiritual communion that Mrs. Moore achieves with India. She accepts Rikki as her master and in all humility receives swimming lessons from him. Rikki is touched by her kind solicitude that he considers himself responsible for her. He keeps a watchful eye on her; dilutes her drink if she has had more than necessary and he returns the money she offers when drunk. His best gifts are always for Tully and Mrs. Pearl. Without any hesitation or fear, she opts for India when the others leave. She takes up residence in a villa built near Shalimar with Kali, the cave child. There is a naturalness and a finality about Mrs. Pearl's choice of India as her home, as though she has returned after the long journey of life to her spiritual abode. The discovery of Kali and the choice of India happen so naturally. For Mrs. Pearl, the journey has come to its end, promising spiritual salvation and ultimate union with the landscape. It is the final discovery of the nature of "man-man, man-land and man-god relationship."[33]

The Indian novelist comes closest to an intuitive portraiture of British character in the depiction of these decolonized whites, who have rejected colonial values. Barriers projected by imperial illusion do not exist here and we find greater understanding and empathy on the part of the novelist. It is significant that such characters are on the increase in the novels written in the seventies and the eighties, indicating the Indian novelist's own progress toward liberation from the colonial hangovers. Chaman Nahal, Kamala Markandaya and Nayantara Sahgal have been remarkably successful in capturing on their canvas the internal conflict in the mind of the passive rejectors of colonialism and in depicting it in all its poignancy. In every novel, they are projected by the novelists as essentially noble and virtuous, in contrast to their imperial opposites. Thus we have Ashby and Dyer; Mark McIvor and Cyril Weatherby; Henry Brewster and Robert Pryor, etc., intended to project the unbridgeable gulf created by ideological differences. Employing the parameter of sympathetic British response to India, their worth is judged and acclaimed and through them the novelists achieve an affirmation of positive human values in a world divided and distraught by the imperial ethics. Markandaya's emigrant stature enables her to unfathom the undercurrents in the alien psyche, revealing its conflicts and the existential angst of non-belonging. Dr. Kenny's character is portrayed with great sympathy, though there is some ambiguity about his relationship with Rukmani. Tully is projected as a spiritual son of India, who was born in the west by accident. Nayantara Sahgal shows remarkable perception in the portrayal of Brewster, Michael Calvert and Rose. However there is a hesitancy to employ the protagonist as narrator in the depiction of English characters. It seems no amount of westernization would give the Indian writer the confidence to reject the omniscient-narrator method or the device of distancing by presenting facts through the perspective of another character. Therefore we can find no Englishmen in the Indian English novel employing the disarming device of the stream-of-consciousness technique, inviting us to share and participate in the unravelling of his thoughts, emotions and dreams. We are always made to view them sifted through the perspective of the narrator. This deliberate distancing is reduced to the minimum in the depiction of the characters under discussion in the chapter. For, they are nearest to the Indian psyche and lend themselves to sympathetic interpretation. As "nowheremen" stranded between two conflicting cultures or decolonized white men seeking a spiritual home in India, these characters stand apart as dignified individuals who have not sacrificed their humanity or moral and spiritual values to an exploiting and money-making political mechanism. There is a universality about them that defies the constricting code of the colonial cult.

In fiction, they form a common thematic concern with Third World writers, who are decolonizing artists attempting a reversal of the imperial rhetoric. The writers attempt what has been termed "racism in reverse" to teach the readers, as Chinua Achebe puts it "that their past—with all its imperfections—was not one long night of savagery from which the first European acting on God's behalf delivered them."[34]

A positive effort is being made by the Indian English novelists like Kamala Markandaya, Chaman Nahal and Nayantara Sahgal to break the myth of white superiority and reassert the worth of oriental culture. Though the Indian novelists do not show the vigour of the African writers in excavating their culture from beneath the debris of the empire, and reinstating it, they have performed the task quite commendably through tracing the journey of decolonization undertaken by the Englishman. The journey undermines the very concept of progress—defined purely in material terms—of the western man and manifests the reverse process of the journey towards spiritual enlightenment. In this journey Helen, Tully and Rose tread back from material civilization to the world of nature, to man's primordial past and to the intuitive knowledge afforded by the instincts. The novelist emerges as the iconoclast or decolonizing artist who breaks the illusory images of the colonial era and shows the growth, development and ultimate liberation of the white man leading to spiritual enlightenment and recognition of a permanent refuge and place.

The iconoclastic function of the post-Indepentent writer manifests most noticeably in the fictional recreation of history and the representation of British historical figures who once held the reins and moved through the corridors of power. The Indian English novelist's approach to them is examined in the next chapter.

NOTES

1. Albert Memmi, *The Colonizer and the Colonized* 19.
2. Peter Alcock, "James K. Baxter and the Terror of History: The Decolonisation of a New Zealander," *Awakened Conscience: Studies in Commonwealth Literature,* ed. C.D. Narasimhaiah (Delhi: Sterling, 1978) 106.
3. Phrase used in the sense in which Frantz Fannon uses it—those who have rejected white destiny.
4. Helen Tiffin, "Towards Place and Placelessness," *Awakened Conscience* 152.
5. Meenakshi Mukherjee, "Inside the Outsider," *Awakened Conscience* 89.
6. Albert Memmi, 36.

7. Arthur Pollard, "Kamala Markandaya's *The Golden Honeycomb*," *The Journal of Indian Writing in English,* 8, Nos. 1 and 2 (Jan.-July I980) 23-25.
8. Leonard Woolf, "Growing," *Autobiography,* Vol. II (1961), p. 111, quoted in Benita Parry, *Delusions and Discoveries: Studies on India in the British Imagination 1880-1930* (New Delhi: Orient Longman, 1974) 30.
9. Albert Memmi, 26.
10. Edward said, *Orientalism* (London: Routledge and Kegan Paul, 1978).
11. Ashis Nandy, *The Intimate Enemy; The Psychology of Colonialism* (Delhi: Oxford Univ. Press, 1983) 71.
12. Lewis D. Wurgaft, *The Imperial Imagination: Magic and Myth in Kipling's India* (Connecticut: Wesleyan Univ. Press, 1983).
13. Kamala Markandaya, *A Silence of Desire* (London: Putnam, 1960) 188.
14. O. Mannoni, *Prospero and Caliban: The Psycology of Colonization,* 158.
15. Gomathi Narayanan, "British Fathers and Indian Sons: Guilt and Pride for the Indian Freedom Movement in the Post-Independence Indian Novel in English," *Journal of South Asian Literature,* XVII, No. 1 (Winter-Spring 1982).
16. Kamala Markandaya, *Nectar in a Sieve* (Bombay: Jaico, 1982).
17. Ann Lowry Weir, "Worlds Apart?—Feminine Consciousness in Markandaya's *Nectar in a Sieve* and *The Coffer Dams,*" CIEFL Bulletin, XIII, No. 2 (1977) 71-85.
18. Quoted in R.S. Pathak, "The Indo-English Novelists' Quest for Identity," *Explorations in Modern Indo-English Fiction*, ed. R.K. Dhawan (New Delhi: Bahri, 1982) 115.
19. K.A. Abbas, *Inquilab* (New Delhi: Indian Paperbacks, 1977) 198.
20. Dieter Riemenschneider, "British Characters in Indo-English Fiction," *Aspects of Indian Writing in English* 137-49.
21. Saros Cowasjee, *So Many Freedoms: A Study of the Major Fiction of Mulk Raj Anand* (Delh: Oxford Univ. Press, 1977) 186.
22. Mulk Raj Anand, *Confession of a Lover* (Delhi: Arnold-Heinemann, 1976) 65.
23. "The Nostalgic Phenomenon and its Exploitation," *Uprooting and After* (New York: Springer-Virlag, 1973) 24.
24. Saros Cowasjee, 186.
25. Helen Tiffin, "Towards Place and Placelessness," 146-63.
26. *Ibid.* 147.
27. "Victims and Virgins: Some Characters in Kamala Markandaya's Novels," *Galaxy of Indian Writing in English* (Delhi: Akshat, 1987) 116.
28. (London: Hodder and Stoughten, 1945) 316.
29. Nayantara Sahgal, A *Situation in New Delhi* (New Delhi: Himalaya, 1977) 13.
30. Timeri Murari, *Last Victory* (Hodder and Stoughten: New English Library, 1989) 12.

31. Mulk Raj Anand, *Private Life of an Indian Prince* (Great Britain: The Bodley Head, 1953) 347.
32. R.K. Narayan, *Waiting for the Mahatma* (Mysore: Indian Thought Publications, 1964) 77.
33. *Awakened Conscience* 152.
34. "The Novelist as Teacher," *Readings in Commonwealth Literature,* ed. William Walsh (Oxford: Clarendon Press, 1973) 185.

The Novelist as Decolonizer

Most of the novels written in the post-Independent era reveal the pressure of history on the consciousness of the writer. This is a phenomenon common to Third World countries who suffer from the received notion of history as "'the few privileged moments' of achievement, which serves either to arrogate 'history' wholesale to the imperial centre or to erase it from the colonial archive and produce, especially in New World Cultures, a condition of 'histroylessness,' of 'no visible history.'"[1] The Indian English novelist, newly liberated from foreign domination, assumes the tremendous responsibility of destructuring history by breaking the idols of the imperial past and reinstating the national heroes, through the new "lenses of language"[2] that bring them into focus. The entire range of post-Independence fiction manifests a conscious or unconscious preoccupation with history and a search for a new vision of the past, free from the clogging images built up by the erstwhile rulers. The process involves not only the rejection of colonial illusions and values, but a deliberate debunking of the myths evolved and sustained by a vast body of western literature and history.

The Indian English novelist launching this new process of emancipation for decolonization evokes the colonial past only to reject it and projects historical figures stripped of the veneer of colonial glory. "Decolonisation," according to Fannon, "is the veritable creation of new men . . . the thing which has become colonized becomes man during the same process by which it frees itself."[3] An attempt is being made in this chapter to make a study of the British historical figures appearing in Indian English fiction of the post-Independence era. They are viewed as part of the cultural strategy of the postcolonial writer to dismantle and demythify imperial heroes and reduce them to the "other,"[4] focusing on them from a different angle. The perspective of the postcolonial writers may not therefore be free from emotional restrictions or prejudices. The British historical figures evolve within the limiting framework of the colonial relationship. They have functional roles in the novels and are found to operate at two levels. Primarily, they are symbols of the imperial value system, of colonial ideals and myths, conjured up by the postcolonial writer with a specific purpose. As figures who have acquired the halo of glory in imperial literature and history, they become icons to be shattered and replaced by the condemned leaders of the once-occupied country. The process involves a reversal of values; a replacing of blind adoration for the ruler by patriotic sentiments; a resurgence of pride in the nation and national values. The British heroes are transformed into anti-heroes during the process.

The British figures recalled from history also help to evoke the bygone era of imperial domination and create a sense of the actuality of the past. The representative role limits the scope of the historical characters, stunts their development and reduces them to symbols indicative of attitudes and beliefs. They seldom grow out of the inhibiting role and remain one-dimensional figures.

The novels chosen for study are *The Devil's Wind*, *The Princes*, *The Golden Honeycomb*, *Private Life of an Indian Prince*, *Azadi*, *The Crown and the Loincloth*, *The English Queens*, *Inquilab*, *The World is My Village*, *The Imperial Agent*, *Last Victory* and *Midnight's Children*. The decolonizing Indian artist employs history in different ways in these novels. History is thematized in *The Devil's Wind*, whereas an interweaving of fact and fiction is attempted in all the other novels. Rushdie writes history as autobiography, allowing an interplay of personal and national histories, so that the odyssey of the Assizes and the Sinais also becomes the odyssey of the nation from the year 1915 to 1977. Like the other novelists dealing with the nation's past, Rushdie too seeks "to make visible/audible what has been pushed to the margins and forcibly silenced."[5] All of them indulge in "revisionist history which subvert the official view and offers a critique of authority."[6]

The novelist as historian has the manifold task of contextualizing the characters, establishing the authenticity of the historical figures and individualizing them. As the decolonizing artist of the Third World, he has the difficult task of demythifying the British heroes and exposing the illusions of imperialism that had blocked impartial judgement.

The Devil's Wind by Manohar Malgonkar is a heroic venture in which the novelist seeks to rewrite the history of the Mutiny of 1857—contemptuously dismissed as the "Sepoy Mutiny" by the British and celebrated as "the First War of independence" by the Indians. It was virtually the first violent reaction to the imperial aspirations of Britain. Malgonkar views the mutiny from the purely Indian perspective. It is a novel written with the deliberate intention of refuting imperial ontology that distorts history to contain the Indian as the "other" or the "native" or the "barbarian." It can be said to be "a radical experiment" in "the deconstruction of European monoliths and the refashioning, through fiction, of the nature of history."[7] In this tremendous task, the Indian novelist's resources are pitted against an intimidating body of English history and literature—about fifty English novels—on the Mutiny. In every one of these novels—*The Afghan Knife, The Touchstone of Peril, The Great White Hand, A Hero of Lucknow, The Devil's Wind* etc., to mention only a few—the principal villain is Nana Saheb, the dethroned heir of Baji Rao II. The heroes are invariably the British civil and military officers whose adventures are described in extravagant terms and whose qualities of heroism and valour are highly eulogised. They illustrate the type of "boastful imperialism" preached by Disraeli, Rhodes and Chamberlain. The British mutiny novels have entrenched the myth of imperialism and British ethnic superiority.

Malgonkar's attempt is to subvert the myth by projecting Nana Saheb, condemned by English historians as "infamous, dastardly, despicable"[8] as the hero of his novel. He declares at the outset that his novel is an attempt to present the story of the revolt and Nana from the Indian point of view. Naturally, the glorification of the Indian leader as hero, offers a different angle of vision that transforms the Sepoy Mutiny—condemned as "the devil's wind" by English writers—into a glorious war for Independence. The altered perspective disturbs the original image of the British hero, casting him into eclipse. The deliberate shifting of stance, involving a toppling of images, is part of the process of "decolonization." The relation between the colonizer and the colonized had always been defined and sustained by a series of images of the white and the non-white. To quote Kamala Markandaya: "Each image carried a counterpart: that is to say the image of the other man, in the colonial mind, was balanced by one of himself: a study in contrasts, if you like, that was as necessary a piece of equipment for tropical foray as pith helmet and rifle."[9]

The image of the native in the colonial mind was that of the depraved, savage and half-beast Caliban. The myth of the mutiny in colonial imagination fostered the images of the valiant, heroic and superior whiteman and the despicable, ungrateful and rebelling sepoy. Nana Saheb, as the leader of the rebels became the natural corollary to the Prospero image of the ruler. The British Empire in India was founded on such myths generated by orientalist discourse, the essence of orientalism being "the ineradicable distinction between Western superiority and Oriental inferiority."[10]

The colonial images are dispelled in *The Devil's Wind* through the exposition of the historical facts long suppressed or mutilated by English historians and novelists. The real villain is revealed to be the East India Company and its officials who found moral justification for their presence in India in self-deluding theories of a beneficent role involving great sacrifice. Trollope had given concrete expression to the popular sentiment: "We are called upon to rule [the colonies], as far as we do rule them, not for our glory, but for their happiness. If we keep them we should keep them—not because they are gems in our diadem, not in order that we may boast that the sun never sets on our dependencies, but because by keeping them we may assist them in developing their own resource."[11]

Malgonkar strikes back at the Empire, revealing the so-called belligerent rulers to be the power-greedy empire-builders, stripping them of the gloss of their imperial ideology that had justified and glorified their actions. He chooses a method of exposition directly opposed to that of the English writer and gives the place of centrality to Nana Saheb who had been reduced to the most despicable villain of the mutiny by the English novelists. The English characters are viewed by the Indian novelist as exponents of imperial ideals and values necessitating a degree of typification. Most of the Englishmen who figure in *The Devil's Wind* thus fall into the pre-fabricated pattern of colonial behaviour. Only slight shades of colour distinguish one from another. They are the stereotyped representatives of an aggressive, exploiting, self-complacent and ethnocentric colonial power.

To this class belongs Sir John Malcolm, who manages through clever and far-sighted manoeuvre the deposition and banishment of Peshwa Baji Rao II of the great Maratha Confederacy. He had employed against the Peshwa, the six thousand strong British garrison stationed within the state at his expense for his protection. Malcolm satisfies his craving for military triumph by finishing off the Peshwa's feudatories one by one and isolating him. Malcolm is described as "business-like but not rapacious or vindictive." (10) In his attitude to the Peshwa he is said to have been "magnanimous" enough to let the exiled and dethorned Peshwa retain his title. But the "magnanimous" Malcolm makes Baji Rao renounce all claims to his heritage for himself as well as for his successors and to undertake that he would never return to his homeland. In return Malcolm consents to let him live with his retinue in the village of Bithoor and grants him a pension of a hundred thousand pounds every year. Lord Hastings, the Governor General, is critical of Malcolm for being too generous to the Peshwa against the interests of the Empire. The author as narrator-protagonist remarks: "Hastings himself, I feel sure, would have liked nothing better than to hang my father like a common felon and declare his wealth to be prize money." (10)

A saga of imperial oppression unfolds itself through the political deeds of the colonials. The self-righteous convictions of a beneficial and better rule vindicated and glorified them. Thus, it is declared by the British, on the death of Baji Rao that his pension would not be continued to his successor. Similar strategies had been employed by Lord Elphinstone towards the Vanchurkars so that they had to rest beholden to the Englishman for the modest holdings left to them. In Nana Saheb's case he realizes only too late that even the rank of the Peshwa was not his to give. Elphinstone had broken and burned the original "guddi" (throne) of the Peshwa when he planted the British flag on his palace in Poona.

All that imperialism signifies is crystallized in the portrait of Lord Dalhousie, who finally shatters Nana Saheb's expectations of a just settlement of the rights of inheritance. He declares: "The GovernorGeneral in council recognises no such person as Maharaja Dhondu Pant Nana Saheb." (45)

The portrait of Dalhousie is one of the darkest and most undiluted among the figures from history. It is interesting to examine Malgonkar's portrait of Dalhousie against English value judgements. Nana Saheb describes Dalhousie as "an enormous giant who spat fire and gave out blood-curdling honks as he went about swallowing kingdom after kingdom as though they were his natural food. His ambition was to clear India of Indian rulers and he all but achieved it with the Doctrine of Lapse." (45-46) The English view about Dalhousie's annexations is presented by Sir John A.R. Marriott in his work *The English in India.* Speaking of the reasons advanced for every annexation, he says: "In every case a vicious and oppressive rule had been replaced by an administration based on principles of justice, impartiality and social order. These 'blessings' had not evoked a vestige of gratitude among the recipients."[12]

If the Doctrine of Lapse was a tyrannical and crude instrument of confiscation in the eyes of the Indian, to the English it was a benevolent measure to redeem the native. Nana Saheb equates him with "the God who rides a buffalo"[13]; the English hail him as one who "had no equal among the rulers of India except Lord Curzon."[14]

Colonial ambition legitimized the annexation of Oudh carried out by Dalhousie in February 1856. (56) He merely serves an order on the king telling him that his country has been taken over and he is bundled off to Calcutta. His Majesty and Nawab is transformed into a private citizen. Dalhousie's galloping annexations cause an uproar even in the British parliament and the press and they advise caution. Dalhousie invents a 'dummy calf' Fakiruddin to serve as heir to the deposed Nawab on condition that he would vacate the Red Fort and renounce all the titles. Dalhousie carries imperial ambitions to unheard-of extents, becoming one of the controversial figures in British Indian history. Malgonkar attributes Dalhousie's feverish urge for empire-expansion to a burning desire for revenge. Hugh Wheeler serves as the authorial voice. "Because Dalhousie has no son of his own, and no heir. Under English law, his estate and titles must lapse after his death." (65) The Doctrine of Lapse was his instrument of revenge. He seeks a form of revenge that victimizes an entire nation, in no way responsible for his personal misfortune. The Company profited by his revenge and an entire nation supported his tyrannical enterprise as is illustrated by the rewards offered by the British government to Dalhousie. He was made a Marquis and granted a special pension of five thousand pounds a year because he had successfully swallowed up Oudh and many other kingdoms.

The trend of aggressive imperialism set by Dalhousie is carried on by Theophilus Metcalfe who turns down Zeenat Mahal's claim to the throne for her son Jawan Bakht. Hodson makes even the question of a Mughal successor irrelevant by finishing off three Mughal princes. Sir Theophilus rounds off the rest—as many as twenty-one of them. British historians have extolled these early 'empire-builders' as romantic adventurists who came to India to establish an empire and to impose a "superior order" on a mass of uncivilised peoples. Their actions were vindicated by the myth of a superior civilization. Jacob Arlow has pointed out the function of the myth in psychic integration. According to him, myth "plays a role in warding off feelings of guilt and anxiety" and "constitutes a form of adaptation to reality and to the group in which the individual lives," and influences "the crystallisation of the individual identity and the formation of the super ego."[15] The shared belief in the myth and the absolute involvement in the emotional medium it created, made the English conquerors impervious to the repercussions of their actions on the colonized mind. Colonialism bred a superiority complex that prevented the British from accepting the Indian as an equal or even as a human being capable of emotional response and organized protest. "The colonizer, who in order to ease his conscience gets into the habit of seeing the other man as an animal, accustoms himself to treating him like an animal and tends objectively to transform himself into an animal."[16] This colonial tendency explains the British failing to understand the religious and moral sentiments of the subjugated nation. It leads to the forceful imposition of greased cartridges on the Indian sepoy—an event that triggers off the Mutiny. The aggressive tactics employed to terrorize the protesting sepoys generates seething undercurrents of anger which finally erupt as the Mutiny. The superego of the British keep them oblivious of the developments around till the Mutiny becomes a violent truth to be reckoned with. The violence of the open confrontation between the colonizer and the colonized bears out the theory of transformation put forward by Aime Cesaire.

Significantly enough, the British characters from history, who escape being paper figures and assume validity in the human context, are those who have preserved basic human values by refusing to freeze into the imperial mould. Major General Sir Hugh Wheeler and Charles Hillersdon are examples. Authorial attitudes are made explicit by the generous and rounded protraiture of these characters. The postcolonial writer, in his effort to throw the colonial baggage overboard, tends to idealize the Englishman who has attained a cultural and spiritual empathy with India. For the English community in India, the worst crime that a colonial could commit was identification with native culture, as illustrated by the pathetic fate of Sir Hugh Wheeler.

Wheeler had first arrived in India as a boy of seventeen and except for a two-year stint with one British column or another in Europe, he had never been out of India and was thus "more Indian than British." (67) At the very first meeting Nana Saheb is pleasantly impressed by Wheeler's behaviour. "Instead of stiff bows and handshakes, there was a warm Indian embrace; instead of the pantomime of betel-nut and rose-water, a musical entertainment." (64) Wheeler had a very pretty Indian wife who was extremely friendly and the two families soon develop a warm intimacy that dissolves racial and political differences. Such an intimacy was hardly warranted by the colonial situation in which they were placed. The differential behaviour becomes his bane. To quote Memmi, "humanitarian romanticism is looked upon in the colonies as a serious illness, the worst of all dangers. It is no more nor less than going over to the side of the enemy."[17]

Wheeler is ostracized by the English community in Kanpur for the crime of "going native." His Indian wife, his fondness for Indian dress and curried meals and his habit of speaking Hindi to his family are condemned as outrageous crimes by the English community. Above all, "he was passionately fond of Indian music and—most shocking of outrages—invite[d] natives to Flagstaff House dinners!" (67) "Fifty-four—or at least fifty-two—Indian summers had burned his skin a dark cinnamon shade, and monsooon upon monsoon had layered his habits and thought processes with mildew so that the pink-faced boy from an impoverished Cornwall rectory who had been sent out into the world to fend for himself had been laid to rest under them." (66) He hardly realizes that this is the main handicap that disqualifies him for the post of Commander-in-Chief though he is the senior-most general in the entire army and his war record reads like the battle honours on some regimental banners. He had earned the sobriquet "Hamlah" among the sepoys, indicating his zest for warfare. Nothing of this prevails with the authorities for the caste system that existed in the English community was more rigid than that among the rabidly orthodox Brahmins of Tanjawar. Even when the post of Commander-in-Chief falls vacant, it is denied to Wheeler, because "Dalhousie had refused to countenance someone like Wheeler, who, according to him, had 'gone native' as his military chief." (64) Six years later, when the post falls vacant, again Wheeler is overlooked and General Anson who knows very little of war, is promoted as Commander-in-Chief. Wheeler waits with undiminished hope for Anson to die or retire, in the meanwhile striving to hide his age. His last hope is crushed when Patrick Grant, fifteen years his junior, is promoted as Commander-in-Chief on the death of Anson.

> It was just that even though old Halmah was of the right caste, he had disqualified himself by marrying that 'ghastly dancing girl from some robber's harem.' The new crop of the Company's officers and, even more so, their ladies would never have suffered a countryborn to be mistress of the Jangi Laat's gleaming palace in Simla. (71)

The English ladies of the Doab club cannot tolerate the fact that Wheeler's "country-born" wife danced, went barefoot in the house, wore saris, chewed paan, stained her lips red and painted the palms of her hands and feet, saffron. What was even more unforgivable was that "she was very beautiful . . . and also the fact that she was just as proud of being Indian as they were of being British." (67)

The qualities for which Wheeler is criticized by the English Community are exactly the traits that exonerate him as an individual. He has nothing but disdain for the racial insolence of his fellow officers who trample on the religious sentiments of the sepoys by imposing on them the greased cartridges. Wheeler writes to George Anson suggesting that the cartridges should be withdrawn or at least the leading drill changed so that they need not be broken with the teeth. "As for me, I'd rather resign than compell my sepoys to bite them," said Wheeler. (101) He realizes the gulf in understanding that separates the English officers from the sepoys. The services of the sepoy are taken for granted and they hardly ever acknowledge his loyalty which has made their conquests in India possible. Wheeler had been a link between the sepoy and the Company because the sepoys respected and admired him for his military prowess. But when he is repeatedly overlooked for promotion, the sepoy too loses his respect for Wheeler because "they cannot venerate an object of ridicule—cannot go on respecting someone dropped by his own side." (137)

Wheeler's predicament is that of the individual who has internalized the culture of the occupied country and in the cross-pull between the divergent cultures, fails to attain complete identification with either. He is compelled to remain an outsider and suffer for both sides because of his incapacity to emotionally detach himself from either.

The English Mutiny novels mention Wheeler as the gullible Englishman who is deceived by Nana Saheb's promise. This led to the murder of a number of Englishmen, women and children. Malgonkar reveals how both Nana Saheb and Wheeler are the victims of the inexorable course of history. Nana Saheb's noble intentions are miscarried at the upsurge of the mob's hostility and Wheeler and the English become silent prey to it. The portrait of Wheeler comes alive as no other English character does, due to his closeness to the Indian sensibility. In British books on history, Wheeler's name is conspicuously absent among the heroes listed. No kudos for the credible English officer who makes the mistake of believing an Indian—Nana Saheb—and brings about the death of several English men, women and children.

The Collector of Kanpur, Charles Hillersdon, is another English officer who seeks to escape the stifling rigidity of the colonial role and establishes a warm relationship with the natives. He becomes a regular weekend visitor in Nana Saheb's palace. Though Nana Saheb feels that there is much in common between them, official restrictions bar intimacy between the Collector and the Peshwa's heir. Nana Saheb even feels that Hillersdon is his exact opposite number, "a cultivated English Brahmin, less interested in hunting and shooting than in abstract learning, the man who wanted to get to know people more than to govern them or even to be a demi-god to them; the sort of man who dreams and talks of his dreams." (17) Their finer sensibilities could soar above confining political and racial boundaries and commune at a higher level. Hillersdon makes a study of Kalidasa as a dramatist which earns him the title "Orientalist" and provokes the suspicion of his compatriots. However Hildersdon can keep his "caste" because he does not suffer from the stigma of a marriage to "a country-born." It seems to be a cruel twist of fate that both these friends of Nana Saheb meet with their tragic end in the entrenchment. The English interpret their deaths as instances of Nana's deliberate deception. Malgonkar reveals how the forces of violence unleashed by the mass rebellion had overpowered the two Englishmen, causing great pain to Nana Saheb.

The heroes celebrated in the English novels on the Mutiny are the British military officers who successfully dealt with the rebellious forces led by Nana Saheb in a ruthless manner, exposing the horrifying brutality that a colonizer-colonized conflict can assume. What is glossed over as instances of heroism and valour are revealed to be a chain of blood-curdling incidents where racial antagonism against the natives finds violent outlet.

The English novelists have created a myth of the Mutiny through the romanticization and glorification of the British heroes. The large number of novels that sprouted on the topic are woven round this myth and fall into a class of propagandist fiction. *Eight Days* by R.E. Forrest, *The Juggler* by G.A. Henty, *The Star of Fortune* and *The Great White Hand* by J.E. Muddock express the prevailing mood of these novels. They create clear outlines of British superiority. The pattern has hardly any variations; the mutiny upsets the placid, comfortable life of the British Cantonment; the British hero takes the hazards of the Mutiny in his stride and by his ability to cope with extreme situations, proves that Indians are no match to his leadership qualities. Invariably, the Indian leaders are hanged or killed and their deaths are given the complexion of retributive punishment. The cult of an ideal British hero emerges—one who is "brave, forceful, daring, honest, active and masculine."[18] Rene Maunier, a French student of imperialism states:

> The legal sources of imperialism are to be sought in the old mood of the Anglo-Saxon soul, in the ideal of the gentleman who was the standard type of culture and good manners. The gentleman is not only the polite and polished man; he is more especially the man who knows how to command, the imperial man in a certain sense, who having powers, makes it his duty and his right to use them for the common welfare. The ideas of authority-as-power and authority-as-duty are the heritage of an aristocratic tradition.[19]

The English novels on the Mutiny are structured round this illusory ideal of the gentleman English officer and the Indian leaders, in contrast, are made to conform to the savage and uncivilized being, often reduced to the despicable image of an animal. To quote Jean-Paul Sartre: "The colonizer can only exonerate himself in the systematic pursuit of the 'dehumanization' of the colonized by identifying himself a little more each day with the colonialist apparatus."[20]

Malgonkar's task is the reversal of the myth and the exposition of historic truth. Unlike most of the postcolonial writers Malgonkar has not chosen allegory as a strategy for transforming inherited notions of history or to transcend or go "beyond history."[21] He only presents history from a different perspective, for history as we know, from the work of Michel Foucault, "is a mode of discourse that is culturally motivated and ideologically conditioned."[22] Malgonkar takes upon himself the task of relating those incidents of history that have been reduced to invisibility by British historians. Racial antagonism is exposed at its worst: the carnal butchery and savage destruction indulged in by the colonizer are revealed to bring out the dehumanization involved in the colonial process. Coverley Jackson, Henry Lawrence, John Lawrence, Neill, Major Renaud, Henry Havelock, Thomas Metcalfe, Colin Campbell, Gen. Hope Grant, Hugh Rose, Lord Clyde and Frederic Cooper—the illustrious heroes of the British are revealed to be unscrupulous oppressors who dismember the host country with deliberate villainy. Coverley Jackson is depicted as a greater villain than Dalhousie himself in his systematic assault on Indian culture and ways of life. He and the Company's men methodically broke down the framework of a city which was the capital of a court renowned for its flamboyance and profligacy, its riches and the arts, the beauty of its women and the elegance of its men. Lucknow was reduced to "merely a property of foreign merchants, a city without a soul." (106) Ministers, heads of departments and talukdars were replaced by the Company's men. Soldiers strutted like nawabs on the streets and their women used the king's carriages. Even the palace of the dowager queens was forcibly taken by the Chief Commissioner, Coverley Jackson, who had the women dragged out. The holy shrine of the Muslims was converted into a military storehouse. Through Nana Saheb, Malgonkar gives expression to the shock suffered by the Indian at this spectacle of the "ruthless uprooting of a civilization." (108) Even Lord Canning was shocked at Coverley Jackson's impudence to the queens and hastily recalled him and gave back the palace to the ex-queens.

The much-celebrated Henry Lawrence who replaces Jackson as Commissioner is revealed to be a vainglorious official who refuses to see Nana Saheb because he is affronted by the size of Nana Saheb's retinue and the flamboyance of his equipage when he arrives in Lucknow. The unbelievable savagery of Commander Neill and Major Renaud, as they confront the mutineers, is described thus: "They kill for sport: they burn for fun. They don't spare any one—not old men or women or children. They go in parties, looking for people to kill, for villages to burn." (170) Major Renaud had made "a practice of killing villagers merely because they happened to be looking the other way when the column passed" and Neill's orders to him were "to slaughter all men and take no prisoners." (171) The vengeance of Neill is endorsed by history.

> Neill put to death all the mutineers who were caught; and in the surrounding country which was placed by the Governor-General

> under the martial law, rebels, subjects and even disorderly boys were executed by infuriated officers and unofficial British Residents, who volunteered to serve as hangmen.[23]

Though the success of the British depended on the loyalty of a major section of the Indian sepoys and labourers they were thrown out of the Enrenchment because they consumed precious food and water. Neill and Renaud carried violent oppression to extreme extents. They selected at random what they termed "guilty villages" to be cordoned off and set on fire. Those who tried to escape were shot down. They organized volunteer hanging parties to hunt for "guilty men" which term included anyone whose behaviour seemed even remotely suspicious to any member of the party. These hunting parties soon "developed a competitive spirit, and bets were laid openly as to which one would spear the highest number of 'pandies' on a given day" (200) ("pandies"—a contemptuous term used by the British for the natives). The gallows and trees had "each day the fresh fruits of rebellion displayed upon them,"[24] admitted F.A.V. Thurburn, who was appointed Deputy Judge Advocate General. Neill's revenge on the mutineers continued for three months during which period eight dead-carts went on their rounds from sunrise to sunset, to take down corpses which hung at the cross-roads, and the market-places and to throw them into the Ganges. In the words of Malleson, the famous historian of the Indian mutiny, Neill had the "energy of one of the most determined characters ever bestowed on man."[25]

Havelock, an embodiment of monstrous cruelty, is a typical British military leader—a commander of exceptional ability as well as a skilled technician who could take in at a glance every aspect of a military situation. He is also audacious, resourceful, crafty and cool-headed. But he seems to derive enjoyment from destruction which had been developed into an art. The military thoroughness with which he sacks a village and dishonours its women gives rise to what comes to be called "the Havelock legend." (202) Fatehpur is cordoned off and set on fire. Those who try to escape, even women and children, are thrown back into the fire or shot while escaping. (202) Havelock does not spare even Nana Saheb's concubine Azijan. She is hanged to death for helping the revolutionaries actively and for inciting the sepoys. It is Havelock's military strategy that finally leads to the overthrow of Nana Saheb and the victory of the British. In spite of the brutality of his measures, English novelists have hailed him as the hero who saved Lucknow. in *The Peril of the Sword*[26] and *Love Besieged*[27] Havelock figures as the hero. What impairs his glory in British fiction is not the horror caused by his atrocities, but the humiliation on being superseded by James Outram. The glorification of the rude facts of history in imperial discourse needs no better evidence.

Malgonkar expresses the unquenched blood-lust of the conquerors through the orgy of violence they indulge in soon after military victory. The most gruesome incidents are the wanton destruction by a British batallion of their unfortunate camp followers—the water carriers, sweepers, porters, grooms, cooks, bearers and bootblacks who had loyally served the British—before the walls of Delhi and the revenge of the Bibighar massacre by Neill. The slaughter of the English men, women and children in Bibighar by the woman, Hussainy Begam is avenged measure for measure by Neill who has been promoted as Brigadier. He shows that he has nothing to learn from Hussainy Begam. "He rounded up Kanpur's most prominent and respectable citizens and ordered them to be hanged. But, before being hanged, they were made to atone for the sin of Bibighar by cleaning its floors" (208) and that too in "as revolting" a manner as possible. Men of the highest learning and lineage who could not conceivably have had anything to do with the massacre, "were made to crawl on all fours and lick off the mess of clotted blood and urine and faeces." (208) History testifies to the truth of the statement. Racial hostility blots out individual distinctions among the colonized and the colonizer is able to view them only as a class—the inferior race to be trampled upon and crushed. It is this savage face of the oppressor-oppressed relationship that comes out through the incidents.

We see the oppressors themselves merging into this indistinguishable class behaviour so that names like Hodson, Metcalfe, Colin Campbell and Hope Grant cease to represent individual entities. They fall into the same pattern of oppressive racism. Only the methods differ. Mannoni has explained this as a natural consequence of the emotional aspect of racism. "The racialist apprehends racial differences emotionally; he is conscious of belonging to a particular race, and in another person he sees the race before he sees the man. For him the race overshadows the individual."[28]

Mannoni's explication of group behaviour under the impact of racism accounts for the barbarities indulged in by the British in the wake of victory. According to Mannoni, the group infected with racism acquires a cheap sense of superiority that causes an inversion of normal values and influences leading to a gradual deterioration of intellectual and moral standards. Christian values are discarded and we find the Englishmen vying with one another to inflict fresh wounds on the defeated natives. Hodson, a subaltern, suddenly emerges a hero by murdering three of the Mughal Emperor's sons and sending their heads on a platter to the bereaved Emperor; Metcalfe organizes a hunt for the

Mughal heirs and hangs them in batches; Sir Colin Campbell personally charges his subordinate Brigadier Hope Grant to destroy Bithoor as thoroughly as his chief has sacked Lucknow; and Frederic Cooper, the British Commissioner of Amritsar locks up his prisoners in a windowless room where they die of suffocation. The well in which Nana Saheb had hidden his gold is emptied and the wealth plundered. The Commanders make fortunes, the privates get only the price of a few bottles of grog. Malgonkar expresses his views on the lust of the English for gold through Azim: "If only we had unlimited gold to throw in their paths. . . . Then they would never go on campaigns. They'd just sit, holding committees over prize money and doing each other down." (236)

The British heroes of the Mutiny are reduced to anti-heroes or villains through the exposure of the bare facts of history. Malgonkar does not tamper with historic truth in presenting the mutiny from the Indian point of view. The kaleidoscope is only shifted slightly to help us focus on a different picture emerging from the collage of historical facts. The irony of contrasting values emanating from the same situation strikes us anew as he records that Frederic Cooper who avenged the crime of Bibighar by killing as many as five hundred, becomes "the hero of Ajnale" to the British. Neill is paid a public tribute by the British citizens of Calcutta who say that "he had filled a page in the annals of history and that he was an honour to his country." (290) To the British the most despised villain of the Mutiny was Nana Saheb. After the Mutiny, Malgonkar depicts Nana making a visit to his native country from Nepal where he was in hiding. He finds the country littered with memorials for the dead English where as there are no souvenirs for the dead Indians, who fought to liberate the country from foreign shackles. He feels pained and hurt at the inscriptions that proclaim him as the man behind the Satichaura incident, whereas in truth he was not present anywhere near the place where the tragedy had occurred. He feels that by the same logic Queen Victoria could be held responsible for all the atrocities committed by the British in her name.

It should be acknowledged that Malgonkar, in the task of demythifying history, does not try to glorify Nana Saheb as a hero; and is content to expose his virtues and lapses as a man and clarify the motives behind his actions. By this technique he has succeeded in bringing him to life. As Best has remarked, Nana emerges neither "a hero nor an anti-hero; he is the kind of ambiguous character that Malgonkar delights in."[29]

Colonials in the first flush of empire, inspired by dreams of power and spurred by the ambition for conquest are introduced in *The Devil's Wind*. Malgonkar has ripped open the colonial baggage to reveal the illusions and myths that sustained these men. Against the backdrop of their oppression and villainy emerges the image of the Nana Saheb as a redeemed hero, who has been wronged, deprived and condemned in imperial history and fiction. The spiritual function of "decolonization" as envisaged by Frantz Fanon is fulfilled. Malgonkar's novel satisfies the liberated writer's urge for a reorientation of national values and perspectives. At the same time *The Devil's Wind* does not fall short of the requirements of a good historical novel. By giving expression to the racial and cultural conflicts that are of perennial interest to the human kind through the immediate experience of the mutiny, he has achieved the ultimate goal of a historical novelist. Stating the critical canons of historical fiction, Lion Feuchtwagner remarks: "The historical data in most historical novels are verifiable only to a certain degree. The fact in no way denigrates their poetic content, for the essence of human kind remains unchanged throughout the ages."[30] Malgonkar has succeeded in conveying this inner truth of human kind, unimpaired by the forbidding mass of historical data. He has achieved a "creative integration of history and art"[31] and "has broadened our understanding of the Sepoy Revolt from a novelist's perspective, probing the protagonist's psyche which, of course, lies beyond the historian's domain.'[32]

The end of the Mutiny marks the beginning of a new era in the history of Indo-British relationships. The rule of the East India Company is replaced by the direct rule of the Crown transforming the concept of an empire acquired temporarily "in a fit of absence of mind"[33] into a permanent possession. There is a sudden surge of popular imperialism, lending a righteous tone to the British enterprise in India. "The abolition of the East India Company and the esatablishment of Crown rule were the assurance the nation required that India did indeed now 'belong' to the nation and not just to a handful of Englishmen."[34]

With this new assurance comes a hardening of values and a crystallization of attitudes. The myth of imperialism axiomatic to the concept of white destiny becomes deeply entrenched in the British consciousness. The historical characters representing this new era of the Raj voice the moral complacency of a divinely ordained "heaven-born" race, carrying out their holy mission in an India firmly established in English consciousness as the quintessence of depravity."[35] The Indian novelists have drawn them as symbolic figures with the functional role of figureheads of power. As the power-symbols of the British Empire, they embody in themselves the evils of the Empire. The excessive opulence and the deliberate exclusiveness of their life in India speak for the attitude of the entire community. The "otherness" of the alien culture and its values excited no healthy curiosity in their insular minds. With a delicate stroke here and there, the novelists have succeeded in lending a certain distinctiveness to their identities, preventing the reduction of the characters to mere formulae.

Silhouettes of the British Viceroys who ruled over the destiny of India, emerge against the political background of the Indo-British relationship. As the representative of the Crown, the Viceroy epitomized power. He had the authority to sanction or annul the succession of a legal heir to the throne. Bawajiraj III (*The Golden Honeycomb*) has to wait anxiously for years for the Viceroy's sanction to hand over the reins to his son Rabi. The Indian princes live in dread of the displeasure of the Viceroy. They have to pay tributes to the Viceroy and please the Vicerienes with presents of jewellery. The Maharajah Ashok Kumar "spent pitcherfuls of money in giving banquets to the Viceroy and the other English officials when they came to shoot in the hunter's paradise which is Sharanpur."[36] The Indian princes are compelled to sing the panegyric of the British Viceroys—virtually their masters—though in private they fume as the chains tighten, curbing every independent move. The Viceroys bind the Indian princes by treaties according to which a British controlled force is always stationed within the princely states to safeguard the ruler from external attack. The ruler in turn, has to pay a subsidy for the upkeep of the garrison which emptied the state treasury. Refusal to pay led to the annexation of the state by the British. The dethroning and banishment of Peshwa Baji Rao II (*The Devil's Wind*) is an instance.

The Viceroys lived in greater opulence than the princes themselves. Their flamboyant style of living and excessive love of pomp and pageantry are dwelt on by most of the Indian novelists. The spectacular Delhi Durbar of 1902, conducted by Lord Curzon who was the Viceroy of India from 1899 to 1905, forms the central set-piece of Kamala Markandaya's *The Golden Honeycomb*. Intended as a celebration of the King's coronation held in England in August, it is virtually a declaration of power on the part of the Viceroy and a direct demand for the allegiance of the princes. The Viceroy decides the number of cannon shots to be fired at the gun-salute to the Indian princes. The pathetic state of servility to which the princes are reduced is exposed at the guard of honour where they have to wait for hours to pay homage to the Viceroy and stand six paces away, bow low and walk respectfully from the "Presence."

The Indian English novelists unravel the entire history of IndoBritish alliance through the delicate subtleties of the princes' relationship with the Viceroys. The Viceroys use the Indian princes as a trustworthy medium through which they could govern the Indian states. The policy was to keep the princes happy by titles, honours and decorations, as they tightened their hold on them by underhand measures. The Princes vie with one another to please the Viceroys. The readiness to supply a tiger for hunt often becomes an indication of loyalty. The Viceroy applauds the Maharajah of Begwad for being the only man in India who could guarantee a tiger (Malgonkar, *The Princes*).[37] T.N. Murari comments: "No man, however rich and powerful he might be in England, could ever dream of the power and glory of being Viceroy of India. The Viceroy led a life even more splendid and magnificent than that of his only superior, the King-Emperor himself, George V." (*Last Victory* 38)

The flamboyant lifestyle of the Viceroy is exposed by Abbas through Anwar's description of the Viceregal lodge.

> Anwar could hardly keep count of the bewildering list of His Excellency's Morning Room, His Excellency's Bed Room, Their Excellencies' private Dining Room, State Dining Room, Banquet Hall, Ball Room, Blue Room, Writing Rooms, Ante-Chambers, Reception Rooms, Guest Rooms, apartments for Secretaries, A.D.C.s., domestic servants, butlers and chauffers, and kitchens as large as bungalows and a row of garages that could accommodate a fleet of cars and cellars that would contain the choicest wines of the world. (*Inquilab* 21)

The stupendous palace was furnished with the costliest furniture made of the finest wood in the world and ordered from England and decorated with Persian carpets on the floors, paintings on the walls and exquisite china and glass ware for the dining rooms and cut-glass chandeliers for the Banquet Hall. All these luxuries were intended exclusively for the use of two people—the Viceroy and the Vicereine. Even the Mughal kings and emperors did not live in such extravagance.

The authorial comment on the exploitation practised by the Viceroy in India is voiced through Mahatma Gandhi: "They are sucking the life-blood out of India. Take the Viceroy's salary. It is over Rs. 21, 000 per month. This means he gets Rs. 700 per day as against India's average income of less times as much. Yet the British Prime Minister gets only Rs. 180 per day against the average British income of Rs. 2 per day. Don't you call that exploitation?" (*Inquilab* 261)

The Viceroys led a deliberately insulated life, as though to guard their cultural identity from any contact with the Indian ethos. They were convinced of their cultural and moral superiority to the Indians. Lord Curzon believed in "England's civilising mission" and was convinced of the seemingly self-evident truth that "India was the strength and greatness of England."[38] Curzon is different from other British Viceroys who ruled India in that he endeavours to keep up his Christian ideals even when functioning as the supreme representative of a colonial power. He wants the British to set an example to the natives and condemns the tendency for sheer self-indulgence. "We are supposed to set a good example to the native. but when he sees us disporting ourselves in this little England. cutting him off. how can he learn?" (*The Imperial Agent* 14) He suffers when his Christian values refuse to make compromises for his imperial role. Abiding by his Christian principles he punishes the British soldiers of the 9th Lancers for causing the death of an Indian cook and coolie who had not been considered as human beings either by them or their officers. Kamala Markandaya portrays him with sympathy and shows how he tries to put an end to the acts of brutality, perpetrated by British soldiery upon the natives of the country, which were occurring with reprehensible frequency. By acting as a Christian, he flouts the unwritten law of a colonial country—not to let the side down. His action incurs the hostility of the British army as well as the entire English community in India. Curzon's faith in benevolent imperialism as a measure to counteract strengthening forces of nationalism is hardly appreciated by his countrymen. His request to proclaim a remission of taxes at the Delhi Durbar is viewed with suspicion and dismissed with disapproval by the Crown. The Christian Viceroy is forced to repeal his decision and to levy the hated salt-tax on an overburdened people.

Curzon's greatest show-piece was the Delhi Durbar of 1902 conducted to mark the accession of King Edward VII. It was the result of a misconceived notion that Indians would respond heartily to regal pomp and pageantry and to the equal status of citizienship that the empire represented. Kamala Markandaya gives an elaborate description of the preparations for the Durbar which involves evacuation of whole masses of people and demolition of hospitals. The extravagance and the spectacular magnificence of the show exceed all bounds. T.N. Murari shows Curzon reminiscing nostalgically about the coronation durbar on the eve of his departure from India. He had planned everything in the Mughal tradition. "If the pageantry was medieval, Curzon had deliberately planned it so. The British were Mughals now, and Curzon had wanted every Indian, from prince to kissan, to grasp the fact." (*The Imperial Agent* 89) T.N. Murari employs an English lady who opposes imperialism and fervently supports the nationalist movement to voice India's bitterness over Curzon's foolish partition of Bengal. Alice remarks: "Look at that pompous ass, Curzon. Sitting in that carriage like a nawab. He's leaving behind the biggest mess ever, with his partition of

Bengal—which no doubt Minto will botch." (91) The Indian novelist's portrayal of Curzon's love for splendour is hardly an exaggeration as the following barbed remark of the historian indicates: "So prominently did the Viceroy himself figure in the entire proceedings that critics nicknamed it as the Curzonation durbar." (*A Dictionary of Modern Indian History* 170)

Against the sweeping transitions of a revolutionary period in Indian history, the figures of Lord Curzon (1899-1905), Lord Minto (1905-1910) and Lord Hardinge II of Penthurst (1910-1916) make their regal appearances. They are depicted by the Indian novelists as figureheads of power, with practically no direct access to the people they rule and therefore easily beguiled by power-drunk British bureaucrats. In *The Imperial Agent* Curzon's departure and Lord Minto's assumption of charge as Viceroy become the occasion for manoeuvring bureaucrats like Col. Creighton to acquire additional powers. A fake attempt on Prince George's life is cleverly arranged by the scheming Colonel in order to impress upon the Viceroy the justice of his demand for greater power. Lord Minto is depicted as a simple, credulous man, easily taken in by their clever schemes. Minto's term of office is marked in history by several Acts including press Acts passed by the imperial machinery against what the British described as 'seditious meetings' and were intended to curb a people who were swept off their feet by the Swadeshi movement and the nationwide call for boycott of foreign goods. But the Viceroy himself is pictured as hardly ambitious, only eager to leave the country in a peaceful and stable state. He doesn't suspect the dishonesty of Colonel Creighton and even recommends his name for Knighthood. Lord Minto's successor, Lord Hardinge II figures in The *Last Victory* (sequel to *The Imperial Agent*) and is shrewd enough to be suspicious of Creighton. But he cuts a pathetic figure as he wallows in self-pity. Murari uses the historical fact of the shifting of India's capital from Calcutta to Delhi to expose the Viceroy's lack of strength. He emerges a weak person, given to a deep sense of self-pity over the responsibilities thrust upon him. It is as though he has a foreboding of the misfortune that is to befall him on the occasion of the inauguration of the new capital which was constructed at the cost of about fourteen crores of rupees. An abortive attempt is made on his life, as he makes his ceremonial entry into the city, forcing him to the indignity of lying on his stomach for two months, to let the wounds caused by the bomb heal. In these two historical novels, one can detect the deft hand of the author, achieving a clever interweaving of fact and fiction. The author provides "lightning strokes of character that bring to life a whole gamut of historical personages."[39] However, it is not through the historical personae alone that

Murari attempts to strike back at the Empire. The task of decolonization is effected by choosing as the chief protagonist of both novels "a character who was very special to the British"[40]—Rudyard Kipling's hero Kim. Kim is an integral part of Britain's imperial literature and in that sense closer to British hearts than any historical figure. In these two novels Kim is made to protest against colonial intemperance and identify himself so completely with the Indian masses—with their culture, religion and even their belief in the elements of fantasy and the supernatural—that eventually he becomes "an Indian who would be willing to die for his country."[41]

The ethnic aloofness and arrogance of the British is driven home by K.A. Abbas through his picture of Lord Irwin, the Viceroy (1926-1931) who enjoys the cool luxury of Simla, blissfully ignorant of what is happening in the country he governs, as the entire country seethes with protests and armed English policemen encounter peaceful, non-violent Indian demonstrators. At a solemn luncheon at the Viceregal lodge, an American correspondent, Webb Miller, tries to shock the Viceroy out of his complacency by telling him of the imperial atrocities he has witnessed—lathi charges on non-violent women demonstrators, violent suppression of revolting peasants and so on. The Viceroy is reduced to a pathetic figure who evokes Miller's sympathy because he knew so little of the country he is supposed to govern. It was partly the fault of the system that kept the highest dignitaries in the delusive bliss of hill-resorts. But Miller admits that for a Viceroy, his assessment of Gandhi was rather shrewd, though not very charitable. In spite of being ill-informed, Lord Irwin feels embarrassed about the methods of suppressing Gandhian non-violence because he too has "to maintain and vindicate his reputation as the Christian Viceroy." (*Inquilab*, 318) The historical evidence of the Gandhi-Irwin pact which brought about the suspension of civil disobedience and Gandhi's participation as the representative of the Congress in the second session of the Round Table Conference of September-December 1931 (318), bear testimony to Lord Irwin's commendable tact in diplomatic negotiation with his political adversary. It has been said that "few pro-consuls other than Irwin could have demonstrated a subtlety of mind to match that of Gandhi or driven so hard a bargain clothed in language of friendship."[42] The Gandhi-Irwin pact marked the climax of his Viceroyalty. In the thirties imperial confidence was waning and gradually resigning itself to the concept of self-rule for India. The shift in attitude is evident in Irwin's own approach. Abbas quotes another incident in his novel, *The World is My Village*, where Lord Linlithgo, the Viceroy, intervenes in haste to avert a crisis, when the Mahatma undertakes a fast unto death against the Rajkot Maharaja

Thakkur Sahib's breach of his promise to give democratic rights to the people of Rajkot. (137)

Mannoni, in his study of the psychology of colonization exposes the dependent attitude of the colonized towards the colonizer, "the prototype of which is to be found in the affective bond between father and son."[43] Gomathi Narayanan perceives the same pattern of dependence in the Indo-British connection. According to her, the parent-child relationship becomes an analogue to the ruler-ruled relationship.[44] This is obvious in the attitude of Lala Kanshi Ram towards the last Viceroy, Lord Mountbatten. The native Indian is swayed by the charisma of Mountbatten's personality. "He fell in love with the new Viceroy the day he saw his picture on the newspaper." (*Azadi* 31) It is his belief that if the British are going to lose India, it is because of the ugly one-eyed Viceroy Wavell with his bulky frame. The new Viceroy, Lord Mountbatten restores the image of dignity and elegance that the title evokes in the Indian mind. What Nehru wrote to Miss Harrison about Mountbatten reflects Lala Kanshi Ram's view. He said he liked Mountbatten and "his energy and desire to get things done . . . a pleasant change from the last Viceroy."[45] R.J. Moore comments on the myths that grew round Mountbatten who was glorified as "the hero of our time"[46] and "a legend in his life time."[47] He was a controversial figure and several historians have tried to explode the myths. Nahal employs an English sergeant to shake Lala Kanshi Ram out of his blind admiration. An Englishman is thus made the decolonizing agent. He says: "You may sing songs in honour of Moutbatten. . . . But he has duped you into a division of the country. Even Gandhi and Nehru failed to hold their balances before him. Jinnah never counted for much. They had fallen for a handy prize." (*Azadi* 123) R.J. Moore records: "Mountbatten cleverly presented the plan [of partition] to Gandhi as combining all possible elements of the Mahatma's own approach to the problem, and there was grudging admiration as well as admonition in Gandhi's chiding words. You and your magic tricks."[48]

Mountbatten is presented in a different light in Nahal's *The English Queens*, a novel intended as a satire on Anglophiles. Here Nahal employs satire, parody and farce to expose the colonized mentality of the educated upper middle classes in India. It is a deliberate effort "to creatively 'teach' readers how and why they should decolonise."[49] Nahal takes liberties with history to present Mountbatten arriving at a shrewd policy to keep India in thrall even after Independence. He detects the gullibility of the Indian and sells the ideas of partition, the advanced date for Independence (from June 1948 to August 1947), the idea of an Englishman as the first Governor General of free India and that of India continuing as a member of the Commonwealth. So far, the facts are supported by history.

> The agents of imperialism, as they appeared to Nehru and Cripps in 1938, became agents of continuity in 1947. Whilst the last Viceroy became India's first Governor General three former British governors remained to serve Pakistan. . . . Some two thousand five hundred British military officers remained in India for a few months. Very few of the I.C.S. Europeans stayed to serve, but their Indian colleagues carried on the traditions of a bureaucratic administration. The continuity of the old agencies, together with the Commonwealth connection, muted the anti-imperialistic rhetoric.[50]

Nahal goes a step further. He describes these historical incidents as the small fireworks built up by Mountbatten. The climatic one is the hoax he plays on gullible Indians by bestowing on them the gift of the English language and appointing an Order of the Queens, consisting of six anglicised Indian females for the preservation, propagation and spread of the English language in India. He hardly bothers to disguise the imperial motive behind his action. "If the Indians continue to speak English and know they will misuse it, misspell it, mispronounce it—they will mutilate their own languages and consequently their thinking capacity." (*The English Queens* 33) He then adds sardonically that if the hoax works, they would have recovered with the other hand what they had given away with one. "India will continue to be tethered to the feet of England for all time to come." (330) Lord Mountbatten appears here like a modern Machiavelli, shaking his head as the curtain is drawn over the British Raj and there is rejoicing at India Gate for he knows that the Raj is not ended. The British Viceroy who took the momentous decision of the partition and watched over the dissolution of the Empire and the emergence of India as an independent nation, is here reduced to a foreign emissary of Machiavellian cunning, manipulating a country's destiny. The device of the farce is employed here with great effect to expose "the British attempt to colonize the native" and to "deculture the native and rob him of his personality, dignity and intellectual capacity."[51]

Rushdie has used the comic epic genre as a strategy of liberation in his *Midnight's Children.*[52] The imposing name of Lord Mountbatten is listed with "the parents of midnight." (126) He is reduced to insignificance and dismissed without ceremony as "Mountbatten with his extraordinary haste and his chicken-breast-eater of a wife." (126) His arrival is anticipated with a foreknowledge of the inevitable—the partition of India—for he is to arrive with "his inexorable ticktick" and "his soldier's knife that could cut subcontinents in three." (71)

The princes of India were virtually pawns in the hands of the British Viceroys. The Viceroys played with them, deluding them with false promises of autonomy in their individual states. Gomathi Narayanan comments: "By preserving the status quo in the princely states, Britain had created a special breed of rulers invested with such power and little responsibility, apparently independent but in reality subject to Britain."[53] Till the eve of Independence they were led on to believe in promises of individual autonomy in their respective states. Finally when the Congress persuades the princely states to join the Indian Union, Lord Mountbatten changes sides and uses his persuasive powers to convince the princes that the Congress offer is generous and not likely to be repeated and by agreeing to it they would not be endangering their internal autonomy, or sovereignty. It strikes the princes as a sudden betrayal of trust, an abrogation of the illusion of safety. The Viceroy, however, seems to be totally impervious to the human dimension of this political crisis dealt powerfully by Malgonkar and Mulk Raj Anand in their novels on the theme.

The Viceroys as portrayed by the Indian English novelists hardly come to life, for they are intended as instruments to evoke the atmosphere of the Empire and fall into the set mould of the ruler-ruled relationship. Even the enigmatic personality of Mountbatten is not allowed to develop fully and our vision is restricted to Lala Kanshi Ram's perspective. The novelist who gives free rein to his imagination in the depiction of historical characters is liable to lose sight of historic truth. This practical difficulty might account for the fragmentary vignettes of the British Viceroys. Their deliberate alienation from Indian culture and society had kept them aloof and uninvolved in the Indian situation arousing much criticism even in England. Sir John A.R. Marriott comments: "On the whole, the Viceroys have been lesser men than the Governor-General. . . . To say that the Viceroy has become a mere 'clerk at the end of a wire' is a palpable exaggeration, but it is the exaggeration of a truth." (*The English in India* 183) If in actual life they had been so self-effacing, it is hardly surprising that they remain partially realized figures in Indian English fiction, standing out of the imperial background as the towering pillars of the empire. The postcolonial novelists have projected them as images of the colonial era, typifying all that the Empire stood for.

In the colonial situation, the colonizer becomes oppressive due to a false and superior race-complex. The extent to which it can corrupt and dehumanize the colonizer is illustrated by the example of Gen. Dyer, the master architect behind the grossest atrocity in Indian history—that of the Jallianwallah Bagh massacre. The horror of Dyer's action is revealed in all its gruesome form in Abbas's *Inquilab* and Nahal's *The Crown and the Loincloth*. The sadistic cruelty of Dyer was later justified by him and vindicated by the British House of Lords. "The latter concluded that the Hunter Committee had unfairly censured him for performing his duty in the maintenance of law and order and had thereby set a bad precedent."[54] Sir John A.R. Marriott admits that the Amritsar incident "was (in Carlyle's phrase) no 'rosewater surgery'", but he goes on to remark that "though it cost hundreds of lives, it saved thousands; that even if Gen. Dyer temporarily lost his head and finally his job, he saved a Province."[55] Dyer received a great deal of sympathy and understanding in England and was awarded a gift of $ 26,000 collected by an English daily. The toppling of values in a colonial situation needs no better evidence. Colonialism undermines human values, extolls moral depravity and lends respectability to the grossest villainy.

It is incumbent on the part of the Indian English novelist to retell the agonizing tale of the Jallianwala Bagh massacre, exposing the villainy of the sadist Dyer. Abbas presents the incident as viewed by Anwar, whose friend Ratan loses his father in the massacre. Anwar is petrified to see Dyer, the red-faced Englishman, indignantly waving his revolver at the Gurkhas and shouting at them in broken Hindustani, ordering them to fire and threatening to shoot if they did not fire long enough. As the English officers point the guns at the Gurkhas, they fire straight at the crowd. The red-faced English officer (none other than Dyer) then orders the rifles to be directed at those who manage to reach the exit. They are shot down before they could pass through to safety. Ajit singh, Ratan's father, pleads with Dyer, in the name of his loyalty to the English government, asking him not to fire at the unarmed people. His plea becomes the stutter of servility and as he raises his hand to salute the English officer, Dyer standing close to him, shoots him and he is transfixed in an eternal salute. (*Inquilab* 42) Two days later when Anwar goes to see the bereaved family, he finds that Dyer's thirst for revenge is not quenched by the massacre. The Indians are made to suffer the additional indignity of crawling through the streets, for Dyer has imposed martial law and confident of support from civil authority, he carries out the crawling order.

Whereas Abbas is content to expose the base dehumanization of the colonizer, Nahal tries to analyze the motives behind such malignity. The dark figure of Dyer that shadows Indian history is brought to life and endowed with human frailties and frustrated desires that have made him what he is. In the eyes of Dyer, the Indians are worse than Caliban—"brown black creatures who could be only called human by an extension of the term." (*The Crown and the Loincloth* 79) In the fifty years of his acquaintance with India, he has only learned to hate India and the Indians. He plans the murder of the hundreds gathering at Jallianwallah Bagh with deliberate, undisguised malice. The disapproval of Kenneth Ashby, the Deputy Commissioner, infuriates him. He is quite convinced that these people are violent seditionists responsible for the murder of the railway guard Robinson and Sergeant Rowlands, the killing of several Europeans, the humiliation of many Englishwomen and many other misdeeds that deserved punishment. "They are here for one and only reason: to upset and overthrow the government by violence. This is an uprising of no less a scale than the Mutiny of 1857. And I suppose to deal with it accordingly." (72)

Dyer's animosity towards Indians is provided with racial, national and personal motives. Apart from racism and constricting sentiments of nationalism, Dyer is activated by personal grievances as well. He feels a grudge against the entire country that resembles, to him, a smouldering cauldron. He feels that the landscape, the people and the seasons are conspiring against him and acting treacherously. The author strikes a very effective contrast in Ashby, the British Deputy Commissioner who finds India with her natural abundance and the varied beauty of its changing seasons, an enriching experience. The distorted working of Dyer's mind is exposed through the ontrast.

Dyer nurses a private grief against India—a regret that he could not father a child on an Indian woman. His puritanical sentiments and the fear of hurting his mother and wife, prevents him from venturing out to win one of the dark beauties for himself. Even though his own dreams remain unfulfilled, he feels a weakness for the offspring of such liaisons, the Eurasians. Another aspect of India that provokes Dyer's ire is the intricate and impenetrable manner in which the Indian towns with their web of narrow alleyways are built. Jallianwallah Bagh, the strip of wasteland lying near the Golden Temple, makes Dyer trigger-happy because it has only one entrance. He considers it his chosen spot to settle old scores. (*The Crown and the Loincloth* 84) The impudence of a Tehsildar of Nowshera smarts like an open wound, craving revenge. The massacre at Jallianwallah Bagh is thus the letting out of old grievances and suppressed frustrations. Dyer's regret is that Gandhi has been made to leave Punjab for Gandhi had always seemed to Dyer as a crooked and scheming person who acted as though he had doubles to act for him. (85) He shows up wherever trouble is brewing and fans it to flames. He would make himself the custodian of all troubles and send ultimatums to the government and the Viceroy. (84) Dyer's ambition is to expunge for ever from the consciousness of the Indians expressions like Home Rule, Swaraj and self-determination.

Nahal uses the stream-of-consciousness technique to lend credibility to a figure whose name has become a synonym for cruelty and colonial oppression. Even in the age of imperialism there were dissenting voices among the British who condemned Dyer's inhuman massacre. The Hunter Committee, appointed to enquire into the matter declared that "the crawling order was indefensible, the firing a great tragedy and their effect on alienating responsible opinion disastrous."[56]

The motivation suggested for Dyer's villainy is not quite inconsistent with historic facts because Datta, a careful student of the Amritsar tragedy has concluded that Dyer was primarily impelled by the desire for revenge.[57]

The ominous name of Dyer is reconstructed by Nahal and made a person in his own right. He remains one of the worst specimens of the oppressive machinery of colonialism. Nahal's attempt is commendable as an approach to understanding this strange phenomenon of unalloyed malice. Rushdie resorts to understatement in the depiction of the gruesome incident. "Brigadier Dyer's fifty men put down their machine guns and go away. They have fired a total of one thousand six hundred and fifty rounds into the unarmed crowd. Of these, one thousand five hundred and sixteen have found their mark, killing or wounding some person. 'Good shooting.' Dyer tells his men, 'We have done a jolly good thing.'" (*Midnight's Children* 35)

Rushdie's prosaic, unemotional statement of facts, is more powerfully affecting than verbose descriptions. As Tariq Rahman points out, "the statement attributed to Dyer, however, brings out his inhumanity in particular and that of the whole phenomenon of colonial rule in general."[58] The innocence of the people, the deliberateness of the killing and the complete lack of human feeling on Dyer's part evoke the emotion and empathy for the victims and indignation against the British.

Sir John Simon, the Chairman of the Simon Commission that visited India in 1928, is another symbol of oppression drawn from the history of British rule. Abbas presents him in *Inquilab* from the point of view of the protagonist Anwar and his friends of the History Association. The game of imperial administration of which Sir John Simon is an integral part, is revealed in all its hollowness in the Assembly where the members voice their carefully thought-out arguments and the government members remain sphinx-like, paying not the slightest attention to the proceedings. Abbas projects the situation—the picture of the British officials, Sir John Simon among them, sitting with a look of studied indifference and the required degree of aloofness as the Indians present their arguments with great fervour—as a challenge to the nation's faith in British liberalism. It needed Bhuta Singh's bomb to shake the officials in the Assembly out of their complacency. His intention "to make the deaf hear" has its desired effect. These unfinished portraits from history invoke the bygone era of imperial domination. The cold indifference of Sir John Simon seems ironical when we consider the purpose of the Commission's visit to India. It had been constituted to study and submit a report on the suitability of holding a Round Table Conference to discuss the issue of Dominion status. The Commission had provoked much resentment because no Indian was included in the body that was dealing with the destiny of India.

Sir Stafford Cripps who headed the Cripps Mission of 1942 is given a more favourable exposition by K.A. Abbas in the fictionalization of a journalist's experiences—*The World is My Village*. The British leader's status as a left-wing Labourite and his pro-Indian attitudes justify the sympathetic portrayal. Cripps had already visited India in 1939 as a Labourite friend of India and had met the national leaders. Newspaper clippings produced by Anwar, the journalist-protagonist of the novel, have recorded parts of Cripps' speeches. In an interview given by him he declares: "I am convinced that India's salvation remains in a constituent assembly of Nehru's conception." (247) Again, in a speech to the House of Commons during wartime, he says: "The new development in the world situation and the avowed objectives of the British government in declaring war, have made the treatment of India a test question in the eyes of the world, as of many people in the country and the people of India itself." (247) He is bold enough to say that if the British professed to be fighting the war for freedom and democracy, they could not justly deny the same to India and warns Britain against allying themselves with reactionary Indian princes and jointly exploiting the Indian people. Eve Curie, the progeny of two Nobel Prize winners describes him as "the British Jawaharlal Nehru." (250) In spite of Cripps's earnest interest in Indian Independence and his friendship with Jawaharlal Nehru, Cripps's mission failed because in Nehru's words, the honest and sincere man had come as "the Devil's Advocate," (253) and what the British government was offering to India through him was control of items like Public Relations, Petroleum, Amenities of Troops, Stationery, Counter Supervision etc. whereas the Defence Ministry was reserved for the British Commander-in-Chief. In an interview with Bob Miller and Anwar, Cripps frankly admits the limitations within which he worked, though personally he had always been for Indian Independence. The modifications suggested by the Congress for Cripps's proposals were turned down by the British government and Cripps returned by "the first plane back" (259) as Gandhi had advised him to do at their first meeting. Later Gandhi is reported to have said: "India had declined to accept the post-dated cheque on a crashing bank." (259) Through Cripps Abbas projects the crippling effect of imperialism even on liberal minds.

The visit to India of Edward, Prince of Wales, in 1921 is of crucial importance to the plot in Nahal's *The Crown and the Loincloth*. The writer has not bothered to give this historical character any importance outside the immediate relevance of the plot. Like Sir John Simon, he too is only a landmark in the Indo-British political alliance and does not achieve the fullness of a rounded character. The visit of the prince of Wales to India was a colonial device to distract and divert the people of India from reactionary movements. It was the product of the misconceived notion of the British that spectacular shows of pomp and splendour could beguile the people of India. The authorities arrange the visit of the Prince to counteract the protest against the MontagueChelmsford reforms. The prince's visit had already been preceded by that of the Duke of Connaught, the son of Queen Victoria. The charisma of the Prince's personality is intended to act against Gandhi's personal hold over the millions of India. In spite of the elaborate paraphernalia accompanying his tour—the regimental bands, the neatly arrayed civil and military officers and the wildly cheering crowds—the Prince is hardly deceived. He is shrewd enough to detect the rumble of protest behind the spectacular shows put up for his welcome. In the states where loyal princes rule, he partakes in the celebrations with gusto; but he cannot retain his childish pride and confidence when he sees the clouds of revolt gathering in the horizon. In Nahal's novel the Prince of Wales is reduced to a pathetic state, as he desperately tries to keep up his appearance according to his training, preferring at heart the security of the train and the protection it affords. He remains ignorant of the fact that even the apparent calm is superficial and has been made possible by the massive arrests made on his behalf, to push the cream of India behind the bars. The attempt to assassinate him at the Fair is the Prince's hour of trial, in which he emerges a passive victim, without any attempt at heroic resistance. He proves himself to be a helpless dignitary, to be protected and taken care of by the security forces. His passive inaction suffers in contrast with the heroic sacrifice of the Indian freedom fighter who gives up his life for his greatest enemy—the living symbol of the British Empire. Sunil's martyrdom makes him a hero in the eyes of the British as well as the Indians and the Prince pales into oblivion, like any insignificant character in a novel. Sunil, the Indian, eclipses the future King of British India, the Prince of Wales, and the artist scores his victory in the march towards emancipation.

Virtually, all the major events of Indian history find thematic expression in Indian English fiction. What has been pushed to the peripheries or made invisible by British historians or the official view, is brought to focus, by the effective combination of fact and fiction. Thus we hear of the speedy and peremptory decision for advancing the date of Indian Independence and the resulting holocaust that ripped the nation in two (*Azadi*); of the unscrupulous tactics of British bureaucrats in employing their Indian allies to spy on the activities of the Congress and destroy the harmony in the organization (*The Imperial Agent*); and of the British policy of divide and rule leading to communal schism in a united nation. One comes upon an Indian Muslim in England colouring parts of India green in the map, to denote the formation of a separate Muslim nation, with the blessings of the English (*The World is My Village* 78). The permanent colonial legacy handed over by the British is caricatured through Mountbatten's move to bequeath the English language to an Order of English Queens, who would ensure India's perennial allegiance to Britain (*The English Queens*). Rushdie exposes the neo-colonial bondage that will tether India permanently to England through Methwold's reluctance to discard his properties in India. The condition insisted on by Methwold on the sale of his Estate—the "conqueror's houses," as they are called—is that they should be purchased with every last thing in them and "the entire contents" are to be retained by "the new owners" (*Midnight's Children* 109). Methwold's deed symbolizes the perpetuation of the colonizer's hold through the legacy handed over. It drives home the fact that the British transfer of power never made India really free from emotional allegiance to the West.

The Indian English novelists offer "revisionist history" which subverts "the official view and offer[s] a critique of authority."[59] Whereas Nahal, Abbas and Kamala Markandaya have chosen the third-person narrator to unfold the story in a realistic vein, Malgonkar and Rushdie write history as autobiography. Malgonkar's narrator is the muchmaligned central figure in the mutiny who is resurrected through debunking of British imperial illusions and the exposure of historical facts. Events are chronologicallly presented with strict adherence to historic truth. On the other hand, Rushdie's narrator-protagonist occupies the position of centrality by the fact of his birth at a historic moment. As the central consciousness in the novel, he takes liberties and lets in an element of fantasy into his narration. External and objective reality is dismissed as "one-dimensional, flattened by certitude,"[60] and memory is allowed to play its tricks, and provide the excuse for unreliability. Rushdie's is a different personal order of reality as evident in the chronological inaccuracy in the date of Gandhiji's assassination. "In my India," he declares, "Gandhi will continue to die at the wrong time." (*Midnight's Children* 198) Rushdie reveals himself to be a liberated writer who has freed himself from the monotony of chronology, from the tyranny of cause and effect and adherence to objective reality. Collingwood states about the nature of event and history: "For history, the object to be discovered is not the mere event, but the thought expressed in it. To discover that thought is already to understand it."[61]

Therefore, the versions of history proliferate endlessly, every version being a provisional reconstruction. Rushdie's attempt is to enter reality from a different angle in order to reinterpret facts and read significance into events within a selected framework of reference. As he blends history and fiction, allowing concocted stories and even elements of fantasy to encroach upon the recorded facts of history, he cannot any longer make any claim to absolute truth. At the same time, since the novelist does not deny the validity of official records, he cannot be condemned for deliberate distortion of facts. The validity of Rushdie's work has therefore to be accepted on the basis of his subjective and different angle of vision. Rushdie himself admits: "And there are so many stories to tell, too many, such an excess of intertwined lives events miracles places rumours, so dense a commingling of the improbable and the mundane!" (*Midnight's Children* 4)

The fictionalization of history makes heavy demands on the novelist and imposes too many restrictions. In the portrayal of character, the fiction-writer runs the risk of sacrificing historicity to imagination. The novelist is torn between "the demands of scholarship and the impulses of his free-wheeling fancy."[62] The characters can be justified within the context of the novel, if they remain consistent and conform to the image provided by history. The Indian English novelist limits himself to presenting a few pivotal figures from the period of British rule, suggestive of the vital incidents in Indo-British relationship. The First War of Independence, the transfer of power from the East India Company to the Crown, the arrival of Gandhi and the emergence of national spirit, the civil disobedience movement, the visit of the Prince of Wales, the non-cooperation movement, the Montague-Chelmsford reforms, the Simon Commission, the Quit India movement, Independence and Partition of India followed by holocaust and bloodshed—these epoch-making incidents form a collage in the Indian English novel, each novel shifting our focus as in a kaleidoscope. The point of view, or the perspective from which history is recapitulated, and the way in which historical data are tackled, are determined by the peculiar placement of the post-colonial writer. As a citizen of a newly Independent nation, a two-fold task is foisted on him "to reject what of his old tradition was inapplicable in the new environment, and secondly, to arrive at some spiritual understanding of his new world by imaginative surrender to it. He must reject the historical past in favour of the geographical present.[63]

In the review of history and the representation of historical characters, the Indian English novelist is involved in the potentially independent process of specific self-definition and national recreation. The figureheads from history, from the colonial past, serve only as symbols to be recast, images to be discarded and living emblems of values to be redefined. As such they are not intended as rounded portraits and their relevance is within the context of the decolonization process undertaken by the Indian novelist.

NOTES

1. Stephen Slemon, "Post-Colonial Allegory and the Transformation of History," *The Journal of Commonwealth Literature*, XXIII, No. 1 (1968) 158.
2. Coral Ann Howells quoted in Stephen Slemon, 159.
3. Frantz Fannon, *The Wretched of the Earth* (London: Macgibbon and Kee, 1965) 29-30.
4. Term used by Frederick Jameson, *The Political Unconscious: Narrative as a Socially Symbolic Act* (Ithaca: Cornell University Press, 1981).
5. Satya Brat Singh, "Ruby Wiebe, Paul Scott and Salman Rushdie: Historians Distanced from History," *The Commonwealth Review,* I, No. 2 (1990) 155.
6. *Ibid.*, 155.
7. Helen Tiffin, "Post-Colonialism, Post-Modernism and the Rehabilitation of Post-Colonial History," *Journal of Commonwealth Literature,* XXIII, No. 1 (1988) 178.
8. Manohar Malgonkar, "Author's Note," *The Devil's Wind* (London: Hamish Hamilton, 1972).
9. Kamala Markandaya, "On Images," a paper presented at the Seminar on Socio-literature at the East-West Centre for Cultural Interchange (Honolulu, August 1973) 2.
10. Edward W. Said, *Orientalism* 42.
11. Quoted in Bonamy Dobree, *Rudyard Kipling* (London: Longman's, 1967) 79.
12. Sir John A.R. Marriott, *The English in India* (Oxford: Calrendon Press, 1932) 161.
13. Manohar Malgonkar, *The Devil's Wind* 46. In Hindu mythology "the god who rides a buffalo" is Yama, the God of Death.
14. Sir John A.R. Marriott, 157.
15. Jacob Arlow, "Ego Psychology and the Study of Mythology," *Journal of the American Psycho-analytic Association*, 9 July 1961, 375.

16. Aime Cesaire, "Discourse on Colonialism," trans. Joan Pinkham (New York and London: Monthly Review Press, 1972) 20, 57-58, quoted in Ashis Nandy, *The Intimate Enemy* (Delhi: Oxford Univ Press, 1983) 29.
17. Albert Memmi, *The Colonizer and the Colonized* 20.
18. Quoted in Allen J. Greenberger, *The British Image of India* 11.
19. Rene Maunier, *The Sociology of Colonies; An Introduction to the Theory of Race Contact,* ed. and trans. from French, E.O. Lorimer (London: Routledge & Kegan Paul, 1949) 31, quoted in Allen J. Greenberger, 11.
20. Jean-Paul Sartre, "Introduction," Albert Memmi, *The Colonizer and the Colonized* xxxvi.
21. Phrase quoted from Coral Ann Howells, in Stephen Slemon, 59.
22. *Ibid.*
23. *Cambridge History of the British Empire*. VI (Cambridge: University Press, 1959) 182.
24. Christopher Hilbert, *The Great Mutiny: India 1857-1978* (England: Penguin Books, 1980) 202.
25. Malleson, *Indian History,* Vol. I, 497, quoted in G. Anderson and M. Subedar, *The Expansion of British India 1818-1858* (London: G. Bell, 1921).
26. A.F.P. Harcourt, *The Peril of the Sword* (London: Skeffington, 1903).
27. C.E. Pearce, *Love Besieged: A Romance of the Residence of Lucknow* (London: Stanley Paul, 1909).
28. O. Mannoni, *Prospero and Caliban: The Psychology of Colonization* 119-120.
29. Marshall A. Best, "Manohar Malgonkar," *The Contemporary Novelists*, ed. James Vinson (London: St. James Press, 1973) 826.
30. Lion Feuchtwagner, *The House of Desdemona or the Laurels and Limitations of Historical Fiction* (Detroit: Wayne State University Press, 1963) 79
31. M. Rajagopalachary, "Malgonkar's Meditation on History: *The Devil's Wind*," *Triveni,* 55, No. 2 (July-Sept. 1986) 53.
32. *Ibid.*
33. Phrase coined by Professor James Seeley, quoted in Francis G. Hutchins, *The Illusion of Permanence: British Imperialism in India* (Princeton: Princeton Univ. Press, 1967) 34.
34. Francis G. Hutchins, 86.
35. *Ibid.*, 85.
36. Mulk Raj Anand, *Private Life of an Indian Prince* 43.
37. Manohar Malgonkar, *The Princes* (1963; rpt. New Delhi: Orient Paperbacks, 1970).
38. Parshotam Mehra, *A Dictionary of Modern Indian History* (Delhi: Oxford Univ. Press, 1985) 167.
39. Geeta Doctor, "Tales from the Raj Retold," *Express Magazine*, 22 January 1989, 5.
40. T.N. Murari, quoted in Geeta Doctor, *Express Magazine*, 5.
41. *Ibid.*
42. Parshotam Mehra, *A Dictionary of Modern Indian History* 352.
43. O. Mannoni, *Prospero and Caliban* 158.

44. Gomathi Narayanan, *The Sahibs and the Natives: A Study of Guilt and Pride in Anglo-Indian and Indo-Anglian Novels* (Delhi: Chanakya, 1986) 12.
45. Nehru to Miss Harrison, 22 May 1947, quoted in R.J. Moore, *Escape from Empire* (Oxford: Clarendon Press, 1983) 236.
46. R.J. Moore; *Escape from Empire* 216.
47. *Ibid.*, 215.
48. Interview, 4 June 1947, Mountbatten 193, quoted in *Escape from Empire*, 287.
49. Viney Kirpal, "The Indian Elite and *The English Queens*," *Three Contemporary Novelists*, ed. R.K. Dhawan (New Delhi: Classical, 1985) 140.
50. R.J. Moore, 354.
51. Viney Kirpal, 140-41.
52. Salman Rushdie, *Midnight's Children* (1980; rpt. New York: Avon, 1982).
53. Gomathi Narayanan, 67.
54. Quoted in Parshotam Mehra, 223.
55. Sir John A.R. Marriott, 273
56. Parshotam Mehra, 222.
57. *Ibid.*
58. Tariq Rahman, "Politics in the Novels of Salman Rushdie," *The Commonwealth Review*, I, No. 2 (1990) 102-17.
59. Quoted earlier, see note 6.
60. *Midnight's Children*, 153, quoted in "*Midnight's Children*—a Fantasy," *The Commonwealth Review*, I, 2 (1990) 37.
61. P.G. Collingwood, *Essays in the Philsophy of History*, 74, quoted in Satya Brat Singh, 147.
62. Harold A. Basilius, "Foreword," Lion Feuchtwagner, *The House of Desdemona or the Laurels and Limitations of Historical Fiction* 5.
63. Helen Tiffin, "Towards Place and Placelessness: Two Journey Patterns in Commonwealth Literature," *Awakened Conscience* 147.

The Cultural Divide

A direct result of the British presence in India has been the impingement of English culture and values on every aspect of Indian life. English education became the medium for the initiation of Indians not only into western culture, literature, science and technology, but also into a new value system which had no relevance to the Indian situation. It is a clear case of what Wole Soyinka has described as "Cultural imperialism."[1] Since India had her ancient treasures of culture, tradition, religion and literature, British cultural imperialism did not bring about a total ethno-cultural supplanting. But the encounter with the British generated cross-cultural tension at all levels. Its reflection is found in the Indian English novel also.

The fact that the Indian English novelist, by accepting the colonial legacy of the English language as his medium of expression, has subjected himself to western cultural domination to a certain extent, makes the enquiry all the more interesting. As a victim of the gradual process of the cultural subjection carried out by the colonizer, he works within restraints that make his authorial task as detached observer enormously difficult. He feels the pull of two entirely different cultural mores—the umbilical pull towards the inherited culture and the attraction of the value system of the West to which he has been constantly exposed. He is trapped in the dilemma of choice and inhabits a cultural limbo which he shares with all Third world writers. His state is aptly described as "a double exile" by Griffiths in his perceptive book on African and West Indian writing. "A colonial writer," he asserts, is "exiled culturally from the sources and traditions of English as used in England" and "linguistically from the landscape and people"[2] he writes about. The attitude of the Indian English writer towards British culture as reflected in the characters, can be identified and categorized thus:

1. An attitude of self-negation and absolute submission to the alien culture (what has come to be called Anglophilism).
2. A state of tormenting dilemma, throwing the person into a limbo. He is, in fiction, the dispossessed man groping for identity. His predicament is close to that of the writer himself, who, being a Third world writer, is "a

very complex and complicated individual, a composite of many variables, a product of conflicting trends and possibilities."[3]

3. An attitude of compromise and possibly a fusion (synthesis) of the two cultures.
4. A complete rejection of English culture, a re-assertion of the superiority of Indian values and an attempt to retrieve the essentials of the native past. The decolonizing artist of the post-Independence era takes more and more to the tendency to break the idols of the imperial nation, reducing them to rubble and reinstating the national idols. The white man is made an anti-hero and the hollowness of his value system is exposed .

Britain, the chief antagonist in the east-west conflict is represented variously in different novels. In some novels, Indo-British conflict is taken up as an issue between two characters, in some as a conflict of attitudes or values. There are writers who have steered clear of the cultural tension in their work and some have tried to delve deep into the depths of the problem, facing the challenge of bi-cultural development squarely and lending it a profound philosophic dimension. The Indian emigrant's encounter with the English in a journey undertaken by him to that "Byzantium across the 'gong-tormented sea'"[4]—England—shifts the location of the clash, with hardly any change in the attitude of the participants. The emigrant experience forms the theme of many Indian English novels and is dealt with in a highly perceptive manner by writers like Kamala Markandaya and Anita Desai.

The attitude of self-negation and absolute submission to the alien culture, is a commonly observed phenomenon in postcolonial nations. Centuries of foreign domination and constant exposure to the foreign language, literature, culture and values obscure and even scorch the fundamental basis of cultural growth—"the discipline of seeking to be most oneself."[5] It entails in some a total alienation from native roots and a blind acceptance of the foreign culture. It need not always be a matter of conscious choice.

The destiny of many Indians was decided when Lord Macaulay declared in his famous Minute of 1853 that the learned Indian should be allowed to absorb English culture and that "a class of persons, Indian in blood and colour, but English in tastes, in opinions, in morals and intellect"[6] should be trained as good efficient administrators within the framework of the Empire. The outcome of the education envisaged by Macaulay and executed by Lord Bentick was the anglicized Indian. With the British Raj as his sole employer and benefactor, he soon became a pillar of the foreign government which sapped his vitality and alienated him from his own culture and ethical values. Kamala Markandaya's Kitsamy (*Some Inner Fury*), Nayantara Sahgal's Harish, Sanad

(*A Time to be Happy*), Ram (*Rich Like Us*), and Vishnu (*This Time of Morning*) and Malgonkar's Kiran Garud (*Distant Drum*) are typical examples of westernised Indians who have lost their cultural and spiritual moorings in the mad pursuit of an alien culture. If anglicization was a matter of choice with them, it was not so with the princes. From a very malleable age, the Residents insisted on the princes being taught by English resident tutors and later on at Princes' colleges, especially devised by the English. It was a type of education that aimed at the gradual alienation of the prince from his cultural anchorage, from the history of his country and from his own real self. Thus Prince Abhayraj, heir-apparent to the Begwad kingdom (*The Princes*) and Bawajiraj III, the Maharajah of Devapur (*The Golden Honeycomb*), turn out to be puppets in English hands, totally alienated from their history and culture and perfectly trained in English customs and manners. Life for the princes becomes simplified into a code that holds team-spirit and manliness above intellectual attainments. Kipling's "If" becomes their daily prayer, the college motto "never give in" their guiding principle. (*The Princes* 82) In both these cases the victims are hardly aware of the deliberate supplanting of their national identity by the super-imposed image of the Englishman. Malgonkar shows Abhayraj struggling to attain an identification with his father in the tragic crisis of his life when he has to face the harsh truth of losing his kingdom. Through Abhayraj's gaining of his cultural identity, Malgonkar exposes the weakness of the superimposed values.

Kamala Markandaya employs Bawajiraj III's son Rabi as a contrast to the king, his father. By rejecting the English tutor and the English systems of education, Rabi achieves an identification with the land and its people, by sharing in their problems and identifying himself with them. Bawajiraj remains the anglicized Indian prince—a dummy figure, unsure of himself, estranged from his land and people and reduced to an attitude of servile adoration of the British. The typecast figure of the king brings out the predicament of the individual who has lost his roots because the very stump of his cultural identity has been undermined.

The alien value system has a stronger hold on the Indians who adopt it by choice. The large-scale infiltration of English customs, ways of life and manners through constant contact and exposure, as well as the increased opportunity to visit the land of the colonizer, resulted in the creation of a brand of blind imitators in the nineteenth century. They subordinated themselves to the alien culture in mind and spirit, losing their national and cultural identity to values totally alien to their milieu. This blind Angolophilism—"whoring after English Gods,"[7] as the Indian poet Parthasarathy calls it—which has continued at least in a minority even after Independence, has been much criticized.

Kamala Markandaya presents a typical England-educated Indian youth in Kitsamy (*Some Inner Fury*). Kitsamy's insolent impatience with the priest performing religious ceremonies, his sense of superiority and contempt for his people's customs, his popularity at the club owing to the glamour of his being freshly returned from England, and his exclusive preference for everything English—including Wilton carpets, wing chairs, cocktail cabinet, English blue china, and English food cooked by butlers trained by English memsahibs—completes the picture of an Anglicized Indian. Of Kit's devotion to the culture of the alien race, Kamala Markandaya comments: "But Kit did not merely participate in it: he was a part of it; his feeling for the west was no cheap flirtation, to be enjoyed so long, no longer, to be put aside thereafter and forgotten, or at best remembered with a faint nostalgia. It went deeper: it was understanding and love." (142) It seems to have exorcised the East out of his system and there is hardly any moment of conflict or dilemma concerning his choice. Premala, who is typically Indian, cannot communicate with him and their marriage fails. As always in Kamala Markandaya, here too incompatibility between partners leads to sterility.

Harish, in Nayantara Sahgal's *A Time to be Happy* and Vishnu in *This Time of Morning*[8] too share Kitsamy's adoration for everything British and the abhorrence for Indian things. Vishnu feels every aspect of Indian life "appalling." He prefers a job in the cities of Bombay or Calcutta because the provinces would be too "ghastly." Harish, Govind Narayan's son (*A Time to be Happy*), is, but for his colour an Englishman. "It was as if the whiteman, weary for a little while of his burden, had passed it on to Harish and he felt it an inestimable privilege to stagnate under it." (19)

He describes himself as one among 'the nearly English of my generation,' who were better qualified to quote Shelley and Shakespeare and discourse on many an aspect of English life and letters than on their own. Like Kitsamy, Harish too never felt the need for his Indian heritage. Govind Narayan's mother makes a very perceptive comment when she remarks: "He is a success, one of the most successful creations of the British Raj." With the unmistakable ring of irony in her tone, she voices the author's comments on the English educated youth of India who seemed to get transformed into aliens, estranged from their nation, its religion and culture. But for his dark complexion, there was nothing about Harish that could arouse the suspicion of being an Indian. His single mistake had been marrying a shy Indian girl who could hardly fit into the western style of living and entertaining. Harish and Kitsamy are very much alike even in the unhappy marriages with women of a divergent cultural vision. They show a total imperviousness to the problems of a bi-cultural environment and they do not outgrow the fascination for the West, in the course of the story.

While the national movement for Independence was seething outside, Ram's (*Rich Like Us*) voluntary withdrawal into the westernized elite who meet in clubs, waltz and talk of painting and operas, is presented subtly through the perspective of his English wife Rose. The cockney-speaking, lower class English woman who was wafted into Ram's sophisticated life by his overpowering love, realizes soon that not she, but Ram is the outsider in his own country. It is she who takes the initiative to introduce Indian goods into Ram's shop and to throw out the foreign goods. She could only pity Ram for his inability to share and participate in the mass struggle for liberty. The war, the Quit India movement, attainment of fredom, and partition leave him spiritually unscathed. His life flows uninterrupted by the stormy events that rock the scum below, in its daily round of diplomatic parties and cooktails. Ironically enough, as Ram drifts in his illusory world of western glamour, cut off from the real India, Rose comes more and more to know India, and to make contact with the poorest of the poor. Keshav, an inspiring Indian youth, wavering between I.C.S. and nationalistic fervour, confesses that Rose had made him realize "it was a see-saw I was on and that I was neither doomed nor dying!"(225) Rose enables him to gather the courage to face his bi-cultural situation squarely and to arrive at an acceptance of life. "If a see-saw is what I've chosen to live on, I'll live on it and make the best of it." (225) Rose helps Keshav to arrive at a recognition of his complex bi-cultural situation; but Ram does not discover his roots to the very end. The British administration in India relied on the staunch support of these black Englishmen who had estranged themselves completely from their own native ethos and could hardly rediscover their roots.

Manohar Malgonkar's *Distant Drum* glorifies the British military code which has been preserved with awe and absolute devotion by the Indian army. The army code is an extension of the English public school code and Kiran Garud's values of the officer class parallel the Rugby code exemplified in Thomas Hughes's *Tom Brown's Schooldays.*[9] His first-hand knowledge of army life and unconcealed admiration for his traditions, enables Malgonkar to document elaborately the customs kept up by the army with scrupulous devotion. In independent India, liberated fom British yoke, one listens with wonder to Kiran Garud, the Indian army officer, declaring with pride of tradition, that "so little had changed that even Kipling might have felt perfectly at home." (51) The Indian's enthusiasm to preserve the mystic halo surrounding the artificial code handed by the Englishman is recorded truthfully. Garud's unstinting devotion to English values makes him the more satisfying symbol of the code than his own English idol Ropey Booker. As G.S. Amur points out, the novel expounds Malcolm Muggeridge's epigram that the last true Englishmen are the Indians.[10] Malgonkar does not pass judgement on the followers of the code. He almost identifies himself with Kiran Garud, whose portrait is done with admiration. In the world of *Distant Drum*, no discordant note of any other value system is heard, as though the reality of India is shut out from it.

Nahal's *The English Queens* is a sharp satire on the blind anglophilism that reduces the educated elite to "mimic men,"[11] as Naipaul calls them. They remain in a state of passivity, ashamed of their own culture and full of adoration for the British. The Indian ladies chosen by Mountbatten as the custodian of the English language in India truly represent the genre to which they belong—that of bind Anglophilism. They take pride in imitating English ways, in cultivating English interests and scoff at ordinary indians. Sumithra Pandey, an English lecturer at Asoka college in Delhi, hopes to secure an English sire as her husband and when her dreams are miscarried, seeks comfort in the works of Lawrence, Shelley and Shakespeare. They brighten up "the dull Indian days" for her and open her eyes to things which do not even exist in India—seasons like autumn, the sound of laughter and the sight of rosy-cheeked children. Renuka Chopra, second in the list, speaks in her "squeaky English dropping the ash of her cigarette in the metal ashtray beside her" snobbishly using "damn" and such other English words of swearing. Caroline Oaks claims to be British because though she no longer has blonde hair, blue eyes or white skin, she prides herself on her English ancestry. A great grandfather, Colonel Thomas Sterns, had sprung from solid Yorkshire stock and had married a Mohammedan lady in India. Their offspring had married a second generation Christian convert from an untouchable Hindu. "Yet that did not take away the quality of the blood in her veins, did it?" asked Caroline. (13) The children were brought up as British, though neither the British nor the Indians considered them as even remotely connected with the British. Nahal's irony sparkles in the authorial comment: "But they were loyal to the far-off motherland still. For the last thirty years, Mr. Oaks had headed the most prestigious boys' public school in New Delhi, turning out faithful servants of the Empire, though the Empire no longer existed and where the boys still dressed up like boys in Harrow." (13)

Crude examples of blind Anglomania are provided by Nahal through Smt. Hemant Mathen and Sardarni Satwant Kaur. Both were chosen for the noble mission by Lord Mountbatten. The former was the wife of a retired judge and functioned as the honorary director of several women's organizations, Sardarni Satwant Kaur came from the newly rich. She shaved her legs and plucked her eyebrows everyday and used only imported make-up for her face and had a remarkable knack for making her English most mellifluous by suffixing "ji" to any word or sentence she spoke. Through the English queens, Nahal typifies the "white cringe"[12] that survives in the Commonwealth countries.

Nahal shows how the idyllic happiness of the ladies in being the sole custodians of the English language is shattered by the first threat to their make-believe English world—the threat of the Chopras' daughter marrying a low class Indian. It is a flimsy world which could burst like balloon at the first prick dealt by Indian culture.

G.V. Desani provides, in his own comic style different patterns of colonial behaviour in *All About H. Hatterr*. An extreme instance of the Anglophilism of the English educated Indian is seen in Hatterr's Indian friend Bannerji who displays a strong addiction to English literature, especially Shakespeare, and quotes profusely from the bard on all occasions. He longs to change his name from Nath to Noel and has adopted English manners and habits of eating. It is his admiration for everything English that makes him an admirer of Hatterr, who has some English blood in him. He declares: "Shakespeare, literature, Michaelangelo Buonarroti, Mr. Shelley's heart, flowers and other beauties is what I live for."[13] His blind admiration remains unimpaired by Hatterr's follies and his cowardice. Another variation of the western-educated colonial is provided in the character of Y. Beliram, who is shrewd enough to make use of his legal training to set up a flourishing practice in India. Later he transforms himself into Yati Rambeli and sells Indian spirituality to the West. The dependence-complex and total subservience to the colonizer is best represented by Desani, through the relationship between Hatterr and his dog, Jenkins. Jenkins is close to Caliban in his dependence, his worthlessness and his sudden switching of loyalties to Bannerji. Desertion by his master does not cure Jenkins of his Anglomania and he is proud to be enrolled as a member of the English Tail Waggers' Association of London when he has "the clean nationalistic choice" to join the Kennel Club of India. According to him, it is "like loving the Mediterranean Sea . . . when having our own Indian Ocean!" (239)

Through these Anglophiles, who cling on to an Empire that is no more, the Indian English novelists expose what Parthasarathy has called "the high fever of colonialitis." ("Whoring after English Gods" 70) It is a natural consequence of the discourse of imperialism-termed "Orientalism"[14] by Edward Said—that assumes and establishes the positional superiority of the westerner to the oriental. The latter, relegated to a position of inferiority, naturally comes to look upon the West as culturally superior and develops a tendency to emulate western ways. Frantz Fannon considers it as a case of psychic conflict resulting in the alienation of individuals from their native ethos. Fannon says that in so far as he conceives of European culture as a means of stripping himself of his race, he becomes alienated.[15] Alienation from one's own community naturally results in the urge to identify oneself with the ruling race, and to adopt the alien culture and to discard one's racial and national identity.

The second type of response to western cultural domination mainly assumes the form of the dilemma caused by cross-cultural tension between the East and the West. It forms an undercurrent in Indian English writing. Sometimes it even becomes the source of inspiration for creative writing. The Indian English writer who has chosen the alien language as his medium inhabits a cultural limbo and it is his own agonizing dilemma that he exposes through "the unanchored souls," "wavering in spirit and without a secure doctrine."[16] The exposure to English culture and the tendency to imitate English ways poses a conflict with the values and traditions derived from native soil. Inter-cultural tension and the dislocated individual in his search for identity form frequent motifs in Indian English fiction. Kamala Markandaya, Nayantara Sahgal and B. Rajan offer a new insight into the problem through their rootless characters. In the socio-political climate of India in the nineteenth century, most of the young men received their education abroad. The anglicized Indian returning to the home-country found himself in a world of dual values where day-to-day realities posed the question of choice between modern western pragmatism and ancient eastern philosophy.

In *A Time to be Happy* and *The Dark Dancer*, the England-educated protagonist faces a predicament of identity as he encounters the cultural conflict within himself. Sanad Shivpal (*A Time to be Happy*), a public school product, brought up in the anglicised atmosphere of a rich family is proficient in tennis and hence accepted in "the glittering cocktail-party-gymkhana-club Government House circuit upon which social recognition in British India depended." (27) Initiation into the inner circle of English social life makes him conscious of the racial discrimination against the ordinary Indian who was permitted entry into the club only once a month, and who was employed for a smaller pay than his British colleagues. He feels disgusted at the superficial nature of his life in India, totally impervious to the harsh realities of a war raging in the world outside and the premonition of famine in Bengal. "It was like a never-never land of inanity, deliberately sealed and barred against an intelligent awareness of the real world." (104) Sanad feels that "an immense masquerade was going on in Calcutta and that if one tore off the masks and finery, all the ugly rotting structure underneath would be exposed." (104) Success in career only makes Sanad feel more alienated from his fellowmen. The nationalistic movement gaining momentum under Gandhiji's leadership, the intensifying of British measures of oppression, atrocities like the murder of Kusum's brother and the beating of Raghubir, the entry of Kusum into his life as the very embodiment of Indian culture and a symbol of ideal Indian womanhood, become significant factors that strengthen the crisis within Sanad. He tells McIvor: "It is a strange feeling to be midway between two worlds, not completely belonging to either." (147)

In the desperate need to identify himself with his countrymen, Sanad makes a deliberate effort to know his country, its language and culture, with the help of Kusum. Nayantara Sahgal depicts the development of Sanad's character from an anglicized puppet to an Indian who respects his country's culture and tradition. The transformed Sanad interprets the basic tenets of Hinduism to McIvor, rejects the Company's offer to send him to England and seriously contemplates resigning from his job. He retrieves the essentials of his native past, regains his roots and cultural identity.

Krishnan's (*The Dark Dancer*) journey to self-awareness reaches the desired end only after passing through the traumatic experience of an unhappy affair with an English girl, Cynthia. Whereas Sanad consciously struggles to retrieve his lost identity, Krishnan is not even aware of the nature of his predicament. It is the encounter with Cynthia, a relic from his western past, that opens his eyes to her essential otherness and the cultural gulf between them. Involvement in the political movement and exposure to the communal holocaust during partition become different stages in his journey to his own cultural identity. Finally, Kamala, his wife, who had chosen service and sacrifice as a way of life accepts her truant husband without a word of reprimand and thus helps him achieve repossession of identity. In his union with Kamala, in a purely Hindu marriage, Krishnan feels the "restoring of a law within himself," "the feeling of a truth suddenly springing to life beside him, of the repression of an ancient resemblance." (235) S.C. Harrex explains: "Repossession is the key word, signifying end in beginning, returning to the opening page of *The Dark Dancer* and accomplishing what was then unaccomplished: 'a creative confronting, which would open his mind to its depths of repossession.'"[17] Krishnan destroys his ties with the West and finds "inward renewal" as Kamala's death destroys the illusion that man is an island and alienation the ultimate reality.

Kamala Markandaya explores the theme of the loss and the recovery of identity in a quite different context in *Possession*. S.C. Harrex calls the novel "a drama of de-Indianization," in which the artist Valmiki, "is not only culturally and psychologically conditioned by the West, but also possessed by it."[18] Caroline's literal possession of Valmiki becomes an allegory of British cultural imperialism. The wealthy and arrogant Englishwoman thinks that by buying Valmiki and virtually possessing him, she can fashion him into the oriental artistic persona that would be acceptable to the West. However, the temptations of Caroline's world do not destroy the spark of identity that Valmiki preserves—"a cold watchful inner eye, as disdainful of others as of himself." (110) It is this vestige of a former identity that refuses to be affected by the overwhelming temptations of Caroline's sensual world, that stirs in sympathy for Ellie. With the Jewish refugee under Caroline's roof, he shares "an under-the-skin-bondage—the joined experience of a calculating, maiming, actively hostile and cruel world; and the joint feeling of being without roots, top-heavy saplings struggling to keep a crazy balance in an earth that quivered and shifted, recorded every move from isolate nobility to a pervading madness." (115) The Swami and India remain live memories in him and he never loses the need for India's "extraordinary confusion" and "passionate agglomeration of colour." (46) Every aggressive move of Caroline to possess Valmiki—like writing fake letters in the name of the Swami to inspire him, ruthlessly expelling Ellie from the house, offering him the attraction of carnal lust and sensual pleasures, and callously destroying the innocent love that sprouts between Annabel and Valmiki—serves to fill him with bitterness and loathing for her world and makes him realize that he can never belong to that world. The monkey that Valmiki had bought to enhance his Indian image before the West remains the last sign of his identity. With its death, his guilt about Ellie and his child, and the confusion of values resulting from what S.C. Harrex calls "his hybrid mask" (70) come into perspective and Valmiki decides to return to his roots—to the Swami and the wilderness where he could dedicate his talents to the divine spirit of the universe. The Swami's non-attachment and dedication of powers to the higher being, is offered as solution to Valmiki's dilemma. Traditional India with her spiritual wealth provides Valmiki his true home. S.C. Harrex comments: "Thus the spectacle of an Indian talent encouraged, seduced, and almost destroyed by the West adds to the East/West, detachment/ possession, reality/illusion structure yet a further level of allegory and another aspect of the identity predicament." (72)

Dual loyalities and conflicting values cause perpectual tension in

Bashiam (*The Coffer Dams*)—the wild aborigine from the tribals who receives western technical training and becomes an outsider in his community. As one who has been exposed to western ways of living and thinking, Bashiam feels a kinship with Clinton. Ann Lowry Weir calls him "a jungly-wallah version of Clinton"[19] for he shares Clinton's love of machinery and his commitment to his job. He takes pride in the technical know-how he has acquired, but the strong natural instincts of the tribal that gives him intuitive knowledge of nature survive in him. It is these eastern instincts in him that have not been affected by the impact of western culture that draw Helen to him. They are both "outsiders"—"he, the skilled and competent technician away from his jungly-wallah tribe, she the No. 1 memsahib who refused to bear the memsahib's load—so that there was an acreage of common rebellion which both were stimulated by and respected in each other." (81) But when Helen comes of her own accord to him, Bashiam is actually aware of the racial difference and it is a wariness he feels because "she was a memsahib, who would use him like a bluejacket upon her white and exquisite body and then leave him." (105) Unlike Valmiki, Bashiam does not let himself be completely possessed by the West. Even in the acceptance of Helen, there is a withdrawal, a hesitancy and an awareness of the different milieus of which they are a part, and which have a claim on them. It is this recognition of the essential dichotomy between East and West that enables Bashiam to accept the fact of Helen's return to England, even after the cruel maimimg of his body by the collapse of the crane. There cannot be a resolving of Bashiam's rootlessness because the West cannot accept him into its fold. With stoic resignation he replies to Helen who asks him what he would do, when she was gone. He tells her he too would go in search of new projects. He accepts the fact that the affair with Helen can only be temporary and the West holds no place for him. P.S. Chauhan comments on the attitudes that turn one's life into rich or poor.[20] Bashiam's worshipping attitude to the river and the crane which is his "Devi" is typically Indian. "It renders the universe more humane and man less arrogant." (144)

Commenting on Kamala Markandaya's continued preoccupation with England's influence on modern India, P.S. Chauhan writes: "Constantly aware of England's influence on modern India, she writes of Indians not merely as Indians but as people touched and toned by the English. Ultimately this interest acquires epic dimensions. She creates individual characters but writes of people. Like James's, Markandaya's stories lead up to cultural transvaluation." (139)

In *Pleasure City*, Kamala Markandaya deals with the predicament of identity faced by the British in India as well as by the westernized Indian, in his native land. The situation is close to *The Coffer Dams* but Kamala Markandaya has travelled a long way from *The Coffer Dams* and here she shows the extraordinary reaching out of two minds, dissolving racial, national and social barriers. As K.A. Abbas has declared in his story "The Man Who did not Want to Remember" the message of the novel seems to be that "being human is the only identity that matters."[21]

The Indian fisher boy, Rikky (*Pleasure City*) comes under the influence of the English missionary couple—the Bridies—at a very young and malleable age. The homeless Bridies, lingering in India as the last remnants of the British empire, find consolation in befriending Rikky, the golden-haired orphan, an anomaly in his own village. From the Bridies he acquires remarkable fluency in the English language. They open up new vistas of knowledge before his insatiable curiosity and his perceptions branch under their influence; he acquires new dreams and high aspirations, alienating him from a community of fishing folk whose relentless battle with the elements have deprived them of dreams and hopes. The nostalgic dreams of the Bridies regarding a lost motherland become shared experience and Rikky waits for the day when he might be able to visit the England of their dreams. The Bridies' influence on Rikky symbolizes the impact of western education, western values and the sophisticated sensibility of the west on the average Indian who becomes a product of two entirely different cultures and feels rootless and non-belonging in either. The arrival of Tully, one of the directors of AIDCORP that has chosen a fishing village to build the pleasure-complex "Shalimar," marks for Rikky a continuation of the acquaintance with England. Tully's separateness from the other officers of the company draws him to the outsider Rikky. Tully becomes to Rikky another link in the contact with England started off by the Bridies. After a life time of waiting, Tully's arrival opens up the gates of communication once more and unknown voids in his individual unconscious are filled once again. The job of a tea-boy at Shalimar, the task of making a boat for Tully and the marble work Tully entrusted to Rikky, boost his morale and weans him away from his folk. But Rikky does not get completely westernized; nor does he sever links with his people. He remains attached to his foster-mother and his sister and gives them gifts. In spite of his brother's resentment at his choosing a civilized man's job, he helps him during the mackerel season. But the gaps in communication and understanding are unbridgeable and he remains an alien in his community. At Shalimar too, he can establish contact only with the outsiders from the white community—Tully and Mrs. Pearl, who could understand him and even love him with personal warmth. The orphaned boy fills the void in their childless, barren existence. Rikki's longing to see the imaginary homeland, England, is a typical urge in the colonized. Loss of identity with one's own culture impels the colonized to go to the imaginary home—the colonizer's country familiarized through its history and literature—in order to seek his roots. Rikky asks Tully whether it would be possible for him to visit England. Tully knows that such a visit could only bring disillusionment because there is a world of difference between the England of Rikky's dreams, filtered into his imagination through the nostalgic longings of the Bridies, and the real England. Parthasarathy's experience is memorable: "My encounter with England only reproduced the by now familiar pattern of Indian experience in England: disenchantment. Here was an England I was unable to come to terms with. The England I had known and loved existed nowhere, except in my mind." (*Whorimg after English Gods* 66)

Rikky is conscious of the cultural differences that separate him from Tully in spite of occasional moments of blissful communion between them. "Rikky felt the division between them—between one man and another; their minds, their reach and sway, the reality of the distance between himself and Tully. He even voiced his thoughts to Tully—'There is an ocean between us; he said flatly.'" (47) Tully too is conscious of the essential dichotomy of race and culture though "there were times, long serene stretches in which they touched." (147) Like Helen and Bashiam, Tully and Rikky also accept the inevitability of parting and the separateness of their racial and cultural moorings. They have to live with the conflict within themselves, as "unanchored souls" in a world to which they cannot belong. Tully offers Rikky a chance to regain his lost identity by suggesting that he would give Rikky a fishing boat if he wanted to go back to fishing. But Rikky says that his job is all fixed up in Shalimar and Tully feels that "his soul was taken bondage." (337)

The Jamesean dilemma of double cultures impinging on the self, is a painful problem with the small group of Eurasians cast in Indian English fiction. Ruby Miranda and Eddie Trevor in *Combat of Shadows* become victims of the culture-conflict—Ruby Miranda, through her thwarted attempt to marry an Englishman and Eddie as the victim of an Englishman's vengeance. Both had striven and aspired to blend with the English community, only to be rejected by it. Hatterr, the protagonist of G.V. Desani's buildungsroman, *All About H. Hatterr*, is rejected unceremoniously by the English community, of which he had considered himself a member. Refection by "native" culture, necessitates a forced reconciliation with the "alien" ethos and this is depicted with great resourcefulness by Desani, through Hatterr's cultural encounter with India. The reluctance of the English community to accept the Eurasians and the latter's inability to be part of Indian Culture brings about the tragic fate of Wheeler's children in *The Devil's Wind*.

The perfect fusion of the East and the West in an Indian (the third type of response) is envisaged almost as an impossibility by the Indian English novelists. Rarely do we come across in fiction a person like Roshan (*Some Inner Fury*) who fits in both the worlds and feels a sense of identification with the whites and the non-whites. Most people envy the dual citizenship that she simply takes for granted. And curiously enough, both worlds are glad to accept her as one among them. At her father's mills, the spinners and weavers speak to her as one among themselves. At the dance parties in the Government guest house she appears in saris as bright as butterfly's wings and Englishmen vie with one another to partner her. The mark of the west which she wears so lightly does not brand her even in Govind's eyes. Under her influence Mira too learns to accept the west, only to realize at the hour of crisis that her roots lay deeper in India. The writers emphasize the fact that liaison with the west can only be a brief infatuation or a temporary flirtation.

The fourth type of response—the complete rejection of the West and the assertion of the superiority of the eastern values over the West, is a common phenomenon in postcolonial Indian English fiction. Here the artist functions as decolonizer, breaking the ideas of the West and reinstating native images. In his task, the writer is pitted against "the sheer knitted-together strength of orientalist discourse" with its "very close ties to the enabling socio-economic and political institutions and its redoubtable durability."[22] Edward Said points out how orientalism —virtually "nothing more than a structure of lies or of myths"—had created a system of knowledge about the orient, an accepted grid steeped in the western consciousness against which the orient is constantly evaluated. (6) In the effort to corrode the dehumanizing effect of the orientalist discourse, commonwealth writers have resorted to systematic methods of idol-breaking. Though the tone of protest and indignation against the West is not too pronounced as in the African novelists, the Indian writers are seen to establish the superiority of eastern values over the West in novel after novel. In the novels of Kamala Markandaya, Nayantara Sahgal, Raja Rao, R.K. Narayan, B. Rajan, and Chaman Nahal, the superiority of eastern values is established over western materialism.

In an analysis of the decolonizing devices used by postcolonial writers the authors of *The Empire Writes Back*[23] cite as a typical example the symbolic replacing of the photograph of the English bureaucrat, Mr. Noble, by the picture of a God in R. K. Narayan's *The Sweet Ven-*

dor.[24] Mr. Noble, the District Collector, was a much-respected Englishman for whom a special chair had been built by Jagan's father when he used to come for lessons in astrology. After independence, the discarded photograph taken out of its glazed frame is reduced to an object of amusement and a plaything for children. It becomes a piece of junk to be dumped in the loft.

The superiority of Indian spiritual values over western materialism is emphasized in novel after novel, in an effort to counteract the imperial centre. It is often exemplified through the conflict between an Indian and an Englishman or woman. Thus, in the encounter with the cool composure and the Brahminic spirituality of the Minister Narasimha Rao, the resident Mr. Buckridge finds himself the loser(*The Golden Honeycomb*). Kamala Markandaya's Premala (*Some Inner Fury*) and B. Rajan's Kamala (*The Dark Dancer*) embody idealized Indian womanhood with its silent endurance, nobility, essential virtue and high sense of duty, against the hollowness of the material values represented by Kitsamy and his English friends (*Some Inner Fury*) and Cynthia (*The Dark Dancer*). Caroline with her imperialistic urge to possess, acts as a foil to the Indian narrator, Anasuya (*Possession*). Just as Caroline cannot comprehend the purpose of artistic creation in a wilderness, away from the admiring eyes of the world, so too Michael Calvert (*A Situation in New Delhi*) fails to understand the consuming sense of duty that makes Devi, Shivraj's sister, dedicate herself to her brother's service. The traditional Indian values of virtue, nobility and self-fulfilment through sacrifice and service or through the dedication of art as a form of worship are glorified as the expression of the great and ancient culture. The anglicized Indian coming home realizes the hollowness of the super-imposed western culture and is shown as returning to his native moorings—like Sanad in *A Time to be Happy* and Krishnan in *The Dark Dancer*. Nahal's English protagonist Kenneth Ashby (*The Crown and the Loincloth*) recieves an insight into the meaningfulness of existence when Sunil reminds him of the enduring value of love as an ethereal experience. In *Nectar in a Sieve* Rukmani's stoic endurance of suffering exasperates the English Dr. Kenny. He has not learned the nobility in silent suffering and he cannot understand the passive acceptance of life. Baba Goray's reply to her American friend Alix Nichol, who speaks about happiness as her goal in life, is perhaps the best expression of the Indian point of view. "In Jalnabad, I thought, no one made a point about happiness. We were given and we accepted without thinking, certain precepts . . . within our framework we could make our happiness . . . it was never suggested that we pursue happiness. We were not encouraged to waste our time."[25]

In most of her novels Kamala Markandaya shows the clash between the conflicting value systems of the East and the West and even advocates a return from the progressive world of the civilized West, to the tradional, conservative East and thence to the primitive world of instincts. Thus in *The Coffer Dams* it is the instinctive knowledge of the tribal about the monsoons that triumphs over the technical expertise of the western world. Helen, the 'Burra Memsahib' of the white building company is engaged in a quest for the lost power of instincts which had been "battered down" "under concrete and mortar." (138) This reverence for the instincts and for natural elements at large can be observed in Tully (*Pleasure City*) also. Rikki's instinctive knowledge of the sea and its elements is always acknowledged without question by Tully. He is filled with wonder at Rikki's traditional methods of finding water with a divining rod. Tully is one who is liberated from colonial prejudice and ethnic feelings and contact with India helps him regain the lowest world of instincts and intuition. He lives through occasional moments of apocalyptic vision that show the development of his spiritual faculties.

Kamala Markandaya suggests through her novels the superiority of the Hindu acceptance and celebration of life as against the privations of Christian religion based on the constricting concept of sin. Indian spirituality invariably scores over western faith. Srinivas—Kamala Markandaya's "nowhereman"—faces the racial animosity in England with philosophic sobriety and makes passive non-violence his weapon. He establishes beyond doubt the strength of the faith that sustains him indicating the superiority of eastern values. Dr. Radcliffe perceives the hidden strength of his frail-looking patient when he accepts the shocking diagnosis of leprosy without qualm. He could never share in the racial animosity that condemned a man like Srinivas and when he dies he openly accuses his compatriots: "He is dead, and we all had a hand in it." Srinivas's death attains the dimensions of Christ's crucifixion in Radcliffe's troubled conscience—for he has been made the unprotesting, passively bold victim of a prejudiced and ethnic community that fails to make room for really great souls. P.S. Chauhan comments: "The English have hauteur, not humility; vigour, not patience; efficiency, not understanding; certitude, not spiritual doubts. Theirs is a young culture in the process of moral evolution. Till they mellow, they can only be pitied and forgiven. Such is the attitude of Srinivas and of an earlier character, the Swami, who contend against the English but who are never less than compassionate even in the contention. Grace and good manners are on the side of the subdued Indian characters."[26]

In Raja Rao's *The Serpent and the Rope*,[27] the cultural schism arises between an Indian and a French lady and is therefore, not strictly relevant to the study. But it is a powerful exposition of the cultural divide between the East and the West. What has been dealt with at the personal and social levels, is given philosophical dimensions in the novel. Ramaswami, the Brahmin protagonist is himself a fusion of the East and the West and his marriage with the French lady leads him to a perception of the dualities of his world and a realization of the superiority of Eastern spirituality over the West. The marriage brings into relief the polarities of the contrasting cultures and Ramaswami finally arives at his own cultural and spiritual moorings. Padmanabha Iyer in Raja Rao's *Comrade Kirillov*[28] is also a schizophrenic personality, in whom the conflict is between Communist ideology and Indian nationalism.

The widespread social changes wrought by British rule in Indian rural life had its cultural reverberations as well. K.A. Abbas and Nayantara Sahgal harp on the economic impoverishment of India because of Britain's policy of sapping her natural resources for manufacture in England. In *Inquilab* Abbas provides a comprehensive picture of how the British had ruined the Indian peasant:

> India has been ruined economically. The revenue derived from our peoples is out of proportion to our income. Our average income is seven pice [sic] per day and of the heavy taxes we pay twenty percent are raised from the land revenue derived from the peasantry and three percent from the salt tax, which falls most heavily on the poor village industries such as hand spinning etc., have been destroyed, leaving the peasantry idle for at least four months in the year, and nothing has been substituted, as in the other countries on the talents thus destroyed. (239)

The impingement of industrialization on Indian rural life finds powerful treatment in Kamala Markandaya's *Nectar in a Sieve*. The peasant who is weaned away from the soil, is reduced to stark poverty. Rukmani's sons drift away from the land where their roots lie, lured by the world of machines, finally uprooting Nathan and Rukmani themselves. The corroding of cultural moorings is evident in Rukmani's daughter Ira's decision to sell her body to make a living. But Kajoli, in Bhabani Bhattacharya's *So Many Hungers*[29] preserves her spirit even in the midst of the hunger and famine that raged through the villages of Bengal in 1943, due to the British policy of scorching fishing boats and surplus grains to keep away the Japanese invaders. The brutal policy of the government, its indifference to the starvation of the millions and the stark poverty that descends on the land have a reaction in the mighty wave of nationalism that gains strength from unabated suffering. The cow and woman become symbols of indian culture, preserved and honoured by this ancient country. The famine subjects both to violent assault and humiliation. The loved and cherished cow is beaten by the desperate mother of Kajoli; Kajoli's purity's attacked by a British soldier; but her spirit refuses to be trampled on by the brute forces of the city. M. Tarinayya comments: "Her will to power, which is the spirit of India, is what gives the novel its place in Indian wiriting in English . . . the novel is a repudiation of the British Empire built on the explosive foundation of the bones of men, women and children and its soulless political and economic system involving the subjection of vast populations."[30]

The influence of English education and the anglicized ways of the teacher Miss Mendoza corrupt Lalitha (*Two Virgins*),[31] dislodging her from her rural upbringing and making her a victim of urban cruelty and indifference. English culture seems to have taken hold of her soul and the loss of a woman's cherished virtue leaves her hard and indifferent. The essentially Indian response of Saroja to city-culture is provided as a contrast.

East-West conflict assumes the form of a confrontation between spiritual faith and materialistic science in *A Silence of Desire* and between technological and traditional values or between industrialism and Gandhism in *Shadow from Ladakh*.[32] Sarojini's compromise at the instigation of the Swami, and her successful operation and Dandekar's own sense of guilt and spiritual confusion leave us in doubt as to what Kamala Markandaya wants to establish in *A Silence of Desire*. Satyajit (*Shadow from Ladakh*) is a virtual shadow of Gandhi who will not tolerate the industrializing of rural economy, which will pollute the peace and harmony of village life. Bhasker, the new embodiment of technological expertise stands for the West that is determined to leave its stamp on the village. The conflict between the two extremes is left unresolved and ambiguous by the novelist with Sunitha providing a fictional link between the two. But Bhabani Bhattacharya makes it clear that if the steeltown were to annex the village, it would mean annexing a way of life. Co-existence would be difficult. He writes: "There could not be two Indias, back to back, gazing at opposite horizons, ready to march off, and get further and further apart." (59)

The Indian's encounter with the English in their own land has become a theme of increasing potential to Indian English writers, with the growing number of coloured immigrants in England. The Englishmen's attitude to the former subjects, making incursions into the social, intellectual and cultural life of the country, is worthy of exploration. A number of outstanding novelists have tried to capture the immigrant perspective and the problems encountered in the clash with the alien ethos. The experience of exile begins as a condition of living and intensifies itself as a condition of mind. Its sources are cultural displacement and cultural shock. Kamala Markandaya's *The Nowhere Man*, Anita Desai's *Bye-Bye. Blackbird* and Timeri Murari's *The Marriage* deal with the theme of exile and the immigrant's encounter with England, in a very powerful manner. The novelists themselves are victims of cultural displacement due to their immigrant status and therefore the protagonists are mostly "projections of their creators and much of the writer's life is gone into their making. These novels grow on the soil of autobiography. The conflict in the condition of these writers is liberated through the dilemma of their protagonist."[33]

The colonized Indian harbours a sense of belonging to the colonizer's country and cherishes a dream of going to the dreamland, nostalgically presented to him through English literature and arts, familiarized during the period of colonial occupation. The emigration to England is therefore, a natural aftermath of the colonial experience. The chasm between the remembered land and the real England, and its total indifference to his being and its reluctance to let him find his roots there, lead to disillusionment, disinheritance, and a sense of futility and estrangement.

Anita Desai's depiction of the social isolation of Adit and Sarah in *Bye-Bye, Blackbird* is a realistic and poignant portrayal of the problems faced by a mixed couple in the hostile English environment. Like many of his fellow immigrants in England, Adit had love and fascination for England right from his school days in India. He had enjoyed English literature and music, had adopted English ways and manners and considered England a land of infinite opportunities. But England does not accept him. The English society is callous and indifferent. He is abused, insulted and humiliated all the time, even by school children. Parthasarathy has described Britain's attitude to the immigrants in his poem "Exile 2" that he read over the B.B.C.

> Dressed in tweeds or grey flannel,
> Its suburban pockets
> bursting with immigrants
> "Coloureds" is what they call us
> Over there.[34]

The attitude to the "coloured" is one of unconcealed contempt and English doors and windows are tightly closed against him. Adit and Sarah are doomed to live alienated from the society, eking out a living on a petty clerical job in a tiny travel agency without any prospect of further promotion. The only company afforded to him is that of fellow immigrants whom, ironically enough, he despises. Sarah too experiences "an anguish of loneliness" (35) and feels lost and unsure of her own identity. Many details from everyday life are thrown in by Anita Desai to bring home the way in which a culture makes itself felt through the trivialities of life which pile up and become an insurmountable bastion between partners in a marriage. However, in the Adit-Sarah relationship, Sarah does not side with the English. She is hurt by the rudeness of her countrymen towards Adit and exclaims, "When I think of all the Millers of England, I could leave at once." (93) What finally makes Adit take the decision to leave England, by driving home "the basic disharmony of the situation" (189) is the attitude of Sarah's parents. "The placidity, munificence and the ease of England" (210) become abhorrent to him and he feels that he could not bear to see "one more pale, expressionless British face. If one were to approach him, he would hit it, hit it." (119) Nahal's *Into Another Dawn*[35] deals with a similar issue, with Ravi Sharma, from a tradition-bound Brahmin household marrying an American girl, Irene in U.S.A. and returning home to his spiritual moorings.

The isolation of the loosely-knit Indian community trapped in a small industrial town in England, the problems faced by Tekchand and his family (mainly his daughter Leena) through relations with the British and the immense cultural void between the English and the Indians are dealt with in Timeri Murari's *The Marriage.*[36] However it is Kamala Markandaya who has succeeded in lending the theme remarkable intensity by making Srinivas's (*The Nowhere Man*) isolation a metaphor for loneliness. Srinivas, the nowhereman, becomes a symbol of the ruthless ostracism of the coloured man in the English society. There is a strong autobiographical element in the novel and we cannot help feeling that the pathos of Srinivas's predicament gains in intensity due to Kamala Markandaya's own expatriate placement. The racial encounter is viewed from different angles and probable solutions suggested through the viewpoints of Abdul, Srinivas and his son Laxman—Abdul thinks that through force, power and money one can find a parity with the English because "The Britons respect power, but no money—no power." (77) Laxman advocates total identification with the British and accordingly he marries an English girl, and brings up his children in the British tradition. He accuses his father of "sticking out like a sore thumb instead of decently integrating." (261) But even Laxman who has decently integrated, is rejected by the English society and is rated as a black for he too is "colonised." Srinivas adopts a typically Indian nonviolent stance that enables him to accept the facts. But he asserts his identity silently but strongly, by wearing a butter-muslin dhoti and walking across the street as though to declare his Indianness. The disease of leprosy becomes another symbol for Srinivas's aloneness—a disease that alienates him not only from the English but from the entire human race. Srinivas's condition illustrates Maria Pfister-Ammende's analysis of the psychopathology of uprooting:

> If the immigrant lives alone in hostile or unfamiliar surroundings and without sympathetic relationships, certain reactions occur which are either of a more active or passive type. These two types of reactions are found also in uprooted people who are not dependent on a particular group. The passively reacting individual freezes: either he will become ill and wither away like a wounded animal, or he remains outwardly adjusted to his environment, hiding his total inner upset . . . behind a perfect front.[37]

Srinivas easily falls into the first category. In portraying the tragic victimization of Srinivas to racial antagonism, Kamala Markandaya adds a new dimension to the culture-conflict suggesting the rootlessness and total alienation of man that it can lead to. "In *Nowhere Man* the experience of immigration becomes the theme of human isolation."[38]

Bhabani Bhatacharya in his *A Dream in Hawaii*[39] examines a different aspect of the East-West problem—the groping for spiritual values in the disillusioned West, and the journey to India, the land of spiritual wisdom. This is a neo-colonial feature. However, Bhattacharya does not deal with the theme in a satisfying manner because he side-steps the main issue and gets engrossed in depicting the Sanyasi Yogananda's dilemma, caused by his obsesive memory of Devyani, and the sexual assault by Sylvia which sends him fleeing back to India. It is a disappointing exploration of the West's need for the spiritual East.

The inter-cultural tension has been of vital interest to the Indian English novelist because of the constant exposure to the west due to political subjection and social and cultural encounters with the ruling community. Whereas pre-Independence writing mainly concentrated on the East-West tension manifesting as the conflict between tradition and modernity, between nature and technology and spirituality and materialism, post-Independence writing focuses on the encounter at the personal and cultural level. This can be explained by the growth of western education, the incursion of the Indian emigrant into the former colonizer's land and a deepening sense of alienation caused by the cultural and racial gulf. Immigrant writers have given poignant expression to the dispossessed and rootless sensibility of the Indian in exile.

Many of these writers have expressed their regret over the racial exclusiveness of the British that prevented an effective interchange or a fruitful integration with Indian thought and culture in the colonial period. Benita Parry writes: "In retrospect, it seems inevitable that the British, represented as they were by Anglo-Indians, would assimilate little from India's rich and varied cultures, and that the ideas and life style of India would be uncongenial to a civilization in the process of revelutionising the material environment and with it the estimate of man's relationship with the universe."[40]

E.M. Forster expressed regret that the task of promoting Indian culture and art and introducing them to Britain was ignored by the imperialist of the utlitarian English middle class. He wrote:

> After two hundred years of political connection with India, we in England know next to nothing about the Indian culture. Our ignorance is disgraceful and is indeed an indictment of our Empire. We have sent our soldiers and administrators and money-makers to the East, but few scholars and fewer artists. It is unwise to suppose that culture is unimportant and that distance in space and differences in idiom are a sufficient excuse for superciliousness and obtuseness.[41]

The privations of a colonial relationship can be offered as an excuse for British reserve and the refusal to interact with India.

It is amazing to note that years after independence even the novels written in the seventies, eg., *Bye-Bye, Blackbird* (1971) and *The Nowhere Man* (1973), still harp on the incompatibility between the East and the West and the cultural schism that snaps personal ties and prevents enduring human relationships. Racial animosity and intolerance have only lessened the possibility of human relationships. But the strong emotional bonds that develop between Helen and Bashiam (*The Coffer Dams*), Tully and Rikky (*Pleasure City*), Richard and Mira (*Some Inner Fury*), Michael Calvert and Devi (*A Situation in New Delhi*), Ashby and Sunil (*The Crown and the Loincloth*), Adit and Sarah (*Bye-Bye, Blackbird*) loudly proclaim the possibility of a cultural synthesis and beautiful human relationships, provided the English alienate themselves from the racism and cultural exclusiveness that engulf their community. As liberated individuals who break from the tangles of race or culture they can stretch an arm of friendship to the coloured, suggesting the possibility of a harmonious relationship. The novelists show how culture and racial barriers are overcome at least temporarily through such relationships.

One is forced to admit that the relationship cannot endure because of the immense gulf in perspective. Even the westernized Indian is encountered by the truth of his cultural premises and inhibitions at every turn, in the effort to co-exist with the West, making even adjustment in the material relationship impossible. The hold of India on the mind of its countrymen is so powerful and enigmatlc that the West can hardly come to grips with it. Jawaharlal Nehru describes the labyrinth that confronted the westerner in his effort to approach India.

> About her there is the elusive quality of a legend long ago; some enchantment seems to hold her mind She is a myth and an idea, a dream and a vision, and yet very real and present and pervasive. There are terrifying glimpses of dark corridors which seem to lead back to primeval night, but also there is the fulness and warmth of day about her. Shameful and repellent, she is occasionally perverse and obstinate, sometimes even a little hysteric, this lady with a past.[42]

Raja Rao's vision of India expounded in *The Serpent and the Rope* coincides with Nehru's concept of India. Ruth Jhabvala views the problem from a different angle and shows the difficulty in the adjustment forced by the westerner in India. "Life plays itself out to a different rhythm here . . . it is fatal to come to India and expect to be able to live to a western rhythm."[43]

The spiritual values of the East invariably triumph in the novels of Raja Rao, Kamala Markandaya, R.K. Narayan, Nayantara Sahgal, B. Rajan and Chaman Nahal. "Eventhough the West/modernity/technology has the 'brute strength' as it were, to take over the village or the valley, or even to claim the time and energy of human beings, it can never overpower values which spring from the East/tradition/humanism."[44] Only Mulk Raj Anand seems to be free of what the Bengali critic and writer, Ananda Sankar Ray has called "the East-past complex."[45]

These beautiful but brief relationships between Indians and the British, depicted in the Indian English novel, sustain hope and point to a future when the West may come to know the East through a relationship founded on parity and a broader and more humane vision. Human minds reach across the barriers projected by race and culture and a man-to-man contact might become possible. Cultural synthesis can become a reality at the personal level, if not at a social and political level.

NOTES

1. Wole Soyinka, "Cross-Currents: The New African after Cultural Encounters," *Writers in East-West Encounter: New Cultural Bearings*, ed. Guy Amrithanayagam (London:Macmillan, 1982) 51.
2. Gareth Griffiths, *A Double Exile: African and West Indlan Writing Between Two Cultures* (London: Marion Boyares, 1978) 9.
3. Kirpal Singh, "Writers in Limbo: The Third World Experience," *The Literary Criterion,* XXIII, No. 4 (1988) 70-79.
4. R. Parthasarathy, "Whoring after English Gods," in Guy Amrithanayagam, 69.
5. Lloyd Fernando, "A Note from the Third World towards the Redefinition of Culture," *Awakened Conscience: Studies in Commonwealth Literature*, ed, C.D. Narasimhaiah (New Delhi: Sterling Publishers, 1978) 329.
6. Quoted in Kai Nicholson, "The Anglicised Indian," *A Presentation of Social Problems in the Indo-Anglian and the Anglo-Indian Novel* 3.
7. R. Parthasarathy, "Whoring after English Gods," 63-64.
8. Nayantara Sahgal, *This Time of Morning* (1965: rpt. Delhi: Hind Pocket Books, n.d.).
9. Thomas Hughes, *Tom Brown's Schooldays* (London: Ward, Lock, 1947).
10. G.S. Amur, *Manohar Malgonkar* 47.
11. V.S. Naipaul, *The Mimic Men* (London: Andre Deutch, 1967).
12. Quoted from C. Vimala Rao, "Patterns of Colonialism in the New Zealand Stories of Katherine Mansfield," *Commonwealth Fiction,* ed. R.K. Dhawan (New Delhi: Classical, 1988) 134.
13. G.V. Desani, *All About H. Hatterr* (1948; rpt. New York: Farrar, Straus and Giroux, 1970) 266.
14. Edward W. Said, *Orientalism* (London: Routledge and Kegan Paul, 1978) 7.
15. Renate Zahar, *Frantz Fannon: Colonialism and Alienation* (New York and London: Ethiope Monthly Review Press, 1974).
16. V.S. Naipaul, *The Middle Passage* (Harmondsworth: Penguin, 1969) 42.
17. S.C. Harrex, "Dancing in the Dark: Balchandra Rajan and T.S. Eliot," *World Literature Writing in English* 14, No. 2 (Nov. 1975) 310-21.
18. S.C. Harrex, "A Sense of Identity: The Early Novels of Kamala Markandaya," *The Journal of Commonwealth Literature*, VI, No. 1 (June 1971) 65-78.
19. *Ann Lowry Weir, "Worlds Apart, Feminine Consciousness in Markandaya's Nectar in a Sieve* and *The Coffer Dams*," *CIEFL Bulletin*, XIII, No. 2 (1977) 71-85.
20. P.S. Chauhan, "Kamala Markandaya: Sense and Sensibility," *Literary Criterion*, XIII, Nos. 2 & 3 (1976) 144.
21. Quoted in S.C. Harrex, "A Sense of Identity," 258.
22. Edward Said, *Orientalism* 6.
23. Bill Ashcroft et al. *The Empire Writes Back: Theory and Practice in*

Post-colonial Literatures (London: Routledge, 1989) 110.

24. R.K. Narayan, *The Sweet-Vendor* (London: The Bodley Head, 1967).
25. Santha Rama Rao, *Remember the House* (London: Victor Gollancz, 1956) 98.
26. P.S. Chauhan, "Kamala Markandaya: Sense and Sensibility," 141.
27. Raja Rao, *The Serpent and the Rope* (London: John Murray, 1960).
28. Raja Rao, *Comrade Kirillov* (New Delhi: Orient 1976).
29. Bhabani Bhattacharya, *So Many Hungers* (1947; rpt. Delhi: Vision, 1978).
30. M.Tarinayya, "Two Novels: 2. Bhabani Bhattacharya's *So Many Hungers*," *Indian Literature*, XIII, 113-21.
31. Kamala Markandaya, *Two Virgins* (London: Chatto and Windus, 1973).
32. Bhabani Bhattacharya, *Shadow from Ladakh* (London: W.H. Allen, 1967)
33. Hari Mohan Prasad, "Theme of Exile in Indo-English Novel," *Alien Voice: Perspectives on Commonwealth Literature*, ed. Avadesh K. Srivastava (Lucknow: Print House, 1981) 210-16.
34. *Rough Passage* (Delhi: Three Campus Books, 1977) 17-18.
35. Chaman Nahal, *Into Another Dawn* (New Delhi: Sterling, 1977).
36. Timeri Murari, *The Marriage* (London: Macmillan, 1973).
37. Maria Pfister-Ammenda, "The Problem of Uprooting," in *Uprooting and After . . .*, ed. Charles Zwingmann and Maria Pfister-Ammenda (New York: Springer-Verlag, 1973)10.
38. Hari Mohan Prasad, "Theme of Exile in Indo-English Novel," 213.
39. Bhabani Bhattacharya, *A Dream in Hawaii* (1983; rpt. New Delhi: Vision, n.d.).
40. Benita Parry, *Delusions and Discoveries: Studies on India in the British Imagination 1880-1930* (Delhi: Orient Longman, 1974) 53.
41. E.M. Forster's Introduction to K. R. Srinivasa Iyengar, *Literature and Authorship in India* (London: G. Allen and Unwin, 1943) 7.
42. Jawaharlal Nehru, *The Discovery of India* (London: Meridian Books, 1956) 485.
43. Ruth Prawer Jhabvala, *A Backward Place* (London: John Murray, 1965) 34.
44. Ann Lowry Weir, "Worlds Apart? Feminine Consciousness in Markandaya's *Nectar in a Sieve* and *The Coffer Dams*," *CIEFL Bulletin*, XIII, No. 2 (1977) 71-85.
45. Ananda Sankar Ray, "East-West Dialogue," *Indian Writers in Conference*, ed. N. Ezekiel (Bombay, 1964) 108.

Conclusion

The preceding chapters have brought out the continuing impact of colonization on Indian consciousness. Indo-British contact has been an impelling force behind the rich output of Indian English fiction. It has exerted pressure on the Indian mind, curbing and colouring the vision of the novelist, as he recapitulates the period of painful history and translates that experience into literature. The significant place assigned to the former colonizers—the Britlsh—in Indian Engish fiction even after Independence is itself an indication of the colonial hangover on the Indian mind.

In the Indian English novelist's approach to the former ruler, it has been noticed that invariably the tendency is to view the British in terms of the colonial relationship. The constricting framework of the colonial hierarchy that imparts moral and cultural superiority to the ruler and reduces the ruled to the level of the savage and uncivilized native, has served the novelist remarkably well. It has helped the writer not only to expose the imperial ethos of British India, but also to attack the inflexible stance of present-day Prosperos who impose the authority of their superior technical know-how on the "undeveloped native." Beneath the veneer of liberty and equality, the master-servant attitude lingers, giving rise to modern Prosperos and Calibans: "At the heart of western expansionism was the growing disparity in technologies. . . . And along with the enormous technical superiority and the colonizing experience itself came important psychological instruments of minority rule by foreigners: racism and arrogance on the part of the colonizers and a resulting spirit of inferiority among the colonized."[1]

Those who had imbibed the imperial ethos have been projected in fiction against the backdrop of the Empire as well as the modern era. The Indian novelists have exposed these imperialists who were nourished by the imperial cult and moulded by public school values, and acted out their roles in India. They alienated themselves from the natives and from their own selves, and led an artificial existence centred round the club, confining themselves to a narrow world of ethnic arrogance. The women have been pictured as even more arrogant and race-conscious than the men, closing their minds to any kind of cultural and spiritual influence from India. The picture presented is hardly exaggerated as the account of British life in India presented by English novelists like Forster, Orwell and Kipling vouchsafe.

The anger, protest, and strong emotional prejudice underlying these portraits, have been identified as the typical response of a newly liberated people to their former colonizers. A sharply divergent attitude coexists with this indignation—a generous appreciation of the system, even love for individual representatives of the British Empire, manifesting itself through the portrayal of the liberal-minded humanists and through authorial remarks that declare the novelist's stance. However, the ambivalence in the attitude to the British is perceptible only in isolated instances in R.K. Narayan and Raja Rao. In Narayan, it is seen in the contrast between the quixotic Indian protagonist Sriram and the dignified and benevolent Englishman, Mathieson (*Waiting for the Mahatma*). In Raja Rao it comes out through a comment of the author. "The whiteman I felt, did not bear his burden but the Englishman did . . . there could be good government on earth and decency and a certain nobility of human behaviour, and all because England was[sic]. That I, an Indian who disliked British rule, should feel this only revealed how England was recovering her spiritual destiny." (*The Serpent and the Rope* 199) The polarities are more pronounced in Malgonkar who adopts the role of the decolonizing artist in the *The Devil's Wind*, but presents rather a contemptuous image of India's freedom struggle in *A Bend in the Ganges*. Kai Nicholson remarks about the novel: "The underlying theme in the novel has been a praise for the British Empire in India and by making Debi realise the flaws in the Congress Party, he [Malgonkarl has turned Debi finally against the idea of Indian Independence."[2] Malgonkar reveals through his novels an ungrudging admiration for the British sense of justice, their lack of corruption and their inflexible military code.

Another writer who has shown an unabated interest in the English and has voiced through her novels an equally strong love and hatred for them is Kamala Markandaya. Hers is a world of infinite variety peopled by English men and women, ranging from hardened and arrogant imperialists to the most liberal humanists and even completely decolonised whitemen and women who transcend racial and cultural barriers. Through the mingling of politics, history, and fiction in her novels, she has given vent to her ire against the British as rulers, at the same time creating several "sterling, strong-minded Britishers." Her attitude is best expressed through the words of the character Roshan Merchant in *Some Inner Fury*. According to her, the English were insufferable as overlords; but humane, civilized and charming as individuals. The ruler-ruled relationship or "the overseer and serf" relationship as Kamala Markandaya calls it in *The Coffer Dams*(37), is shown as continuing in the postcolonial era, with the English assuming the role of the masters by virtue of their superior technical knowledge. The persisting animosity between the races has been traced by her to "the noxious emotional cauldron that Britain the ruler and India the ruled had kept on the boil throughout the term of an imposed overlordship to the humiliation of being an undeveloped pauper nation"(*The Coffer Dams*). S.K. Aithal sums up her attitude thus: "She shows deep intimacy with the British as can be seen from her numerous detailed and vivid portraits. She does unmask their hypocrisy and arrogance and related faults in a bold and forthright manner, but does so as someone who deeply loves them."[3]

Nayantara Saghal too has been fluctuating between the emotional polarities of the colonized mentality. But she has adopted a mildly sarcastic tone in the portrayal of the British, which hardly ever shows the bitterness of Kamala Markandaya's darts against the ruling class. The strong emotional undercurrents that had been dormant in the Indian mind, surface through Sahgal's portraits of the British.

Another major problem encountered by the Indian English novelists in the fictionalization of the British has been their inability to bring the linguistic nuances of native English speech into the dialogue of their British characters. Even those novelists who show a remarkable command of the English language as the medium of narration, have found it difficult to capture the rhythm and the cadence of actual English speech. This cannot be viewed as a serious drawback in non-native writers of English. The Indian English novelists should be given credit for using a correct and intelligible variety of English for the dialogues, where the contrast in speech is driven home through the Indianisms of the Indian characters. In some cases when the author tries to make an English character his own mouthpiece, the language tends to become pompous and artificial. Thus in Mulk Raj Anand's *Confession of a Lover*, the loud proclamations of anti-imperialistic sentiments by Prof. Henry, Marmaduke Pickthall and Rev. Williams have been cast in the same propagandist style. To provide a few specimens,

Prof. Henry: I am for the wisdom of the Rishis of the Vedas and the Upanishads. I am with Mrs. Annie Besant. I am against Imperialism, the White Man's burden-stuff and Western civilization, which has staged a giant world war. (65)

Rev. Williams: Money is the Whiteman's God. Exploitation is his religion. They have sapped the energy of the people everywhere! Climate does the rest. And the old bad habits of the people! (186)

The language used by the British characters in *The Bubble* is, however, more natural and easy, which might be due to the sense of freedom that Anand experienced when he did not feel obliged to portray them against the Indian settings. K. Nagarajan's English is full of stale idioms and cliches and it even forms a deliberate device for the characterization of his pompous narrator. But he has taken care to keep them away from the speech of his English characters. Though Nagarajan suavely drops the comment that Cole is an Englishman endowed with "a happy gift of phrase" (*Chronicies of Kedaram* 92) we are relieved to find the language employed free from the stylistic naivete of Gokarna Sastri's speech. In B. Rajan's *The Dark Dancer*, the echoes of Eliot that pervade the narrator's language have been carefully avoided in the language used by the English character, Cynthia. Rajan has succeeded in making language blend and fuse with character and the contrast between the independent arrogant English lady and the quiet and dignified Kamala is very well conveyed through the language put into their mouths. Cynthia's terse and assertive utterancess like "A plane is not drawn on paper. It's drawn by the difference it makes to millions of people"[4] and "Don't let him [Krishnan] sink himself in being Indian" (73) have a bold and haughty tone as against the sedate, mature and even poetic style of Kamala's speech. To quote one example, "It's in all of us, in the many many years of occupation, submission to the state, obedience to the family, every inch of our lives completely calculated, every step down to the relief of the grave. And if we wanted to protest, there was only the pitiless discipline of nonviolence." (74) Here the difference in speech is an authorial device for characterization.

The Taylors in Khushwant Singh's *I Shall Not Hear the Nightingale* speak a natural style of English, with an occasional Indian word thrown in, which was quite commonplace among the British in India. Thus we have John Taylor remark: "The English are his Mai-Bap, Father-Mother when they are about: when they are not, he is more himself." (218) Chaman Nahal and Abbas have managed to acquire a smooth flow and ease in writing conversational passages for their English characters. Nahal has succeeded in building up warm and friendly moments of emotional rapport between his English and Indian characters through fine dialogue. The conversation between Kenneth Ashby and Sunil in *The Crown and the Loincloth* is an instance. (388-89)

Malgonkar has made the subtle difference between the pucca sahib's speech and the dialect of the Anglo-Indian race, one of the thematic concerns of his novel, *Combat of Shadows*. Henry Winton displays the typical Englishman's embarrassment and uneasiness when Ruby Miranda indulges in expressions common to the Anglo-Indian race, like "he was really jay!" (102) "Give's a fag" (99) etc. When she pronounces "thanks" correctly, Winton is astonished at her overcoming "this almost insurmountable linguistic handicap of her race." (149) When she calls Christmas "exmas," Henry muses: "O Pygmalion! How difficult, how heart-breaking it was to unlearn a way of speech! So much more difficult than learning an altogether new language." (187) Malgonkar's novels afford several examples of perfectly turned-out conversations between English and Indian characters, revealing "his command of the medium comparable to that of a gifted native speaker of English."[5]

As an expatriate writer, Kamala Markandaya has become so familiar with native English speech that it is the language used by her Indian characters that has provoked criticism. Margaret P. Joseph comments: "It is very significant that the novelist is far more successful in rendering the conversation of Sir Arthur and Lady Mary Copeland. Their speech is realistic, as the Indian character's speech is not."[6] The language of the country that she has made her home has become part of her and it seems to be difficult for her to recapture the rhythm and clang of Indian local speech.

Though a resident writer, Nayantara Sahgal's language responds to the rhythm of native English speech and her English characters converse with natural fluency. By making Rose a cockney speaker from England her protagonist in *Rich Like Us*, she has attempted something unprecedented in the Indian English novel. She has succeeded in rendering quite effectively the broad accent, rambling tone and the embarrassing mannerisms of cockney speech and making it the cause of the incompatibility between Rose and Ram, and the enmity of Dev. To cite a few examples: "Don't long-time-ago me. What you call entreprenner-ship now, or however you pronounce it, is one minute you are nothing and the next minute you're an enter-prenner and a bloomin' millionaire." (10) Again, "And I suppose it would be all the same to you if a bulldozer come along and levelled this 'ouse and you were given Compungsaytion. Compungsaytion! 'Ow do we know it was enough compungsaytion?" (13) The author's intention in making a cockney-speaking English lady the victim of the Emergency is rather vague. Yet, one has to admit that Nayantara Sahgal has made a daring experiment with language for here she encroaches into the dialectical variations of native English speech, which non-native speakers seldom attempt to present.

The brief survey of the Indian English novelists' use of alien speech as a device for characterization, is intended only to show how language has not become a barrier in the effective portrayal of English characters. The need to come to terms with the imperial experience has proved to be the motivating force behind the portrayal of the British in post-Independence fiction. Though the distance of time has lessened the bitterness of the post-Independence novelists and given him greater psychological insight into the working of the imperial psyche, he still tends to place the British in the imperialist group or in the anti-imperialist class. The anathema for the former who had been instruments of oppression, has found expression in the idealization of the later. An implied value system has been found operating in Indian English fiction, invariably glorifying the English man who has rejected imperial values and sought identification with Indian cultural and spiritual mores. To the post-Independence writer, nobility and virtue have thus become synonymous with an anti-imperialistic attitude and sympathy for the Indian cause. The Indian English novelists have shown remarkable insight into the problem of alienation suffered by them, because of their inability to identify themselves with the imperial culture and the natives' reluctance to accept them. The predicament of these nowheremen has been brought home with remarkable poignancy by most of the Indian English novelists. The sensitive perception and sympathy in the portrayal of these unhoused beings have lent them a rare brilliance totally absent in the characterization of the imperialists.

This itself can be viewed as a decolonizing device employed by the newly independent Indian writer. An unmistakable note of protest is audible through the entire range of post-Independence Indian fiction in English, manifesting itself in a tendency to demythify the Empire and its values, to reject received images of history and define and glorify one's own cultural and spiritual mores. The process has been found operating in Indian English fiction through demythification of British heroes and the glorification of those who have rejected the imperial cult. It involves the upholding of Indian womanhood and the reinstating of national heroes. The exemplary way in which Malgonkar, Nahal, Kamala Markandaya, Abbas, Timeri Murari, Nayantara Sahgal and Salman Rushdie have effected this, establishes their identity with postcolonial writers all over the world. Helen Tiffin remarks: "such establishing or rehabilitation of an independent identity involves the radical interrogation and fracturing of these imposed European perspectives and their systematic (in Wasserman's sense) replacement of an alternative vision, or the attack on or erosion of the very notion of system and hegemonic control itself.[7]

The task of restructuring "the active sense of self"[8] which has been destroyed by cultural imperialism, has been mainly achieved in fiction by re-enacting the cultural encounters between Indians and the British and bringing out through fictional reconstructs, the unmistakable superiority of the East. The outright condemnation of Anglophilism, the exposition of ineffective attempts at total assimilation and identification as in inter-racial marriages, and the portrayal of the existential angst of those caught in a cultural limbo, are the methods that have been adopted by the Indian English novelists to proclaim the need to discover one's roots and to seek one's identity. Self-realization in most cases is achieved through a return to India's spiritual wealth. Thus we find that Rajan's protagonist returns to the virtuous Kamala from the glamorous Cynthia; T.N. Murari's Kim opts for India and its values; Anita Desai's Adit and Sarah return to India, leaving a hostile Britain; Nahal's Ashby receives spiritual insights from his friend Sunil; Markandaya's Valmiki, Helen, Mackendrik, Tully and Mrs. Pearl turn to India for spiritual sustenance; and Ramaswami comes to India on a spiritual quest seeking his Guru. The message seems to be what Nayantara Sahgal has expressed through the title of her novel, *Rich Like Us*, proclaiming the superiority of India's spiritual riches against the poverty of the material wealth of the western countries.

Language itself has been made to function as a powerful decolonizing device by the Indian English novelists. Deliberate efforts to Indianize the alien medium chosen for narration have been identified in the works of all the major Indian English novelists. As William Walsh remarks, their achievement involves "hacking out an area of freedom and manouvre from a choked jungle of inheritance," in order to construct "a fresh identity,"[9] and to achieve a fusion of Indian thought with the English language.

The concept of Indian English as the medium for narration is well expounded by Raja Rao: "The tempo of Indian life must be fused into our English expression, even as the tempo of American or Irish life has gone into the making of theirs. We, in India think quickly, and we talk quickly, when we move, we move quickly."[10]

Like Synge who brings in the authentic ring of the speech of Aaron Island into his plays, or O'Neill who dabbles in the dialect of the downtrodden Negroes, Raja Rao has captured the rich rhythm of Indian speech into the very structure of his languages, making it unique and highly individualistic. Anand has resorted to a liberal use of Punjabi swear words and literal translations of Punjabi terms into his English. This is a marked feature of the dialogue of his Indian characters. Though he struggles to keep the language used in the narrative part of his fiction correct and idiomatic, the language continues to be aggressively Indian. M.K. Naik comments: "It has certain distinct peculiarities which makes its Indian origins unmistakably clear. Its oriental opulence, its passion to use more words than are absolutely necessary, its fast, galloping tempo, typical of the speech of a race which perhaps talks too fast, too loud and too much."[11]

In the hands of these writers English is shorn of its alienness and made Indian. R.K. Narayan has achieved this with remarkable ease, in a quite unobtrusive manner. His language is disarmingly simple, stripped of all embellishment and perfectly suited to the directness and authenticity of the vision he wants to convey. Language and the theme have been blended so well that the Indianness of the locale, of the theme, character and philosophy make the English he uses more and more Indian. Meenakshi Mukerjee speaks of "Narayan's artlessness"[12] which really conceals art.

Chaman Nahal and Khushwant Singh also hail from the Punjab and have enriched their English with the flavour of Punjabi. As in the novels of Mulk Raj Anand, their pages are also littered with Punjabi swear words and expressions. Nahal has been able to impart the vigour, strength and savour of Punjabi life to his styles. Occasionally the attempt at Indianization is carried to extreme extents by these writers, with a generous use of obscene expressions drawn from the local tongue. It is doubtful whether this device creates the desired impression as it often seems to result only in producing a nauseating effect.

Though B. Rajan's style in *The Dark Dancer* has been said to be academic and literary with echoes from Eliot pervading the novel, the imagery is unmistakably Indian. The title itself refers to Lord Shiva, *The Dark Dancer*, who is engaged in the perpetual dance of creation and destruction. The language as well as the theme is infused with the spirit of the *Gita*, which makes it obviously Indian.

English language has become a flexible medium in the hands of writers like Malgonkar and Kamala Markandaya. They effortlessly bend and modulate the language so as to convey the local colour of the fictional settings. Thus Malgonkar brings in the rich flavour of Indian rural life when he speaks of the feud between "The Big House" and "The Little House," and the "Pooja" and Aji's superstitious ceremonies, in *A Bend in the Ganges*. The richness and variety of life in India is brought home through the use of Indian words—"chota-pegs" and "ekdum" in the speech of the sahibs and revolutionary slogans of "chale jao" from plantation labours. The heavy drawl of the Bengali Police inspector, "We bheel habh to separate the leaders farst"[13] also suggests the ingenuity of the writer who wants to make the language his own.

Though Kamala Markandaya does not seem to have made a deliberate attempt to Indianize her English, she too has let in a lot of local colour when the setting has demanded it. Thus in a novel like *Nectar in a Sieve* or *Two Virgins*, any passage chosen at random, brings in the spirit of an Indian village. "Krishna was a personification of God, cried Amma, are you daring to compare him with this gutter lout? Who said I was, I'm only saying, said Lalitha." (*Two Virgins* 20) The rhythm of local speech is virtually caught into the English translation. Expressions like "masala dosai," "puttani" etc. lend the Indian touch to the language of *A Handful of Rice*. Through a language richly laden with the fragrance of local colour, and through symbols and images evocative of the Indian background, she makes her English distinct from native English speech. Deliberate experimentation is absent in Nayantara Sahgal and Anita Desai.

The attempt at decolonizing the language takes the form of a deliberate assault in the works of G.V. Desani and Salman Rushdie. Desani's protagonist, H. Hatterr exists on the fringe of three cultures, being the offering of a European merchant seaman and a Malay lady, brought up in India. He claims that he has gone completely Indian "to an extent few pure non-Indian blood sahib fellers have done." (*All About H. Hatterr* 33). A polyglot style of language is used, which suits the hybrid nature of the hero. About the language used by Desani, Anthony Burgess remarks: "It is what may be termed whole language, in which philosophical terms, the colloquialisms of Calcutta and London, Shakespearean archaisms, bazar whinings, quick spiels, reference to the HIndu pantheon, the jargon of Indian litigation, and shrill babu irritability seethe together. It is not pure English, it is like the English of Shakespeare, Joyce and Kipling, gloriously impure."[14] Desani has freed his language from the conventions of orthodox English and uses a variety of babu, sahib, cockney, pidgin, learned, oratorical and rhetorical idioms. Hatterr's adventures are arranged in the format of a Hindu treatise under seven titles following the "digest," "instruction," "presumption," "life-encounter" pattern, showing a kind of dialectical progression from illusion, through defeat to enlightenment.

Desani's virtuosity as a literary artist is seen in the dialectical variants employed for Hatterr, Bannerji and Beliram-Rambeli. Hatterr's colloquial style is a mixture of the slang used by Anglo-Indians of little formal education and "pidgin and bastard-brand Hindustani." (*All About H. Hatterr* 82) Hatterr tells Bannerji: "Bannerji, don't worry, old feller. I won't take the drastic step. To hell with the sahibs! Not an anna-piece for the drink-chits! Not a ruddy chip! Damme, I will go Indian!" (47) Hatterr's encounter with the sage who was a dealer in second hand clothes, calls forth the following speech: "I spit at thy unwashed beard! I spill dust at thee! I shall expose thee and thy crafty brother! Son of a merciless cheetah! Tyrant! Pathos-promoter! Unspeakable materialist! Shame upon Hindus!" (59) Hatterr refers to his own "dialect" on more than one occasion. It is an idiom of his own creation.

Bannerji's style is intended to expose the tendency of the educated Indian Anglophiles, who quote profusely from Shakespeare and revel in universals and generalizations. A typical passage reads thus: "The Bard has said, who steals my purse, steals trash! Nevertheless, Mr. H. Hatterr, ahead of us is Double, double, toil and trouble; fire burn and cauldron bubble! I am not a sob-sister, but excuse me, the situation reminds me of Hamlet. To be! But firstly, let us be calm, honest Iago." (114) The Babu English used by him and Beliram is the artificial and stiff variety of English, generously sprinkled with wrong usages, characteristic of colonial speech. The jargon of Hindu spiritual and religious literature is also liberally used—very often in half-serious, half-comic style. Her English language is dislodged from its imperial centre and becomes the medium to assert the author's essential Indianness through original concepts, principles, usage and style.

The experimentation with language as a decolonizing device is equally bold in Salman Rushdie's *Midnight's Children*. Rushdie himself has spoken about the current waves of decolonizing in erstwhile colonies where "English no longer an English language, grows from many roots; and those whom it once colonised are carving out large territories within the language for themselves."[15] Rushdie recognizes with admiration how G.V. Desani has "bent and kneaded" English "until it spoke in an authentically Indian voice."[16] In Rushdie, the wide range of characters, drawn from diferent social classes have their social and class hierarchy and their cultural background. There are specimens of mission-school English, club-jargon, vernacular idioms and Goanese English—all the varieties prevalent in India. Using translations that retain the touch of the vernacular, Rushdie gives the flavour of the local language used by the characters—Hindi or Urdu. The narrative voice starting in the traditional way with "I was born in the city of Bombay . . . once upon a time," draws frequent parallels between national and domestic life and occasionally aquires breathless haste to indicate the quick succession of events in the national scene or to suggest the confusion in the narrator-protagonist's brain. Then Rushdie's protagonist pours out long narratives at one go, in large paragraphs without full stops; but with capitals to show where the full stop ought to have been. Symbols, repetitive images and compound forms coined by clubbing words together, are used profusely to bring together people and incidents spread out over a long period of time. To quote a typical passage,

> Years ticking away—and my inheritance grows, because now I have the mythical golden teeth of the boatman Tai, and his brandy bottle which foretold my father's alcoholic dzinns; I have Ilse Lubin for suicide and pickled snakes for virility; I have Tai-for-changelessness opposed to Adam-for-progress; and I have too, the odours of the unwashed boatman which drove my grandparents south, and made Bombay a possibility. (124)

Rushdie has sabotaged all the rules of English grammar and syntax and, wrestles with the language, making it move with an amazing speed and fluency, combining in itself, elements of magic and fantasy and stark realism. William Walsh remarks: "All this is indelibly stamped into unity by a powerful personality, which wrestles the language and the fiction down and masters it to serve a large purpose, namely the personification of India and the realization of Indian life."[17] The language is uniquely Indian, completely liberated from imperial ontology and acquiring a strength and astonishing energy produced by the fiction between the instinct for flow and control, looseness and tightness.

An important feature of the fiction of the seventies and eighties, seems to be the increased occurrence of decolonized whitemen. They can be a pointer to the writers' own gradual release from the colonial hang-over. Tully in *The Pleasure City* is a typical decolonized being. Tully, the progeny of imperial ancestors who built pleasure palaces in India, reveals a totally liberated mind that can lose itself in the natural beauty of an Indian fishing village and even establish a perfect emotional rapport with a fisher boy of the village, who had received the legacy of the English language from an old missionary couple who have lived in the village. Tully thus combines in him the past and the future. The small group of decolonized Englishmen in fiction suggests the possibility of the British being viewed apart from the colonial framework and its inhibiting values, in the future. Through them, the Indian English novelists have uniformly envisaged the West turning to the East, in a quest for spiritual mores and human values, in a depressingly materialistic world. They are, however, not content to counteract with the British on a level of parity, but display a genuine eagerness to tilt the balance and establish the essential superiority of the east. These can be recognized as concerted efforts on the part of postcolonial writers to wrest language and theme from the cultural hegemony of the dominant European centre.

The Indian English novelists' attempt to re-evaluate colonial experience and the relationship between the Indians and British forms a part of his endeavour to strike against the imperial centre. The dominant feature of post-Independance fiction—the displacement of the idols of the Empire by national heroes, the appropriating of frames of power, the reversal of the colonial perspective and even the liberation of the linguistic medium from the emotional tags of the colonial authority—establish its oneness with other postcolonial literatures.

NOTES

1. Viney Kirpal, *The Third World Novel of Expatriation* (New Delhi: Sterling, 1989) 20
2. Kai Nicholson, *A Presentation of Social Problems in the Indo-Anglian and the Anglo-Indian Novels* (Bombay: Jaico, 1972) 158.
3. S.K. Aithal, "Indo-British Encounter in Kamala Markandaya's Novels," *Journal of South Asian Literature*, 22, No. 2 (Summer-Fall 1987) 58.
4. B. Rajan, *The Dark Dancer* (New York: Simon and Schuster,1958) 72.
5. K. Ayyappa Paniker, "Manohar Malgonkar: The Predictable Posture," *Indian Literature in English* (Madras: Anu Chitra, 1989) 66.
6. Margaret P. Joseph, *Kamala Markandaya* (New Delhi: Arnold-Heinemann, 1980) 209.
7. Helen Tiffin, "Post-Colonialism, Post-Modernism and the Rehabilitation of Post-Colonial History," *JCL*, 23, 1 (1988) 172.
8. Bill Ashcroft, Gareth Griffith and Helen Tiffin, "Introduction," *The Empire Writes Back: Theory and Cractise in Post-Colonial Literature* (London: Routledge, 1989) 9.
9. William Walsh, "The Indian Sensibility in English," *Awakened Conscience*, ed. C.D. Narasimhaiah (New Delhi: Sterling, 1978) 65.
10. Raja Rao, "Foreword," *Kanthapura* (1938; rpt. New York: New Directions, 1963) 7.
11. M.K. Naik, *Mulk Raj Anand* (London: Arnold-Heinemann, 1973) 164.
12. Meenakshi Mukkerjee, *Twice-Born Fiction* (1971; rpt. New Delhi: Arnold-Heinemann, 1974) 193.
13. Manohar Malgonkar, *Combat of Shadows* (1962; rpt. New Delhi: Orient Paperbacks, 1968) 193.
14. Anthony Burgess, "Introduction," *All About H. Hatterr* (London: The Bodley Head, 1970) 10.
15. Salman Rushdie, "The Empire Writes Back with a Vengeance," *The Times* (3rd July 1982).
16. *Ibid.*
17. William Walsh, "India and the Novel," *The New Pelican Guide to English Literature: The Present*, ed. Boris Ford (1956; England: Penguin, 1984) vol. 8, 245-60.

Bibliography

Primary Sources

Abbas, K.A. *Inquilab*. New Delhi: Indian Paperbacks, 1977.
_____. *The World is My Village*. 1983; rpt. New Delhi: Ajanta, 1984.
Anand, Mulk Raj. *Seven Summers*. London: Hutchinson's International Authors, 1951.
_____. *Private Life of an Indian Prince*. Great Britain: The Bodley Head,1953.
_____. *Morning Face*. 1968; rpt. India: Arnold Heinemann, 1976
_____. *Confession of a Lover*. Delhi: Arnold Heinemann, 1976.
_____. *The Bubble*. New Delhi: Arnold Heinemann, 1980.
Desai, Anita. *Bye-Bye, Blackbird*. Delhi: Hind Pocket Books,1970.
Desani, G.V. *All About H. Hatterr*. 1948; rpt. New York: Farrar, Strauss and Giroux,1970.
Malgonkar, Manohar, *Distant Drum*. 1960; rpt. Bombay; Asia, 1970
_____. *Combat of Shadows*. 1962; rpt. Delhi: Orient Paperbacks, 1968.
_____. *The Princes*. 1963; rpt. Delhi: Orient Paperbacks, 1970.
_____. *A Bend in the Ganges*. 1964; rpt. London: Pan Books,1967.
Malgonkar, Manohar. *The Devil's Wind*. London: Hamish Hamilton,1972
_____. *The Bandicoot Run*. Delhi: Vision Books, 1982.
Markandaya, Kamala. *Nectar in a Sieve*. 1954; rpt. Bombay: Jaico, 1971.
_____. *Some Inner Fury*. 1957; rpt. Bombay: Jaico, 1971.
_____. *A Silence of Desire*. 1960; rpt. London: Four Square, 1966.
_____. *Possession*. 1963; rpt. Bombay: Jaico, 1984.
_____. *A Handful of Rice*. 1966; rpt. New Delhi: Orient Paperbacks, 1985.
_____. *The Coffer Dams*. London: Hamish Hamilton, 1969.
_____. *The Nowhere Man*. 1972; rpt. London: Allan Lane, 1973.
_____. *Two Virgins*. 1973; rpt. London: Chatto and Windus, 1974
_____. *The Golden Honeycomb*. New York: Thomas Y. Cromwell, 1977.
_____. *Pleasure City*. London: Chatto and Windus, 1982.
Murari, Timeri. *The Imperial Agent*. Great Britain: New English Library, 1987.
_____. *Last Victory*. Hodder and Stoughton: New English Library, 1989.
Nagarajan, K. *Chronicles of Kedaram*. Bombay: Asia, 1961.
Nahal, Chaman, *Azadi*. New Delhi: Arnold Heinemann, 1975.
_____. *The English Queens*. New Delhi: Vision Books, 1979.
_____. *The Crown and the Lioncloth*. Delhi: Vikas, 1981.
Narayan, R.K. *Waiting for the Mahatma*. 1955: rpt. Mysore: Indian Thought Publications, 1964.
Rajan, Balachandra. *The Dark Dancer*. New York: Simon and Schuster, 1958.
Rushdie, Salman. *Midnight's Children*. 1980; rpt. New York: Avon Books, 1982.
Sahgal, Nayantara. *A Time to be Happy*. 1957; rpt. Delhi: Sterling, 1975.
_____. *A Situation in New Delhi*. New Delhi: Himalaya Books, 1977.
_____. *Rich Like Us*. London: Heinemann, 1985.
_____. *Plans for Departure*. London: Heinemann, 1986.
Singh, Khushwant. *I Shall Not Hear the Nightingale*. 1959; rpt. Bombay: India Books House, 1979.

Secondary Sources

Achebe, Chinua. "The Truth of Fiction." *The Literary Half-Yearly*, 22, 2 (July 1981) 2-15.
Afzal-Khan, Fawzia. "Myth Debunked: Genre and Ideology in Rushdie's *Midnight's Children* and *Shame*." *The Journal of Indian Writing in English*, 14, No. 1 (Jan. 1986) 49-59.
Aithal, S. Krishnamoorthy. "Inter-racial and Inter-cultural Relationships in Anita Desai's *Bye-Bye, Blackbird*." *Commonwealth Novel in English*, 3, No.1 (Spring-Summer 1984) 101-7.
_____. "Indo-British Encounter in Kamala Markandaya's Novels." *Journal of South Asian*

Literature, 22, No. 2 (Summer-Fall 1987) 49-59.

Alcock, Peter. "James K. Baxter and the *Terror of History*: The Decolonisation of a New Zealander." *Awakened Conscience*. Ed. C.D. Narasimhaiah. Delhi: Sterling, 1978, 92-110.

Allen, Charles. *Raj: A Scrapbook of British India 1877-1947*. Andre Deutsch: Indian Book Company, 1977.

Alter, Robert. *Motives for Fiction*. Cambridge: Harvard University Press, 1984.

Amrithnayagam, Guy. *Writers in East-West Encounter*. London: Macmillan, 1982.

Amur, G.S. *Manohar Malgonkar*. London: Arnold-Heinemann, 1973.

_____. Ed. *Indian Readings in Commonwealth Literature*. New Delhi: Sterling, 1985.

_____. "Forbidden Fruits," *Indian Literature*, 6, 30 (Nov-Dec. 1987) 49-62.

Anderson, G. and M. Subedar. *The Expansion of British India, 1818-58*. London: G. Bell, 1921.

Anjaneyulu, D. "Indian Writing in English from K.S. Venkataramani to Kamala Markandaya." *Triveni*, 22 (April 1963) 19-28.

Appasamy, S.P. "*The Golden Honeycomb*: A Saga of Princely Life in India by Kamala Markandaya." *The Journal of Indian Writing in English*, 6, 2 (July 1978) 56-63.

Arora, Nina, "*Rich Like Us*: A Note." *The Commonwealth Review*, 1, 1 (1989) 130-32.

Atkins, John. *George Orwell*. 1954; rpt. Great Britain: John Calder, 1971.

Ashcroft, Bill, et al. *The Empire Writes Back: Theory and Practice in Post-Colonial Literature*. London: Routledge, 1989.

Banerjie, Ashutosh. "Narrative Technique in *Midnight's Children*." *Commonwealth Review*, 1, 2 (1990) 23-32.

Barr, Pat. *The Memsahibs: The Women of Victorian India*. London: Martin Secker and Warburg, 1976.

Basu, Aparna. *Imperialism, Nationalism and Regionalism in Canadian and Modern Indian History*. Delhi: Manchar, 1989.

Beliappa, Meena, "East-West Encounter: Indian Women Writers of Fiction in English." *The Literary Criterion*, 7, 3 (Winter 1966), 18-27.

Bennett, George. *The Concept of Empire: Burke to Atlee, 1774-1947*. London: Plack, 1953.

Benians, E.A., et al., ed. *The Cambridge History of the British Empire*. Vol. 3. *The Empire—Commonwealth 1870-1919*. Cambridge: Cambridge Univ. Press, 1959.

Bergonzi, Bernard. *The Contemporary English Novel*. London: Edward Arnold, 1979.

Berry, Ralph. *The Shakespearian Metaphor: Studies in Language and Form*. London: Macmillan, 1978.

Best, Marshall, A. *The Contempary Novelists*. Ed. James Vinson. London: St. James Press, 1973.

Bakhtiyar, Iqbal, ed. *The Novel in Modern India*. Bombay: The PEN, All India Centre, 1964.

Bhatt, P.N. "R.K. Narayan and Politics." *Triveni*, 50, 1 (April-June 1981) 42-45.

Bhattacharya, Bhabani. "The Hybrid Indo-Anglian Novel." *The Indian PEN*, 21 March 1955, 70-72.

Bhattacharya, B. *Glimpses of Indian History*. New Delhi: Sterling, 1976.

Blaber, Ron. "Salman Rushdie: *Midnight's Children*" *The CRNLE Review Journal*, 2 (1982), 33-35.

Bowle, John. *The Imperial Achievement: The Rise and Transformation of the British Empire*. London: Secker and Warburg, 1974.

Brata, Sasthi. *India: Labyrinths in the Lotusland*. New York: William Morrow, 1985.

Bruce-Jones, Mark. *The Viceroys of India*. London: Constable, 1982.

Calderwood, James L. and Harold E. Toliver. *Perspectives on Fiction*. New York: Oxford Univ. Press, 1968.

Calmer, John. *E.M. Forster: The Personal Voice*. London: Routledge and Kegan Paul, 1975.

Chaddha, Ramesh. "*Heat and Dust* and *The Coffer Dams*: A Comparative Study." *Comparative Literature*. Ed. R.K. Dhawan. New Delhi: Bahri, 1987, 146-52.

Chand, Tara. *History of the Freedom Movement in India*. 1967; rpt. New Delhi: Publications Division, 1983.

Chandrasekhar, K.R. "East and West in the Novels of Kamala Markandaya." *Critical Essays on Indian Writing in English*. Ed. M.K. Naik. Dharwar. Karnataka Univ., 1968,

62-85.

Chaudhuri, Nirad C. *The Continent of Circe*. 1965; rpt. Bombay: Jaico, 1978.

Chauhan, P.S. "Kamala Markandaya: Sense and Sensibility." *Literary Criterion*, 12, 2 & 3 (1976), 134-47.

Chew, Shirley. "Fictions of Princely States and Empire." *Ariel*, 17, 3 (July 1984) 103-17.

Churchill, Winston S. *History of the English Speaking Peoples*. Vol. III. *The Age of Revolution*. London Cassell, 1957.

Conto, Maria. "The Raj in Fiction and Film." *Narrative Forms and Transformations*. Eds. Sudhakar Marathe and Meenakshi Mukherjee. Delhi: Chanakya, 1986, 120-36.

Cowasjee, Saros. *So Many Freedoms: A Study of the Major Fiction of Mulk Raj Anand*. Delhi: Oxford Univ. Press, 1977.

_____. Review of *The Confession of a Lover*. *The Journal of Commonwealth Literature*, 12,1 (Aug. 1977) 75-76.

_____. "Mulk Raj Anand: The Fusion of History and Fiction." *The Toronto South Asian Review*, 6,1 (Summer 1987) 39-48.

_____. "Mulk Raj Anand's *The Sword and the Sickle*." *World Literature Written in English*, 14, 2 (Nov. 1975) 269-77.

Davies, Bryan M. "British and Indian Images of India." *Ariel*, 1, 4 (Oct. 1970) 48-52.

Dell, Ethel M. *The Way of an Eagle*. London: T. Fisher Unwin, 1914.

_____. "The Safety Curtain." *The Safety Curtain and Other Stories*. London: T. Fisher Unwin, 1917.

Derrett, M.E. *The Modern Indian Novel in English: A Comparative Approach*. Bruxelles: University Libre de Bruxulles, 1966.

Desai, K. Shantinath. "Indian Writing in English: The Predicament of Marginality," *The Indian Journal of English Studies*, 26 (1987) 29-39.

Detaller, Roger. *The Plain Man and the Novel*. London: Thomas Nelson, 1940.

Dhawan, R.K., ed. *Explorations in Modern Indo-English Fiction*. Delhi: Bahri, 1982.

_____, ed. *Three Contemporary Novelists*. New Delhi: Classical, 1985.

_____, ed. *Commonwealth Fiction*. 3 Vols. New Delhi: Classical, 1988.

_____. "The Artist as Historian: Some New Writers." *Commonwealth Fiction*. Vol. 3, 227-37.

Dobree, Bonamy. *Rudyard Kipling*. London: Longman's. 1967.

Doctor, Geeta. "Tales from the Raj Retold." *Express Magazine*, 22 Jan. 1989, 5.

Dwivedi, A.N. "The Dark Dancer: A Critique." *Studies in Indian Fiction in English*. Ed. G.S. Balarama Gupta. Gulbarga: JIWE Publishers, 1987, 68-76.

Edwardes, Michael. *Battles of the Indian Mutiny*. London: B.T. Batsford, 1963.

_____. *Glorious Sahibs: The Romantic as Empire-builder 1799-1838*. London: Eyre and Spottiswoode, 1968.

_____. *Raj*. London: Pan Books, 1969.

_____. *Bound to Exile: The Victorians in India*. London: Sidgwick and Jackson, 1969.

_____. *A Season in Hell: The Defence of the Lucknow Residency*. Great Britain: Hamish Hamilton, 1973.

_____. *The Myth of the Mahatma: Gandhi, the British and the Raj*. Great Britain: Constable, 1986.

Fannon, Frantz. *The Wretched of the Earth*. London: Macgibbon and Kee, 1965.

Feiling, Keith. *A History of England*. London: Macmillan, 1966.

Fernando, Lloyd. "A Note from the Third World towards the Redefinition of Culture." *Awakened Conscience: Studies in Commonwealth Literature*. Ed. C.D. Narasimhaiah. 227-38.

Feuchtwagner, Lion. *The House of Desdemona or the Laurels and Limitations of Historical Fiction*. Detroit: Wayne State University Press, 1963.

Fieldhouse, D.K. *Colonialism 1870-1945: An Introduction*. London: Weidenfeld and Nicolson, 1981.

Fisher, Marlene. "Mulk Raj Anand's Confessional Novels." *The Journal of Indian Writing in English*, 4, 2 (July 1976) 39-45.

Ford, Boris. *The New Pelican Guide to English Literature: The Present*. Vol. 8. 1983; rpt. England: Penguin, 1986.

Forster, E.M. "Reflections on India, I—Too Late?" *The Nation and the Atheaneum*, 30 (21 Jan. 1922) 612-16.

_____. *A Passage to India.* London: Arnold, 1924.
_____. "Notes on the English Character." *Abinger Harvest.* London: Edward Arnold, 1936, 3-14.
Gondal, Yogesh. "Unreal Situation." *The Indian Literary Review,* 1, 4 (Aug. 1978) 42-43.
Goodwin, K.L. *National Identity.* London: Heinemann, 1970.
Gooneratne, Yasmine. "Traditional Elements in the Fiction of Kamala Markandaya, R.K. Narayan and Ruth Prawer Jhabvala." *World Literature Written in English,* 15, 1 (April 1976) 121-34.
Gordon, Ian, ed. *Undiscovered Country: The New Zealand Stories of Katherine Mansfield.* London: Longman's, 1974.
Gowda, H.H. Anniah, ed. *The Colonial and Neo-Colonial Encounters in Commonwealth Literature.* Mysore: University of Mysore, 1983.
Goyal, Bhagwat S. *Culture and Commitment: Aspects of Indian Literature in English.* Meerut: Shalabh, 1984.
Greenberger, Allen J. *The British Image of India: A Study in the Literature of Imperialism 1880-1960.* London: Oxford Univ. Press, 1969.
Griffiths, Gareth. *A Double Exile: African and West Indian Writing Between Two Cultures.* London: Marion Boyares, 1978.
Gupta, Neena. "The Memsahibs of Anglo-Indian Fiction." *The Literary Half-Yearly,* 29, 1 (Jan. 1988) 55-67.
Harcourt, A.F.P. *The Peril of the Sword.* London: Skeffington, 1903.
Harrex, S.C. "A Sense of Identity: The Novels of Kamala Markandaya." *The Journal of Commonwealth Literature,* 6, 1 (Jan. 1971) 65-78.
_____. "The Novels of Kamala Markandaya." *Indian Literature,* 18, 2 (1975) 36-43.
_____. "Dancing in the Dark: Balachandra Rajan and T.S. Eliot." *World Literature Written in English,* 14, 2 (Nov. 1975) 310-21.
_____. *The Fire and the Offering: The English Language Novel of India 1935-1970.* Vol. I. Calcutta: Writers Workshop, 1977.
_____. "The Novel as Gesture: *All About H. Hatterr.*" *Awakened Conscience.* New Delhi: Sterling, 1978, 73-85.
Harvey, W.J. *Character and the Novel.* 1965; rpt. U.S.A.: Cornell Univ. Press, 1966.
Hasib, Ahmad. *The Novels of Khwaja Ahmed Abbas: A Study in His Art and Vision.* Delhi: Seema, 1987.
Hemenway, Stephen Ignatius. *The Novel of India.* Calcutta: Writers Workshop, 1975.
Hilbert, Christopher. *The Great Mutiny: India 1858-1978.* 1978; rpt. England: Penguin, 1982.
Hughes, Thomas. *Tom Brown's Schooldays.* London: Ward, Lock, 1947.
Hutchins, Francis G. *The Illusion of Permanence: British Imperialism in India.* Princeton: Princeton Univ. Press, 1967.
Indira, C.T. "The Dark Dancer: Characterisation, Images and Meaning in the Novel." *The Commonwealth Novel in English,* 1, 2 (July 1982) 147-55.
Islam, Shamsul. *Chronicles of the Raj.* London: Macmillan, 1979.
Iyengar, K.R. Srinivasa. *Literature and Authorship in India.* London: George Allen and Unwin, 1943.
_____. "The Lure of India." *The Commonwealth Pen: An Introduction to the Literature of the British Commonwealth.* Ed. Alan L. McLeod. Ithaca: The Cornwall Univ. Press, 1961, 115-41.
_____. *Indian Writing in English.* 1962, 5 eds. New Delhi: Sterling, 1985.
_____. Review of *Morning Face. Kakatiya Journal of English Studies.* 3,1 (Spring 1977) 241-43.
_____. "The Colonial and Neo-Colonial Encounters in Commonwealth Literature." *The Colonial and Neo-Colonial Encounters in Commonwealth Literature.* Ed. Anniah Gowda, 9-20.
_____. *The Adventure of Criticism.* New Delhi: Sterling, 1985.
Jain, Jasbir. "The Novels of Kamala Markandaya." *Indian Literature,* 18, 2 (April-June 1975) 36-43.
_____. *Nayantara Sahgal.* Delhi: Arnold-Heinemann, 1978.
Jain, Jasbir, "Strange in Enemy Territory: Expatriate and Exile." *Littcrit,* 4, 2 (Dec. 1978), 31-35.

_____. "The Emperor's New Clothes: The Emergency and Sahgal's *Rich Like Us." The New Indian Novel in English: A Study of the 1980s.* Ed. Viney Kirpal. 27-36.

James, Henry. *The Art of Fiction and Other Essays.* New York: Oxford Univ. Press, 1948.

James, Robert Rhodes. *Ambitions and Realities: British Politics 1964-'70.* London: Wendenfeld and Nicholson, 1972.

Jameson, Frederick. *The Political Unconscious: Narrative as a Socially Symbolic Act.* Ithaca: Cornell Univ. Press, 1981.

Jena, Seema. *Voice and Vision of Anita Desai.* New Delhi: Ashish, 1989.

Jha, Rekha. *The Novels of Kamala Markandaya and Ruth Jhabvala: A Study in East-West Encounter.* New Delhi: Prestige, 1990.

Jhabvala, Ruth Prawer. *A Backward Place.* London: John Murray, 1965.

_____. *Heat and Dust.* London: John Murray, 1975.

Joseph, Margaret. *Kamala Markandaya.* New Delhi: Arnold-Heinemann, 1980.

Juneja, Punim. "The East-West Theme: *Some Inner Fury, The Serpent and the Rope* and *A Dream in Hawaii." Commonwealth Fiction.* Vol. I. Ed. R.K. Dhawan. 178-97.

Juneja, O.P. "Prospero in Caliban's Free State: Margaret Laurence's African Short Stories." *Commonwealth Fiction.* Vol. III. Ed. R.K. Dhawan. 187-97.

Jussawalla, Feroza. "Of Cabbages and Kings: *This Time of Morning* and *Storm in Chandigarh* by Nayantara Sahgal." *The Journal of Indian Writing in English,* 5, 1 (Jan. 1977) 43-50.

Kabir, Humayun. *Britain and India.* Calcutta: Orient Longman's, 1960.

Kachru, Braj B., ed. *The Other Tongue: English Across Cultures.* Illinois: The University of Illinois Press, 1982.

Kalinikova, Elena J. *Indian English Literature: A Perspective.* Ed. K.K. Sharma. Ghaziabad: Vimal, 1982.

Karanth, K.A. "How Deep is Western Influence on Indian Writers of Fiction?" *Literary Criterion,* 7, 2 (Summer 1966), 33-40.

Kettle, Arnold. *An Introduction to the English Novel,* Vol. 2. London: Hutchinson, 1953.

Key, C.E. *A History of the British Empire.* 1936; 5 rpts. London: George G. Herrap, 1946.

Kincaid, Dennis. *British Social Life in India, 1608-1937.* 1938; rpt. London: Routledge and Kegan Paul, 1973.

Kipling, Rudyard. *Kim.* London: Macmillan.

Kirpal, Viney. "The Indian Elite and *The English Queens" The Three Contemporary Novelists.* Ed. R.K. Dhawan. 139-47.

_____. "What is the Modern Third World Novel?" *The Journal of Commonwealth Literature,* 23, 1 (1988) 144-56.

_____. *The Third World Novel of Expatriation.* New Delhi: Sterling, 1989.

_____, ed. *The New Indian Novel in English: A Study of the 1980s.* New York: Allied, 1990.

Krishnaswamy, Shantha. *The Woman in Indian Fiction in English 1950-80.* New Delhi: Ashish, 1984.

Kumar, Shiv K. and Keith McKean. *Critical Approaches to Fiction.* New York: McGraw-Hill, 1968.

Lal, P. *The Alien Insiders; Essays on Indian Writing in English.* Calcutta: Writers Workshop, 1985.

Lamba, B.P. "Chaman Nahal: *The Crown and the Loincloth." World Literature Today,* 56, 2 (Spring 1982) 405-6.

Liu, Marcia P. "Continuity and Development in the Novels of Nayantara Sahgal." *The Journal of Indian Writing in English,* 8, 1 and 2 (Jan.-July 1980) 45-52.

Macmillan, Margaret. *Women of the Raj.* USA: Thames and Hudson, 1988.

Majumdar, R.C., et al. *An Advanced History of India.* 2nd ed. London: Macmillan, 1958.

Majumdar, Swapan. *Comparative Literature: Indian Dimensions.* Calcutta: Papyrus, 1987.

Mannoni, O. *Prospero and Caliban: The Psychology of Colonization.* trans. Pamela Powesland. 1956; rpt. London: Metheun, 1960.

Markandaya, Kamala "On Images." Paper read at the Seminar on Socioliterature at the East West Centre for Cultural Interchange. Honolulu: August 1973, 1-18.

_____. "One Pair of Eyes: Some Random Reflections." *The Literary Criterion,* 11, 4 (Summer 1975), 13-25.

Marriott, Sir John A.R. *The English in India.* Oxford: Clarendon Press, 1932.

Masters, John. *Nightrunners of Bengal.* 1951; rpt. London: Michael Joseph, 1962.

Maunier, Rene. *The Sociology of Colonies: An Introduction to the Study of Race Contact.* Ed. and trans. E.D. Lorimer. London: Routledge and Kegan Paul, 1949.

Mead, Henry. *The Sepoy Revolt: Its Causes and its Consequences.* Delhi: Gian, 1986.

Mehra, Parshotam. *A Dictionary of Modern Indian History.* Delhi: Oxford Univ. Press, 1985.

Mehrotra, Raja Ram. "The Language of Indian Writing in English: Some Sociolinguistic Evidence." *Journal of South Asian Literature,* 22, 2 (Summer-Fall 1987), 103-12.

Mehta, P.P. *Indo-Anglian Fiction: An Assessment.* Bareilly: Prakash, 1979.

Melwani, Mulk Das. *Themes in Indo-Anglian Literature.* Bareilly: Prakash, 1977.

Memmi, Albert. *The Colonizer and the Colonized.* New York: The Orion Press, 1965.

Menon, K.P.K. *K. Nagarajan's Writings: An Introduction.* Madras: Emerald, 1984.

Mill, James. *The History of British India.* Vol. VI. London: Baldwin, Gradock and Joy Paternoster-Row, 1820.

Mohini, V. "Writer at Work: Nayantara Sahgal." *The Literary Criterion,* 25, 1 (1990) 60-70.

Moore, R.J. *Escape from Empire.* Oxford: Clarendon Press, 1983.

Mukherjee, Arun. P. "Characterization in Salman Rushdie's *Midnight's Children*: Breaking out of the Hold of Realism and Seeking the 'Alienation Effect.'" *The New Indian Novel in English: A Study of the 1980s.* Ed. Viney Kirpal, 109-20.

Mukherjee, Meenakshi. *The Twice-Born Fiction: Themes and Techniques of the Indian Novel in English.* 1971; New Delhi: Arnold-Heinemann, 1974.

_____. "Inside the Outsider." *Awakened Conscience: Studies in Commonwealth Literature.* New Delhi: Sterling, 1978, 86-91.

_____. *Reality and Realism: The Novel and Society in India.* Delhi: Oxford Univ. Press, 1985.

Murphy, Rhoads. *The Outsiders: The Western Experience in India and China.* USA: University of Michigan Press, 1977.

Murti, K.V. Suryanarayana. "*Seven Summers:* Anand's Fictional Matrix." *Kakatiya Journal of English Studies,* 4, 1 (Spring 1977), 71-84.

Nahal, Chaman. *The New Literatures in English.* New Delhi: Allied, 1985.

_____. "The Writer and the 'Convenience' of History: A Reading of *Midnight's Children." Yearly Review,* 3 (Dec. 1989) 114-30.

Naik, M.K., ed. *Critical Essays on Indian Writing in English.* Dharwar: Karnataka University, 1968.

_____. *Mulk Raj Anand.* London: Arnold-Heinemann, 1973.

_____, et al. *Critical Essays on Indian Writing in English.* Delhi: Macmillan, 1977.

_____, ed. *Aspects of Indian Writing in English.* Delhi: Macmillan, 1979.

_____. *A History of Indian English Literature.* Delhi: Sahitya Akademi, 1982.

_____. *Dimensions of Indian English Literature.* New Delhi: Sterling, 1984.

_____. *Perspectives on Indian Fiction in English.* New Delhi: Abhinav, 1985.

_____. *Studies in Indian English Literature.* New Delhi: Sterling, 1987.

Naipaul, V.S. *The Mimic Men.* London: Andre Deutsch, 1967.

_____. *The Middle Passage.* Harmondsworth: Penguin, 1969.

Nandakumar, Prema. "Indian Writing in English: 1972-73." *Indian Literature,* 17, 4 (Oct.-Dec. 1974) 94-96.

Nandy, Ashis. *The Intimate Enemy.* Delhi: Oxford Univ. Press, 1983.

Narasimhan, Raji. "Indian Writing in English, 1962." *Indian Literature,* 6, 2 (1963) 81-86.

Narasimhaiah, C.D. *Fiction and the Reading Public in India.* Mysore: University of Mysore, 1965.

_____. "Indian Writing in English: An Introduction." *The Journal of Commonwealth Literature,* 5 (July 1968) 3-15.

_____, ed. *The Swan and the Eagle: Essays on Indian English Literature.* 1968; Simla: Indian Institute of Advanced Study, 1987.

_____, ed. *Awakened Conscience: Studies in Commonwealth Literature.* New Delhi: Sterling, 1978.

_____ and C.N. Srinath, eds. *Kipling's India.* Mysore: Dhvanyaloka, n.d.

Narayanan, Gomathy. "British Fathers and Indian Sons: Guilt and Pride for the Indian Freedom Movement in the Post-Independence Indian Novel in English." *The Journal of South Asian Literature*, 17, 1 (Winter-Spring 1982) 207-21.

_____. *The Sahibs and the Natives: A Study of Guilt and Pride in Anglo-Indian and Indo-Anglian Novels.* Delhi: Chanakya, 1986.

Narayan, Shyamala A. *Raja Rao: Man and His Works*. New Delhi: Sterling, 1988.

Nehru, Jawaharlal. *The Discovery of India*. London: Meridian, 1965.

Newman, Judie. "Prospero's Complex: Race and Sex in Nadine Gordimer's *Burger's Daughter*." *The Journal of Commonwealth Literature*, 20, 1 (1985) 81-99.

Nicholson, Kai. *A Presentation of Social Problems in the Indo-Anglian and Anglo-Indian Novel.* Bombay: Jaico, 1972.

Niranjan, Shiva. *Raja Rao: Novelist as Sadhaka.* Ghazibad: Vimal, 1985.

Nivan, Alistair, ed. *The Commonwealth Writer Overseas*. Bruxelles: Dieter, 1976.

Nodel, George A. and Perry Curbs. *Imperialism and Colonialism*. London: Macmillan, 1964.

Orwell, George. *Burmese Days. The Complete Works of George Orwell*. Vol. 2. 1949; rpt. London: Secker and Warburg, 1986.

Pallan, Rajesh K. "Encounter with the Self: A Study of the Confessional Mode in Mulk Raj Anand's *The Bubble*." *The New Indian Novel in English: A Study of the 1980s.* Ed. Viney Kirpal. 11-23.

Pandeya, S.M. "In the International Style Immerse—A Note on the Shape of Commonwealth Fiction." *Commonwealth Literature: Problems of Response*. Ed. C.D. Narasimhaiah. 20-29.

_____. *Studies in Modern Fiction*. Delhi: Vikas, 1983.

Paniker, K. Ayyappa, ed. *Contemporary Indian Fiction in English.* Trivandrum: University of Kerala, Institute of English, 1985.

_____. *Indian Literature in English.* Madras: Anu Chitra, 1989.

_____. "Manohar Malgonkar: The Predictable Posture." *Indian Literature in English.* Madras: Anu Chithra, 1989, 58-70.

Panikkar, K.M. *A Survey of Indian History*. 2nd ed. Bombay: Asia, 1954.

Parameswaran, Uma. *A Study of Representative Indo-English Novelists*. New Delhi: Vikas, 1976.

_____. "Salman Rushdie in Indo-English Literature." *The Journal of Indian Writing in English*, 12, 2 (July 1984) 15-25.

_____. "Review of *Rich Like Us*." *World Literature Today*, 60, 2 (Spring 1986), 361-62.

Paranjape, Makarand R. "Inside and Outside the Whale: Politics and the New Indian English Novel." *The New Indian Novel in English: A Study of the 1980s*. Ed. Viney Kirpal. 213-26.

Parry, Benita. *Delusions and Discoveries: Studies on India in the British Imagination, 1880-1930*. 1972; rpt. New Delhi: Orient Longman, 1974.

Parry, Graham. "Anand, Orwell and the War." *Commonwealth Fiction*. Vol. 1. Ed. R.K. Dhawan. 112-21.

Parthasarathy, R. "Exile 2." *Rough Passage*. Delhi: Three Campus Booms, 1977, 17-18.

_____. "Whoring After English Gods." *Writers in East-West Encounter: New Cultural Bearings*. Ed. Guy Amrithnayagam. London: Macmillan, 1982.

Pathak, R.S. "The Indo-English Novelists' Quest for Identity." *Explorations in Modern Indo-English Fiction*. Ed. R.K. Dhawan.

Pathan, B.A. *Gandhian Myth in English Literature in India*. New Delhi: Deep and Deep, 1987.

Paul, Premila. *The Novels of Mulk Raj Anand: A Thematic Study*. New Delhi: Sterling, 1983.

Pearce, C.E. *Love Besieged: A Romance of the Presidency of Lucknow*. London: Stanley Paul, 1909.

Pollard, Arthur. "Kamala Markandaya's *The Golden Honeycomb*." *The Journal of Indian Writing in English*, 8, 1 & 2 (Jan.-July 1980) 23-25.

Pontes, Hilda. *Nayantara Sahgal*. New Delhi: Concept, 1985.

Prasad, Hari Mohan. "Theme of Exile in Indo-English Novel." *Alien Voice: Perspectives on Commonwealth Literature*. ed. Avadesh K. Srivastava. Lucknow: Print House, 1981, 210-16.

Prasad Madhusudan, ed. *Indian English Novelists: An Anthology of Critical Essays*. New Delhi: Sterling, 1982.

_____. *Perspectives on Kamala Markandaya.* Delhi: Vimal, 1984.
Radha, K. "The English in *Azadi* and *The Crown and the Loincloth.*" *Three Contemporary Novelists.* Ed. R.K. Dhawan, 148-71.
Radhakrishnan, N. *Indo-Anglian Fiction: Major Trends and Themes.* Madras: Emerald, 1984.
Rahman, Tariq. "Politics in the Novels of Salman Rushdie." *The Commonwealth Review,* 1, 2 (1990) 102-17.
Rajagopalachary, M. "Malgonkar's Meditation on History: *The Devil's Wind.*" *Triveni,* 55, 2 (July-Sept. 1986) 53-56.
Rajan, P.K. *Studies in Mulk Raj Anand.* New Delhi: Abhinav, 1986.
Ramakrishna, D. "Academics and Yogis: Reflections on the Present Indo-English Fiction." *The Journal of Indian Writing in English,* 7, 2 (July 1979) 89-96.
Ramamurthy, K.S. "Patterns of Distinctiveness in the Language of Commonwealth Fiction—A Comparative Study of the Language of Achebe, Naipaul, Narayan and Nagarajan." *The Literary Half-Yearly,* 22, 2 (July 1981) 85-100.
_____. *The Rise of the Indian Novel in English.* Delhi: Sterling, 1987.
Rao, Kolar Suryanarayana. "Some Notes on the Plots of Kamala Markandaya." *Indian Literature,* 12, 1 (1970) 102-12.
Rao, A.V. Krishna. *Nayantara Sahgal: A Study of Her Fiction and Non-Fiction.* Madras: M. Seshachalam, 1976.
Rao, Raja. "Foreword." *Kanthapura.* 1938; rpt. Bombay: Oxford University Press, 1947.
Rao, Santha Rama. *Remember the House.* London: Victor Gollancz, 1956.
Rao, Susheela N. "England in the Novels of Kamala Markandaya." *The Journal of Indian Writing in English,* 15, 1 (Jan. 1987) 1-10.
Riemenschneider, Dieter. "British Characters in Indo-English Fiction." *Aspects of Indian Writing in English.* Ed. M.K. Naik. 137-49.
_____. "G.V. Desani's *All About H. Hatterr* and the Problem of Cultural Alienation." *The Literary Criterion,* 20, 2 (1985) 23.
_____. "History and Individual in Anita Desai's *Clear Light of Day* and Salman Rushdie's *Midnight's Children.*" *The New Indian Novel in English: A Study of the 1980s.* New Delhi: Allied, 1990, 187-200.
Rimmon-Kenan, Shlomith. *Narrative Fiction: Contemporary Poetics.* London: Metheun, 1983.
Ruddock, Ralph. *Roles and Relationships.* London: Routledge and Kegan Paul, 1969.
Rushdie, Salman. "The Empire Writes Back with a Vengeance." *The Times,* 3 July 1982.
Said, Edward W. *Orientalism.* London: Routledge and Kegan Paul, 1978.
Sarma, G.P. *Nationalism in Indo-Anglian Fiction.* Calcutta: Sterling, 1978.
Sastri, K.A. Nilakanta, et al. *Advanced History of India.* Bombay: Allied, 1970.
Sastry, L.S.R. Krishna. "The East-West Theme in the Indo-Anglian Novel." *The Indian Journal of English Studies,* 26 (1987), 62-67.
Sathianathier, R. *A Political and Cultural History of India.* Vol. 3. *Modern India.* 2nd ed. Madras: Central Art Press, 1952.
Scott, Paul. *Staying On.* 1977; rpt. London: Heinemann, 1979.
_____. *The Raj Quartet.* London: Heinemann, 1978.
Shahane, Vasant A. *Khushwant Singh.* New York: Twayne, 1972.
Sharma, K.K. *Perspectives on Raja Rao.* Ghaziabad: Vimal, 1980.
Sharma, Sudarshan. "Gandhian Ideology and Nayantara Sahgal." *The Influence of Gandhian Ideology on Indo-Anglian Fiction.* New Delhi: Soni, 1982, 133-60.
Shepherd, Ron. "*Midnight's Children* as Fantasy." *Commonwealth Review,* 1, 2 (1960) 33-45.
Shifman, Alexander. *Tolstoy and India.* 1969; rpt. New Delhi: Sahitya Akademi, 1978.
Shirdwadkar, Meena. *Image of Woman in Indo-Anglian Fiction.* New Delhi: Sterling, 1979.
Singh, Bhupal. *A Survey of Anglo-Indian Fiction.* London: Oxford Univ. Press, 1934.
Singh Kirpal, "Writers in Limbo: The Third World Experience." *The Literary Criterion,* 23, 4 (1988) 70-79.
Singh, R.S. "Manohar Malgonkar, the Novelist." *Indian Literature,* 13, 1, 2 (1970) 122-31.
_____. "From Resentment to Social Protest: Mulk Raj Anand." *Indian Novel in English.*

Delhi: Arnold-Heinemann, 1977, 38-54.

_____. *Indian Novel in English: A Critical Study*. Delhi: Arnold-Heinemann, 1977.

Singh, Satya Brat. "Rudy Wiebe, Paul Scott and Salman Rushdie: Historians Distanced from History." *The Commonwealth Review*, 1, 2 (1990) 146-56.

Singh, S.D. *Novels on the Indian Mutiny*. New Delhi: Arnold Heinemann, 1973.

Slemon, Stephen, "Post-Colonial Allegory and the Transformation of History." *The Journal of Commonwealth Literature*, 23, 1 (1988) 157-68.

Smith, V.A. *The Oxford History of India*. Oxford: Clarendon Press, 1923.

Southgate, George W. *The British Empire*. 1936: rpt. London: J.M. Dent, 1939.

Soyinka, Wole. "Cross Currents: The New African After Cultural Encounters." *Writers in East-West Encounter: New Cultural Bearings*. Ed. Guy Amrithnayagam. 51-63.

Strachey, Sir John. *India: Its Administration and Progress*. 1888; rpt. London: Macmillan, 1911.

Tarinayya, M. "Two Novels," *Indian Literature*, 13, 1 (1970), 113-21.

Thumboo, Edwin. "Kamala Markandaya's *The Silence of Desire*." *The Journal of Indian Writing in English*, 8 (1980) 108-36.

Tiffin, Helen. "Towards Place and Placelessness." *Awakened Conscience*. Ed. C.D. Narasimhaiah. New Delhi: Sterling, 1978. 146-63.

_____. "Post-Colonialism, Post-Modernism and the Rehabilitation of Post-Colonial History." *The Journal of Commonwealth Literature*, 23, 1 (1988) 69-81.

Trevelyan, Humphrey. *The India We Left*. London: Macmillan, 1972.

Venkatachari, K. "R.K. Narayan's Novels: Acceptance of Life." *Indian Literature*, 13, 1 (1970) 73-87.

Verghese, Paul C. "Indian English and Man in Indo-Anglian Fiction." *Indian Literature,. 13 (1970) 6-25.*

_____. "Two Novels in English—reviewed." *Indian Writing Today*, 4, 4 (Oct.-Dec. 1970) 236-38.

_____. *Problems of the Indian Creative Writer in English*. Bombay: Somaiya, 1971.

Verma, Rajiv, "The Indian Novel in English: Recent Titles." *Yearly Review*, 1 (Dec. 1987) 97-100.

Viswanathan, K. *India in English Fiction*. Waltair: Andhra University Press, 1971.

Walsh, William. *A Manifold Voice: Studies in Commonwealth Literature*. London: Chatto and Windus, 1964.

_____. *Commonwealth Literature*. London: Oxford Univ. Press, 1973.

_____. "The Indian Sensibility in English." *Awakened Conscience*. Ed. C.D. Narasimhaiah. New Delhi: Sterling, 1978, 63-72.

_____. "India and the Novel." *The New Pelican Guide to English Literature: The Present*. Vol. 8. Ed. Boris Ford. 1956; England: Penguin, 1984, 245-60.

Weir, Ann Lowry. "Worlds Apart?—Feminine Consciousness in Markandaya's *Nectar in a Sieve* and *The Coffer Dams*," *CIEFL Bulletin*, 13, No. 2 (1977), 71-85.

Wendt, Allen. "Babu to Sahib: Contemporary Indian Literature." *English and India*. Ed. M. Manuel and K. Ayyappa Paniker. Delhi: Macmillan, 1978, 94-107.

Williams, Haydon Moore. *Studies in Modern Indian Fiction in English*. Vols. 1 & 2. Calcutta: Writers Workshop, 1973.

_____. "Manohar Malgonkar: The Captains and the Kings," *The Journal of Indian Writing in English*. 8, Nos. 1 & 2 (Jan.-July 1980) 35-44.

_____. "Victims and Virgins: Some Characters in Kamala Markandaya's Novels." *Galaxy of Indian Writings in English*. Delhi: Akshat, 1987, 11-121.

_____. *Galaxy of Indian Writings in English*. Delhi: Akshat, 1987.

Woodford, Peggy. *Rise of the Raj*. Kent: Midas Books, 1978.

Wurgaft, Lewis D. *The Imperial Imagination: Magic and Myth in Kipling's India*. Connecticut: Wesleyan Univ. Press, 1983.

Zahar, Renate. *Frantz Fannon: Colonialism and Alienation*. New York: Ethiope Publishing Corporation, Monthly Review Press, 1974.

Zwingmann, Charles and Maria Prister-Ammende. *Uprooting and After*. New York: Springer-Verlag, 1973.

Index